lonely planet

PARIS

ENCOUNTER

CATHERINE LE NEVEZ

Paris Encounter

Published by Lonely Planet Publications Pty Ltd
ABN 36 005 607 983

Australia	Head Office,
	Locked Bag 1, Footscray, Vic 3011
	☎ 03 8379 8000 fax 03 8379 8111
	talk2us@lonelyplanet.com.au
USA	150 Linden St, Oakland, CA 94607
	☎ 510 250 6400
	toll free 800 275 8555
	fax 510 893 8572
	info@lonelyplanet.com
UK	2nd fl, 186 City Rd
	London EC1V 2NT
	☎ 020 7106 2100 fax 020 7106 2101
	go@lonelyplanet.co.uk

This title was commissioned in Lonely Planet's London office and produced by: **Commissioning Editors** Caroline Sieg, Michala Green, Clifton Wilkinson **Coordinating Editor** Alison Ridgway **Coordinating Cartographer** Brendan Streager **Layout Designer** Jim Hsu **Assisting Editor** Andrea Dobbin **Managing Editors** Sasha Baskett, Brigitte Ellemor **Managing Cartographer** Alison Lyall **Managing Layout Designer** Celia Wood **Project Manager** Glenn van der Knijff **Cover Designer** Pepi Bluck **Thanks to** Yvonne Bischofberger, Katrina Browning, Mark Griffiths, Imogen Hall, Debra Herrmann, Laura Jane, Chris Lee Ack, Wayne Murphy, Trent Paton, Lyahna Spencer

ISBN 978 1 74059 848 4

Printed by Hang Tai Printing Company, Hong Kong. Printed in China.

Acknowledgement Paris Metro Map © 2008 RATP.

Lonely Planet and the Lonely Planet logo are trademarks of Lonely Planet and are registered in the US Patent and Trademark Office and in other countries.

Lonely Planet does not allow its name or logo to be appropriated by commercial establishments, such as retailers, restaurants or hotels. Please let us know of any misuses: www.lonelyplanet.com/ip.

HOW TO USE THIS BOOK
Colour-Coding & Maps
Colour-coding is used for symbols on maps and in the text that they relate to (eg all eating venues on the maps and in the text are given a green knife and fork symbol). Each neighbourhood also gets its own colour, and this is used down the edge of the page and throughout that neighbourhood section.

Shaded yellow areas on the maps denote 'areas of interest' – for their historical significance, their attractive architecture or their great bars and restaurants. We encourage you to head to these areas and just start exploring!

Prices
Multiple prices listed with reviews (eg €10/5 or €10/5/20) indicate adult/child, adult/concession or adult/child/family.

Send us your feedback We love to hear from readers – your comments help make our books better. We read every word you send us, and we always guarantee that your feedback goes straight to the appropriate authors. The most useful submissions are rewarded with a free book. To send us your updates and find out about Lonely Planet events, newsletters and travel news visit our award-winning website: **lonelyplanet.com/contact**.

Note: We may edit, reproduce and incorporate your comments in Lonely Planet products such as guidebooks, websites and digital products, so let us know if you don't want your comments reproduced or your name acknowledged. For a copy of our privacy policy visit **lonelyplanet.com/privacy**.

CATHERINE LE NEVEZ

Catherine first lived in Paris aged four and has been returning at every opportunity since, completing her Doctorate of Creative Arts in Writing, her Masters in Professional Writing, and post-graduate qualifications in editing and publishing along the way. In between revisiting her favourite Parisian haunts and uncovering new ones, she wrote this book in a tiny (but charming) garret in the city's heart.

Catherine's writing on Paris includes the previous (1st) edition of this book, and newspaper and radio reportage covering the city's literary scene. Beyond Paris, she's written numerous Lonely Planet guidebooks and web reviews, including Lonely Planet's *France* and *Provence & the Côte d'Azur* guidebooks. Wanderlust aside, Paris remains her favourite city on earth.

CATHERINE'S THANKS

Merci beaucoup to the innumerable Parisians who offered insights and inspiration. At LP, cheers to Caroline Sieg, Alison Ridgway and Mark Griffiths. And *merci surtout* to my family for instilling in me my lifelong love of Paris.

Our Readers Many thanks to the travellers who wrote to us with helpful hints, useful advice and interesting anecdotes. Barry Butchard, Gwen Christini, Katherine Craigs, Jay Geller, Gordon Grams, Tomislav Krajcer, Robert Martin, Rene Rodgers, Rosie Sontheimer.

Cover photograph Rue Vieille du Temple, Marais, Steven Greaves. This image was selected as one of the winners of a competition to find four unique travellers' photos that really convey the experience of using an Encounter guide. Entrants were challenged to submit eye-catching photos that get right to the heart of the city and give the impression of seeing and experiencing it for themselves. Check out the other winning images on *Istanbul*, *London* and *Barcelona Encounter* covers. **Internal photographs** p27 David A. Barnes/Alamy; p24 Erick Nguyen/Alamy; p25 Ted Pink/Alamy. All other photographs by Lonely Planet Images, and by Glenn Beanland p18, p131, p135, p153, p181; Bruce Bi p44, p54, p55; Karl Blackwell p144; Jean-Bernard Carillet p6 (top left), p12, p15, p19, p22, p30 (top right), p39, p43, p63, p69, p76, p117, p128, p176, p183, p187, p189, p190, p191; Ann Cecil p86; Olivier Cirendini p100, p114; Kevin Clogstoun p20; Juliet Coombe p89; John Elk III p30 (bottom), p95; Greg Elms p60; Dan Herrick p23; Dennis Jones p17; Kevin Levesque p11, p195; Martin Moos p30 (top left); Russell Mountford p6 (top right); Christine Osborne p125; Will Salter p6 (bottom), p8, p16, p34, p53, p122, p140, p170, p186; Neil Setchfield p158; Jonathan Smith p13, p21, p29, p58, p105, p160, p174, p178, p185; Oliver Strewe p14, p163.

All images are copyright of the photographers unless otherwise indicated. Many of the images in this guide are available for licensing from **Lonely Planet Images:** www.lonelyplanetimages.com.

Exterior of the Institut du Monde Arabe (p140), Latin Quarter

CONTENTS

THE AUTHOR	03	> ROMANTIC PARIS	184
THIS IS PARIS	07	> PANORAMAS	185
HIGHLIGHTS	08	> MONDIAL PARIS	186
PARIS DIARY	23	> JAZZ, CHANSONS &	
ITINERARIES	29	CABARET	187
QUARTERS	34	> COOKING & WINE-	
> INVALIDES &		TASTING COURSES	188
EIFFEL TOWER	38	> CLASSICAL MUSIC,	
> ARC DE TRIOMPHE,		OPERA, DANCE &	
CHAMPS-ÉLYSÉES &		THEATRE	189
GRANDS BOULEVARDS	48	> GAY & LESBIAN	190
> LOUVRE & LES HALLES	68	> WALKING (FLÂNERIE)	191
> MONTMARTRE	84	> CYCLING	192
> BELLEVILLE &		> KIDS	193
SURROUNDS	96	> CINEMA	194
> MARAIS & BASTILLE	110	**BACKGROUND**	195
> THE ISLANDS	130	**DIRECTORY**	204
> LATIN QUARTER	138	**INDEX**	217
> ST-GERMAIN DES PRÉS			
& MONTPARNASSE	150		
FURTHER AFIELD	165		
SNAPSHOTS	170		
> ACCOMMODATION	172		
> FOOD	174		
> DRINKING & NIGHTLIFE	176		
> SHOPPING	178		
> ARTISTIC PARIS	180		
> PARKS & GARDENS	181		
> LITERARY PARIS	182		
> ARCHITECTURE	183		

THIS IS PARIS

On the surface, Paris' tree-shaded boulevards, romantic bridges illuminated by wrought-iron lamps and wicker chair–lined café terraces – not to mention more recognisable monuments than any other city – all have a timeless familiarity, whether it's your first visit in a while or your first altogether.

Scratching the surface, however, reveals that France's fashion-conscious capital continually evolves. Strict regulations have preserved its villagelike layout and architectural treasures, and have ensured an almost total absence of high-rises. This gives rise instead to innovative conversions of existing structures into everything from galleries to hip bars to green spaces. Plans are currently unfolding for the *Périphérique* (ring road) to provide a pedestrian link between central Paris and the *banlieues* (suburbs) with parklands grassing over the traffic flowing beneath. Even brand-new buildings, such as the Musée Quai Branly, intuitively connect with the existing cityscape.

Paris' changes are most apparent in its regenerated *quartiers* (quarters), particularly around Canal St-Martin, home to emerging artists and designers; the colourful multicultural districts in the north and northeast; and the reinvigorated southeast, particularly along the riverbanks.

The Seine itself forms part of changes to the city's public transport system, with the 2008 debut of the Voguéo 'metro boat' service. And low-cost-to-free bicycle rental is now available from pick-up/drop-off stations all over the city following the success of the Vélib' service.

Paris also takes on a different atmosphere depending on the season. But Cole Porter was spot on, meteorology and all: whether you're here in the springtime, the fall, the winter (when it drizzles) or the summer (when it sizzles!), the world's most romanticised city has a way of seducing you every moment of the year. Some things never change.

Top left Fruits of the sea, La Grande Épicerie de Paris at Le Bon Marché (p158), Left Bank **Top right** Musée d'Orsay's impressive old station clock keeps watch over the impressionist masters (p42) **Bottom** The Marais' fashion boutiques (p119) along rue des Francs Bourgeois

>HIGHLIGHTS

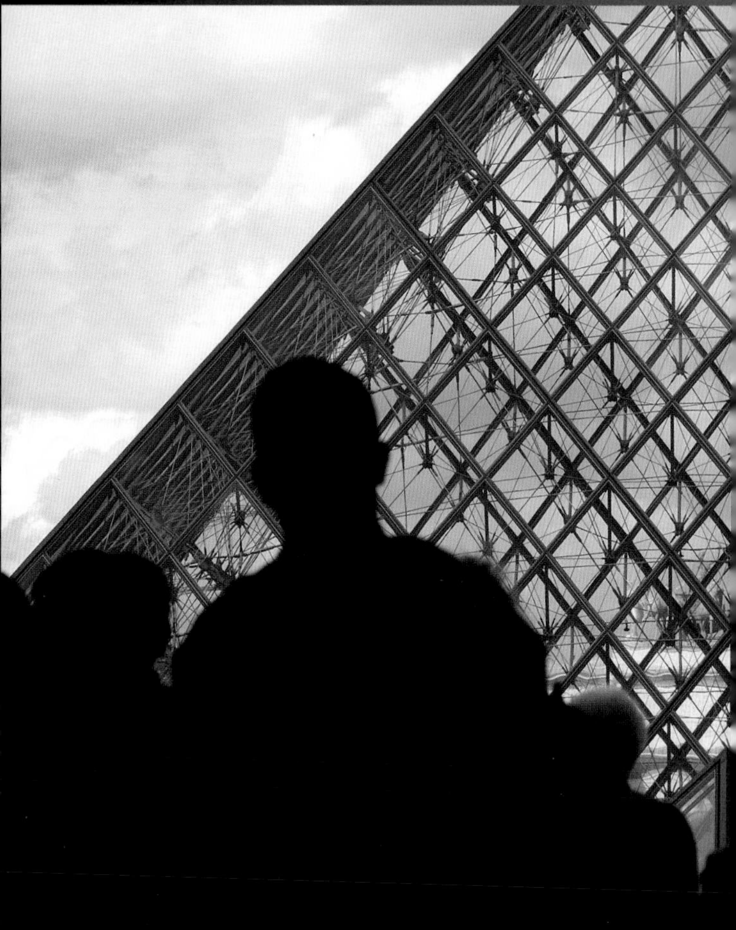

>1 See the City of Light at night from the Eiffel Tower 10

>2 View impressionist, postimpressionist and art nouveau works by a roll-call of masters 12

>3 Join Parisians at play in the city's most popular gardens 13

>4 Feast your senses during a wander through Paris' markets 14

>5 Revitalise your mind, body and soul at Paris' 1920s mosque 15

>6 Browse the shelves of a legendary Paris bookshop 16

>7 Stroll around Paris' prettiest island with a Berthillon ice cream 17

>8 Navigate the labyrinthine Louvre 18

>9 Take a romantic promenade along Paris' elevated park 19

>10 Pay homage to the departed at Cimetière du Père Lachaise 20

>11 Spend a Sunday afternoon exploring Paris' photogenic canal 21

>12 Head up to Paris' landmark basilica 22

>1 EIFFEL TOWER

SEE THE CITY OF LIGHT AT NIGHT FROM THE EIFFEL TOWER

The second-most mesmerising view of the 'city of light' by night is from the tip of the city's iconic spire, with its 360-degree panoramas over Paris. (The most mesmerising night-time view is, of course, from an aeroplane – preferably one that's landing.)

Over 250 million people have ascended the tower to date – around seven million each year. Most visit its three platforms (57m, 115m and 276m) in daytime hours, when, on a clear day, views from the top extend up to 60km. Far fewer visitors make the pilgrimage after sunset. Although you're unlikely to have it to yourself, come nightfall the queues are significantly shorter, and the illuminated boulevards and floodlit monuments spread out before you.

Gustave Eiffel constructed the tower initially as a temporary exhibit for the Exposition Universelle (World Fair) in 1889. Until the completion of Manhattan's Chrysler Building in 1930, it remained the world's tallest structure, at 320m (varying by up to 15cm when its 7000 tonnes of iron and 2.5 million rivets expand in warm weather and contract when it's cold). Its popularity assured its survival beyond the fair and its elegant architectural design became a defining fixture of the city's skyline.

Each night, the tower's twin searchlight beacons beam an 80km radius around the city (look up from the top platform to see the 6000-watt lamps). And every hour, for 10 minutes on the hour, the entire tower sparkles with 20,000 gold-toned lights. It took 25 mountain climbers five months to install the bulbs, and the glittering, diamondlike effect when viewed from within the tower is dazzling.

Night-time at the top can be breezy – bring a jacket.

LA VILLE LUMIÈRE

Paris was dubbed *la Ville Lumière* (the City of Light) in the 19th century, when it was the first Continental European city to install gas lamps along its streets – although some believe the nickname derives from the soft light captured by the impressionists' paintings. Either way, it remains a fitting description of the shimmering French capital.

To prolong the panoramas, book dinner at one of the tower's restaurants: Altitude 95, on the 1st level; or Le Jules Verne, the sublime 2nd-level restaurant, accessed by private lift (see p45).

Day or night, queues are set to be slashed with the 2009 introduction of online ticketing for groups, which should speed things up significantly for individual visitors. And queuing in the wind and rain will be a thing of the past when the area between its four feet is refurbished, although renovations aren't due to wrap up until 2015. Topping off the overhaul, a 3rd-floor champagne bar is also in the works.

See also p39.

>2 MUSÉE D'ORSAY

VIEW IMPRESSIONIST, POSTIMPRESSIONIST AND ART NOUVEAU WORKS BY A ROLL-CALL OF MASTERS

The home of France's national collection from the impressionist, postimpressionist and art nouveau movements is, appropriately, the glorious former Gare d'Orsay art nouveau railway station. Built in time for the 1900 Exposition Universelle, by 1939 the station's platforms were too short for mainline trains, and within a few years all rail services ceased. In 1962 Orson Welles filmed Kafka's *The Trial* in the then-abandoned building. Over the following two decades the government set about transforming it into the country's premier showcase for art from 1848 to 1914.

On the ground floor you'll find earlier works of the era, while the middle level has some stunning art nouveau rooms and sculptures. On the dazzling skylit upper level, masterpieces include Manet's *On The Beach;* Monet's gardens at Giverny and *Rue Montorgueil, Paris, Festival of June 30, 1878;* Cézanne's card players, *Green Apples* and *Blue Vase;* Renoir's *Ball at the Moulin de la Galette* and *Girls at the Piano;* Degas' ballerinas; Toulouse-Lautrec's cabaret dancers; Pissarro's *The Harvest;* Sisley's *View of the Canal St-Martin;* and Van Gogh's scenes of Auvers-sur-Oise just outside Paris (where he died and is buried).

See also p42.

>3 JARDIN DU LUXEMBOURG

JOIN PARISIANS AT PLAY IN THE CITY'S MOST POPULAR GARDENS

The merest ray of sunshine is enough to draw apartment-dwelling Parisians outdoors. You'll see locals unwinding throughout the city: in parks, on bridges and on the banks of the Seine. But the Luxembourg Gardens have a special place in the hearts of Parisians.

Napoleon dedicated the gardens to the children of Paris, and many residents spent their childhood prodding little wooden sailboats with long sticks on the octagonal pond, watching marionettes perform Punch & Judy–type shows, and riding the *carrousel* (merry-go-round) or ponies.

All those activities are still here today, as well as a modern playground and sporting and games venues.

If you're planning on picnicking, forget bringing a blanket – the elegantly manicured lawns are off-limits apart from a small wedge on the southern boundary. Instead, do as Parisians do, and corral one of the iconic 1923-designed sage-green metal chairs and find your own favourite part of the park.

See also p154.

>4 MARKETS

FEAST YOUR SENSES DURING A WANDER THROUGH PARIS' MARKETS

Nowhere encapsulates Paris' village atmosphere more than its street markets. Not simply places to shop, the markets are social gatherings for the entire neighbourhood, where residents toting quintessentially Parisian canvas shopping bags on wheels chat with stallholders and pick up culinary tips.

Nearly every little quarter has its own street market at least once a week (never Mondays), where trestle tables topped by tarpaulins groan under the weight of spit-roasted chickens, geese and ducks; seafood on beds of crushed ice; freshly killed meat; huge cheese wheels; boiled sweets; whole cakes; sun-ripened fruit and vegetables; and pâtés, preserves and countless other delicacies. Many markets also sell clothes, belts, bags, shoes, baskets, homewares and much more.

Marchés biologiques (organic markets) are also sprouting up all over Paris, while stalls in the city's more multicultural quarters brim with exotic fruits, vegetables, herbs and spices imported from all over the world.

Antiques, vintage and retro clothing, jewellery, bric-a-brac, racks of cheap brand-name jeans, denim and leather jackets, footwear, African carvings, woven Rastafarian caps, CDs, DVDs and electronic items are laid out at the city's sprawling flea markets.

See listings under Shop in the Quarters chapter, and p178.

>5 MOSQUÉE DE PARIS

REVITALISE YOUR MIND, BODY AND SOUL AT PARIS' 1920S MOSQUE

Built between 1922 and 1926 and topped by a 26m-high minaret, Paris' art deco–Moorish mosque is a treat off the beaten track. Provided you're modestly dressed, you can wander through the colonnaded courtyards – with incredible acoustics during the Call to Prayer – and leaf through ancient Arabic texts in the library.

The visual, physical and spiritual replenishment extends to a mosaic-and-marble *hammam* (a series of Turkish steam baths, each successively hotter), with various treatments also on offer, such as a *gommage* (black-soap scrub down) or massage. Also here is an authentic souk (Moroccan-style market) overflowing with colourful fabrics, crockery and trinkets, and an elaborately tiled restaurant serving *tajines* (slow-cooked meat), couscous and sweet, flaky North African pastries such as pistachio-and-honey *baklawas*. If all that sounds too decadent, you can simply sip a peppermint tea in its tearoom's tent-lined, cushion-strewn courtyard.

See also p141.

>6 SHAKESPEARE & COMPANY

BROWSE THE SHELVES OF A LEGENDARY PARIS BOOKSHOP

A kind of spell descends as you enter this cluttered, charming bookshop opposite Notre Dame. Its enchanting nooks and crannies overflow with new and secondhand English-language books, while amid handpainted quotations and a wishing well, a miniature staircase leads to an atticlike reading library.

The bookshop is the stuff of legends. The original shop (12 rue l'Odeon; closed by the Nazis in 1941) was run by Sylvia Beach and became the meeting point for Hemingway's 'Lost Generation'. Beach published James Joyce's *Ulysses* there in 1922, when no-one else would. In 1951 George Whitman opened the present incarnation, attracting a beat poet clientele. Scores of authors have since passed through its doors. At night its couches turn into beds where writers stay for free in exchange for working behind the till or stacking shelves. George is now aged in his 90s, and today his daughter, Sylvia Beach Whitman, maintains Shakespeare & Co's serendipitous magic.

See also p145.

>7 ÎLE ST-LOUIS

STROLL AROUND PARIS' PRETTIEST ISLAND WITH A BERTHILLON ICE CREAM

The Île St-Louis' tiny streets – where you'll still see the odd Citroën 2CV among its few cars – are a quiet respite from the city's hubbub. Quaint shops, selling everything from marionettes to old travel books, are dotted around the island, while its riverbanks and bridges are idyllic for listening to buskers or just watching the riverboats glide by. A stroll here is a favourite pastime for Parisians as well as visitors, but it wouldn't be complete without a cone of Berthillon ice cream in hand.

Just as champagne is synonymous with the Champagne region where it's produced, Berthillon is synonymous with the Île St-Louis. This esteemed *glacier* (ice-cream maker) was founded here in 1954, and is still run by the same family today. Among the 70 flavours are fruit sorbets such as blackcurrant, pink grapefruit, rhubarb and fig, as well as much richer ice creams, made from fresh milk and eggs, like honey nougat, white chocolate and Grand Marnier. In typical Parisian style, it's never slathered onto the cone but meticulously set in place in a petite, perfectly rounded scoop.

In addition to Maison Berthillon's own premises, several other establishments selling these all-natural, chemical-free ice creams are sprinkled around the island. See also p136.

>8 THE LOUVRE

NAVIGATE THE LABYRINTHINE LOUVRE

Stretching a whopping 700m along the Seine, it's estimated it would take nine months just to *glance* at every artwork in the world's largest museum.

And the Louvre keeps getting bigger. Constructed as a fortress by Philippe-Auguste in the early 13th century, the Palais du Louvre was rebuilt in the mid-16th century as a royal residence. In 1793 the Revolutionary Convention turned it into France's first national museum. The late President Mitterrand doubled its exhibition space, and new and renovated galleries see some 35,000 works now displayed.

And – with a bit of planning – it doesn't disappoint.

Save time by purchasing your ticket beforehand. Tickets are available from the Louvre's website, ticket agencies (p211), or machines in the Carrousel du Louvre. The Paris Museum Pass (p210) is valid here. To avoid the queues at the pyramid (the main entrance), enter via the Carrousel du Louvre (99 rue de Rivoli), or the Musée du Louvre exit from the Palais Royal–Musée du Louvre metro station. Museum tickets are valid all day, so you can take a break any time.

Before setting off down the endless corridors, rough out an itinerary based around what you most want to see by picking up a free English-language map from the information desk in the Hall Napoléon. Guided tours (available in English) are an info-packed option to make the most of your visit. Otherwise, multilanguage audioguides can help you self-navigate.

See also p73.

>9 PROMENADE PLANTÉE

TAKE A ROMANTIC PROMENADE ALONG PARIS' ELEVATED PARK

Seduction springs up in the most unlikely places in Paris, and perhaps none are more unlikely than a disued 19th-century railway viaduct carving through the busy Bastille quarter.

Climbing the stairs from Bastille's av Daumesnil brings you out on top of the viaduct that has been turned into the tranquil Promenade Plantée. Planted with a fragrant profusion of cherry trees, maples, rosebushes and lavender, it's a haven that feels far from the madding crowds four storeys below.

The walking path offers views over the surrounding *quartiers* (quarters) as well as intimate glimpses of wrought-iron balconies and rooftops including an art deco police station crowned by a dozen marble torsos.

At the end of the viaduct, the Promenade Plantée continues at ground level almost to the *Périphérique* (ring road), a total distance of 4.5km. If you're not ready to return to the urban jungle just yet, there are signs directing you east to the nearby woods, the Bois de Vincennes (see p118).

See also p117.

>10 CIMETIÈRE DU PÈRE LACHAISE

PAY HOMAGE TO THE DEPARTED AT CIMETIÈRE DU PÈRE LACHAISE

Paris is a collection of villages, and this 48-hectare cemetery of cobbled lanes and elaborate tombs the size of small houses qualifies as one in its own right.

The cemetery was founded in 1804, and initially attracted few funerals because of its distance from the city centre. The authorities' response was to exhume famous remains and resettle them here. The marketing ploy worked and Père Lachaise has been the city's most fashionable final address ever since.

With a population (as it were) of one million, among the cemetery's celebrity residents are the composer Chopin; writers Molière, Apollinaire, Balzac, Proust, Wilde, Gertrude Stein (and Alice B Toklas) and Colette; artists Delacroix, Pissarro, Seurat and Modigliani; singers Édith Piaf and rock god Jim Morrison; and tragic 12th-century lovers Abélard and Héloïse, who in 1817 were disinterred and reburied here together beneath a neogothic tombstone.

Maps locating noteworthy graves are posted around the cemetery, but it's worth purchasing a detailed map from one of the nearby newsstands.

See also p97, and p97 for long-standing tomb traditions.

>11 CANAL ST-MARTIN

SPEND A SUNDAY AFTERNOON EXPLORING PARIS' PHOTOGENIC CANAL

Sunday afternoons are ideal for discovering the charms of Paris' lesser-known waterway, when its shops open up and the surrounding streets are closed to traffic, giving it a street-party atmosphere.

Bordered by shaded towpaths and traversed by iron footbridges, the 4.5km-long canal was originally dug out as a water supply in 1825. By the time Marcel Carné's 1938 film *Hôtel du Nord* was set in the canalside hotel (now restaurant) of the same name, it was a major cargo thoroughfare.

The canal's fortunes fell in the 1960s when barge transportation declined. It was slated to be concreted over and turned into a road-way until local residents rallied to save it. When the title character of *Amélie* skipped stones here in 2001, the cheap rents and quaint setting were just starting to lure artists, designers and students, who set up artists' collectives, vintage and offbeat boutiques and a bevy of neoretro cafés and bars.

Today Canal St-Martin is the centre of Paris' *bobo* (bohemian bour-geois) life, but maritime legacies endure, including old swing-bridges that still pivot 90 degrees when barges pass through the canal's double-locks. Boarding a barge offers a completely different perspective of the canal (including underground sections with artistic projections and music) – see p214 for cruise details.

See also p96 for the best places to eat, drink, shop and party in the area.

>12 SACRÉ-CŒUR

HEAD UP TO PARIS' LANDMARK BASILICA

The Eiffel Tower doesn't have a monopoly on panoramas over Paris. Dizzying vistas of the city's rooftops unfurl from the front steps of the Basilique du Sacré-Cœur (Sacred Heart Basilica) atop the 130m-high Butte de Montmartre (Montmartre Hill). And the views just get better when you climb the 234 steps inside the basilica's Roman-Byzantine dome: from up here you can see for 30km on a clear day.

The chapel-lined basilica was built in 1873 to atone for the Franco-Prussian War (1870–71), but wasn't consecrated until 1919. In a sense, atonement here has never stopped: a perpetual prayer 'cycle' that began at the consecration of the basilica continues round the clock to this day.

To save you from at least some of the climb, a funicular railway shuttles up and down a 36m hillside track, offering some stunning views of its own during the 90-second ride.

See also p86.

>PARIS DIARY

Pomp and ceremony have been part and parcel of Parisian culture for centuries. A vast array of cultural and sporting events animate the French capital, and no matter what time of year you visit, you're bound to encounter the city's festive spirit. Extensive event listings appear weekly in the publications *Pariscope* and *L'Officiel des Spectacles,* available from kiosks, newsagents and bookshops each Wednesday. Both are in French but easily navigable. Listings also appear under the 'What's On' section of the tourist office's website (www.parisinfo.fr). See p211 for a list of public holidays.

White cap *(képi blanc)* soldiers of the French Foreign Legion marching in the Bastille Day parade (p26)

PARIS DIARY

Chinese New Year celebrations

JANUARY

Festival des Musiques du Nouvel An

www.parisparade.com

Marching and carnival bands, dance acts and more take over the Palais de Chaillot (p54), Trocadéro, on New Year's Day.

FEBRUARY

Paris, Capitale de la Creation

www.pariscapitaledelacreation.com

Prêt-à-porter (fashion salons, held in January/February and September/October) joins forces with trade shows spanning all aspects of fashion and interior design.

Chinese New Year

www.paris.fr

Dragon parades and lantern-lit festivities are held in late January/early February in Paris' main Chinese districts: the 13e (see p146) and the 3e.

MARCH

Banlieues Bleues

www.banlieuesbleues.org

Paris' outskirts swing to the tunes of jazz, blues, world, soul, funk and R&B during the 'Suburban Blues' festival, with big-name talent taking to the stages and streets over five weeks.

APRIL

Marathon International de Paris

www.parismarathon.com

On your marks... The Paris International Marathon, in early April, starts on the av des Champs-Élysées, 8e, and finishes on av Foch, in the 16e.

Foire du Trône

www.paris.fr

This giant funfair's 350 attractions spread over 10 hectares at the pelouse de Reuilly on the edge of the Bois de Vincennes for eight weeks from late March to mid-May.

The Marathon International de Paris charges down the av des Champs-Élysées

MAY

Internationaux de France de Tennis

www.frenchopen.org in French

The only Grand Slam played on clay, the glamorous French Open tennis tournament hits up from late May to mid-June at Stade Roland Garros (p59).

JUNE

Gay Pride March

www.gaypride.fr in French

Over-the-top floats and costumes parade through the Marais.

Paris Jazz Festival

www.parcfloraldeparis.com

Free jazz concerts take place in the park on weekend afternoons in June and July.

JULY

La Goutte d'Or en Fête

www.gouttedorenfete.org

Raï, reggae, rap and more infuses the multicultural 18e during this week-long world-music festival from around late June to early July.

Bastille Day (14 July)

Flag-waving festivities marking France's national day kick off at 10am with a military

FOOD & WINE FESTIVALS

Food and wine are celebrated with gusto at Paris' gastronomical and oenological festivals. The biggie is the **Salon International de l'Agriculture** (www.salon-agriculture.com), a 10-day agricultural (read: food) fair, held at the Parc des Expositions at Porte de Versailles, 15e, from late February to early March. In June you can try chef-prepared dishes for a mere €5 or so during **Le Grand Fooding de l'Été** (http://lefooding.com in French), with proceeds going to charity. Honey harvested from the Jardin du Luxembourg's apiary is available to taste and buy during late September's two-day **Fête du Miel** (Honey Festival; www.paris.fr).

Wine-wise, the **Fête des Vendages de Montmartre** (www.fetedesvendangesde montmartre.com) sees the minuscule Close du Montmartre vineyard herald its harvest on the second weekend in October. On the third Thursday in November, Parisians debate the merits of the Beaujolais vintage in cafés and bars throughout town during the **Fête du Beaujolais** (www.beaujolaisgourmand.com).

And waiters and waitresses race through central Paris balancing a glass and bottle on a tray during June's **La Course des Garçons de Café** (www.paris.fr).

Racers on the final stage of the Tour de France

and fire-brigade parade along av des Champs-Élysées. At around 11pm, fireworks light up the sky above the Champ de Mars.

Tour de France

www.letour.fr

This prestigious international cycling event culminates with a final dash up the av des Champs-Élysées on the third or fourth Sunday of July.

Paris Plages

www.paris.fr

Paris may be a long way from St-Tropez but from mid-July to mid-August, the ever-expanding 'Paris Beaches' – complete with

sun beds, palm trees and even trucked-in sand – see landlocked Parisians lounge on the banks of the Seine.

Paris Cinéma

www.pariscinema.org

Rare and restored films screen in selected cinemas across the city over two weeks.

AUGUST

Rock en Seine

www.rockenseine.com

Big-name acts rock the Domaine National de St-Cloud on the city's southwestern edge.

Cinéma au Clair de Lune
www.parisinfo.fr
Themed nondubbed film screenings take place under the stars around town during Paris' free 'moonlight cinema'.

SEPTEMBER

Festival d'Automne
www.festival-automne.com
The tourist hordes leave, Parisians return from their holidays and the 'Autumn Festival' of arts mounts citywide exhibitions, concerts, dance and theatre productions from mid-September to December.

European Heritage Days
www.journeesdupatrimoine.culture.fr
During the third weekend in September, step inside otherwise off-limits buildings like the Palais de Élysée.

OCTOBER

Nuit Blanche
www.paris.fr
For one 'White Night', museums across town stay open till the *very* wee hours.

Foire Internationale d'Art Contemporain
www.fiacparis.com
Avant-garde art stars at this five-day contemporary art fair held in late October.

NOVEMBER

Mois de la Photo
www.mep-fr.org
'Photography month' sees exhibitions (some free) set up in galleries, museums and cultural centres.

DECEMBER

Patinoire de l'Hôtel de Ville
www.paris.fr
From early December to early March, twirl on the free outdoor ice-skating rink in front of Paris' town hall (skate hire extra).

New Year's Eve
www.paris.fr
Join in the revelry at blvd St-Michel (5e), place de la Bastille (11e), the Eiffel Tower (7e) and especially the av des Champs-Élysées (8e).

Sculpture in Jardin des Tuileries (p72)

ITINERARIES

The ultimate Parisian itinerary is no itinerary at all, but simply letting yourself be enticed by the city's boulevards and backstreets. Alternatively, try the following suggestions, or cherry-pick amongst them. Start any long weekend on a Friday, as many museums, shops and restaurants – and all street markets – are shut on Monday.

ONE DAY

A 360-degree panorama of Paris' most famous sights makes place de la Concorde (p58) the perfect spot to kick off your visit. Stop at the nearby the Musée de l'Orangerie (p72) to see Monet's *Waterlilies,* before crossing the river to the Musée d'Orsay (p42) for more Monet and other impressionist masters; and the sculpture-filled rose garden at the Musée Rodin (p43). Afterwards, wander west along the Seine to the Eiffel Tower (p39), and catch a Batobus (p214) through the heart of the city to the Jardin des Plantes (p141). Poke around the Latin Quarter (p138) and St-Germain des Prés (p150), taking a break at a historic café (p182) before dinner (p159) and drinks (p162). Book-end your day with a stroll over the lamplit bridges (p184).

TWO DAYS

On your second day, be awed by the Gothic splendour of Notre Dame (p131) and the ethereal Ste-Chapelle (p134), tackle the Musée du Louvre (p73) and amble through the Jardin des Tuileries (p72) and along the av des Champs-Élysées (p53), to the Arc de Triomphe (p52). Cross town via the Église de la Madeleine (p53) to the Centre Pompidou (p69) for avant-garde art and architecture, then browse the boutiques in the Marais (p119) before capping the night off in its bars (p125).

THREE DAYS

Spend your third day winding through the cobbled streets of the artists' enclave Montmartre (p87) up to Sacré-Cœur (p86), then across to the spirited quarter of Belleville (p96) and its surrounds. Try Passage Brady for lunch (p104), trawl Canal St-Martin's canal-banks and backstreets for

---

Top left Mural at the Bastille Metro station **Top right** Detail of sculpture on the Arc de Triomphe (p52)
Bottom A painter captures outdoor café life, Île St-Louis (p130)

ITINERARIES

vintage and new fashions (p102) and arty cafés (p106) before hopping on a canal cruise (p214). Check out the legendary tombs at Cimetière du Père Lachaise (p97) then make your way back to Montmartre for a cabaret spectacle (p92).

FOUR DAYS
With four days you'll have time to make a foray further afield to the gilded palace of Versailles (p166), to the gardens planted and painted by Monet at his house in Giverny (p168), or to sip champagne on its home soil in the city of Reims (p169). Otherwise, check out the skyscrapers at La Défense (see p52), or ramble in one of the city's two forests (Bois de Boulogne, see p59; Bois de Vincennes, see p118). For an evening of grandeur, take in an opera or ballet (p189) – or if you haven't yet had the chance, ascend the Eiffel Tower at night (p10) for glittering views of the City of Light.

RAINY DAY
Buy a chic, handmade Parisian umbrella at Alexandra Sojfer (p156) or a cheap one at Monoprix (p178), then scout out the ornate covered *passages* (arcades; see p62). If you're game, escape the rain below ground in the chilling skull- and bone-lined catacombs (p140). Plan an afternoon in the city's myriad museums and galleries (see p180) before holing up in a café (p176), or cosying up at a jazz club (p187).

FORWARD PLANNING
One month before you go Nail down your accommodation (p172), subscribe to newsletter *Secrets of Paris* (p212), book in for a cooking or wine-tasting course (p188), organise tickets for an opera or ballet (p189) and make reservations for a gastronomic feast (see the Eat sections of the Quarters chapter) or a dinner-and-cabaret (p187).

One week before you go Check the 'What's On' section of www.parisinfo.fr and line up tickets for one of Paris' many festivities, sign up for a free, local-led tour (p42), book a sightseeing 'flight' on the Ballon Eutelsat (p39) and start narrowing down your choice of museums (p180).

One day before you go Pack your comfiest pair of shoes – and a bike helmet if you're planning to use the Vélib' system (p208).

ON A BUDGET

Soak up the atmosphere of the street markets (p14), and take a stroll along the Promenade Plantée (p19), before browsing the bookshops (p182) on the left bank. Feast on a crêpe at Chez Nicos (p145) on historic rue Mouffetard (see p148), and stop in for a drink at the street's lively bars. Pick up half-price tickets (p211) for a concert or theatre production, and hit the city's free museums (p180). If you're here on the first Sunday of the month, you can also catch the national museums for free. For more freebies, see p142.

ON A SUNDAY

Sure, it's Sunday, so most shops are shut, but exceptions include those around Canal St-Martin (p21), and sprawling flea markets (p14) such as the Marché aux Puces de St-Ouen (p88), where you can also catch entertainers performing *chansons* over lunch at Chez Louisette (p92). Otherwise, enjoy a languid brunch (p124), then grab a Berthillon ice cream (p17) and stroll around Île St-Louis (p130), before lounging along with Parisians in the Jardin du Luxembourg (p154). Make your dinner plans (p174) early in the day to avoid being caught short, as many restaurants close.

>QUARTERS

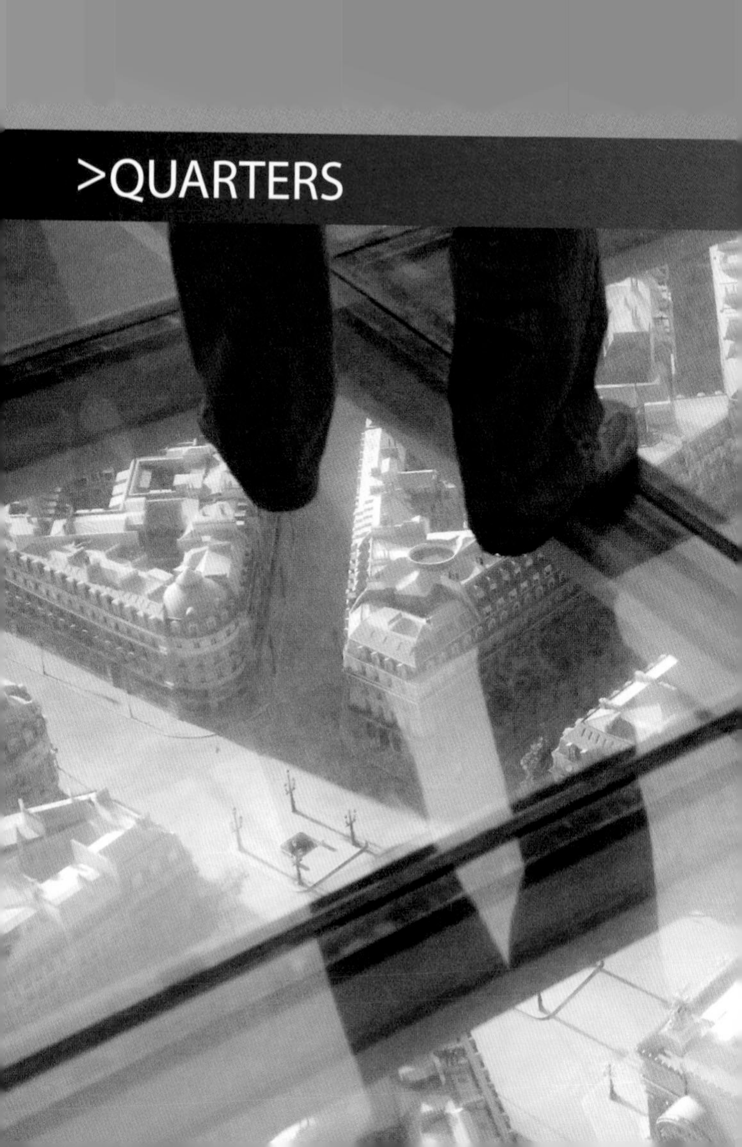

>1 Invalides & Eiffel Tower 38
>2 Arc de Triomphe, Champs-Élysées &
Grands Boulevards 48
>3 Louvre & Les Halles 68
>4 Montmartre 84
>5 Belleville & Surrounds 96
>6 Marais & Bastille 110
>7 The Islands 130
>8 Latin Quarter 138
>9 St-Germain des Prés & Montparnasse 150

Model of Paris on display under the glass floor in the Musée d'Orsay (p42)

QUARTERS

In between Paris' sweeping boulevards and architectural icons is an enchanting maze of backstreets that resemble a very unmetropolis-like collection of villages. Exploring these quarters draws you into the city's true heart. It's this village life that gives Paris its magic.

Best of all, for anyone coming to Paris for a good time, not a long time, is that the city's compact size, mostly flat terrain and efficient public transport make it easy to cover a lot of ground during the most fleeting visit.

Central Paris is split into 20 *arrondissements,* which spiral like a snailshell clockwise from the centre to the *Périphérique* (ring road). *Arrondissement* numbers (1er, 2e etc) form part of all Parisian addresses and are included throughout this book. Overlapping these administrative boundaries are Paris' localised quarters. This chapter pieces the main quarters together in nine interlocked, easily explored sections.

The Invalides and Eiffel Tower area boasts majestic monuments and museums. To its north, on the river's right bank, more major landmarks and ultraluxe shops line the Arc de Triomphe, Champs-Élysées and Grands Boulevards precinct. The postmodern Centre Pompidou, colourful commercial streets and the mecca of all museums make up the Louvre and Les Halles district. Uphill, past sexy, seedy Pigalle, nostalgic Montmartre is crowned by the Sacré Cœur's dove-white domes. Heading east brings you to the rapidly gentrifying Belleville and its surrounds, incorporating Père Lachaise cemetery and hip Canal St-Martin. South towards the Seine you'll find the funky boutiques and bars of the Marais and Bastille. Within the river itself sit the city's two islands, Île de la Cité, guarded by Notre Dame's gargoyles; and intimate, exclusive Île St-Louis. Opposite, the Seine's Left Bank shelters the student cafés and campuses of the Latin Quarter to the east; and the historic literary hangouts gracing chic St-Germain des Prés and Montparnasse to the west and southwest.

In and around these quarters are several fascinating detours worth the trip.

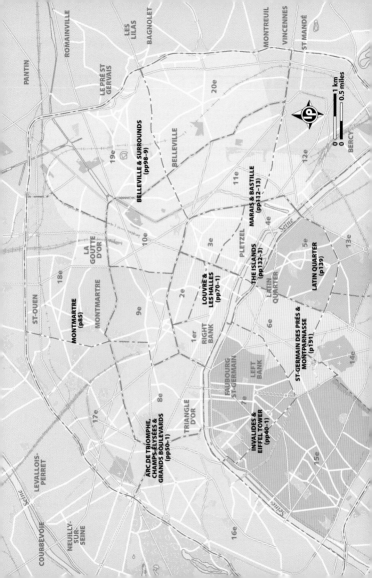

>INVALIDES & EIFFEL TOWER

Stretching west along the Seine's southern bank, the broad boulevards and imposing architecture of the Invalides and Eiffel Tower quarter are Paris at its most bombastic.

This is where you can get up close and personal with the city's symbolic tower, and promenade through the sprawling grounds of the Hôtel des Invalides, the 17th-century war veterans' residence which includes a military museum and Napoleon's tomb. It's where you'll find the private mansion housing the Musée Rodin and its tranquil rose gardens filled with Rodin's sculptures including *The Thinker*. And it's where you can eye the Musée d'Orsay's incredible impressionist art, and peer out over Paris through this art nouveau railway station's glass clockface.

But time hasn't entirely stood still in this *grande dame* of a quarter, as evidenced by the recent opening of Jean Nouvel's black-and-burgundy boxlike masterpiece containing the Musée du Quai Branly, which showcases indigenous art.

INVALIDES & EIFFEL TOWER

◉ SEE
Ballon Eutelsat 1 A6
Champ de Mars 2 D3
Église du Dôme............... 3 F3
Eiffel Tower 4 C2
Hôtel des
  Invalides.................... 5 F3
Musée de
  l'Armée....................... 6 F2
Musée des Égouts
  de Paris...................... 7 E1
Musée d'Orsay............... 8 H2
Musée du Quai Branly 9 D1

Musée Rodin................. 10 F3
Tombeau de
  Napoléon 1er............(see 3)

⚆ DO
École Le Cordon
  Bleu 11 D6

⑪ EAT
Altitude 95 ....(see 13)
L'Arpège..................... 12 G3
Le Jules Verne............. 13 C2
Les Deux Abeilles 14 D1
Les Ombres................(see 8)

Poilâne 15 C3
Restaurant
  Musée d'Orsay ....(see 7)
Rue Cler 16 E2

❦ DRINK
Café Branly ....(see 8)
Café des
  Hauteurs.................(see 7)

★ PLAY
La Pagode................... 17 F3

Please see over for map

The Eiffel Tower rises above an avenue of trees

👁 SEE

🔵 BALLON EUTELSAT

☎ 01 44 26 20 00; www.aeroparis.com
in French; Parc André Citroën, 2 rue de
la Montagne de la Fage, 15e; admission Mon-Fri €10/9, Sat & Sun €12/10;
🕑 9am-9.30pm summer, to 5.30pm
winter; Ⓜ Balard or Lourmel

Drift up and up but not away – this
helium-filled balloon remains teth-
ered to the ground as it lifts you
150m for panoramas of Paris. Confirm ahead as the balloon doesn't
ascend in windy conditions.

🔵 EIFFEL TOWER

☎ 01 44 11 23 23; www.tour-eiffel.fr;
Champ de Mars, 7e; lift 1st fl €4.80/2.50,
2nd fl €7.80/4.30, 3rd fl €12/6, stairs
€4/3.10; 🕑 lifts 9am-12.45am mid-
Jun–Aug (final ascension to top 11pm,
to other levels midnight), 9.30am-
11.45pm Sep–mid-Jun (final ascension
to top 10.30pm, to other levels 11pm),
stairs 9am-12.30am mid-Jun–Aug (final
admittance midnight), 9.30am-6.30pm
Sep–mid-Jun (final admittance 6pm);
Ⓜ Champ de Mars–Tour Eiffel or Bir
Hakeim; ♿

Lifts yo-yo up and down the
north, west and east pillars of
Paris' signature tower (p10);
change lifts on the 2nd floor for
the final ascent to the top. (Anyone nervous will be relieved to
know that the lifts are monitored
by computer, and in the event of
overloading they're automatically
immobilised and unable to leave.)
If you're feeling athletic, you can
take the south pillar's stairs –
some 1665 of them – as far as the
2nd floor. There's wheelchair access to the 1st and 2nd floors.

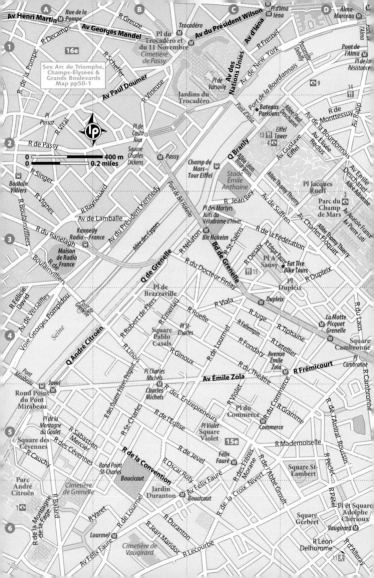

HÔTEL DES INVALIDES

☎ 08 10 11 33 99; www.invalides.org; Esplanade des Invalides, 7e; admission €8/6; ⏱ 10am-6pm Apr-Sep, to 5pm Oct-Mar, closed 1st Mon of month; Ⓜ Invalides; ♿

Built in the 1670s to provide housing for thousands of *invalides* (infirm veterans), this immense complex screens sobering war-time footage at its **Musée de l'Armée** (Military Museum), with weaponry, flag and medal displays. In the Cour de Valeur wing, a new multi-media area is dedicated to former French president Charles de Gaulle (1890–1970). The **Église du Dôme**, which is visible throughout the city, receives its name for its gilded dome. Beneath it, Napoleon's remains lie in the **Tombeau de Napoléon 1er** (Napoleon I's Tomb).

MUSÉE DES ÉGOUTS DE PARIS

☎ 01 53 68 27 81; www.paris.fr; opposite 93 Quai d'Orsay, 7e; admission €4.20/3.40; ⏱ 11am-5pm Sat-Wed

May-Sep, to 4pm Sat-Wed Oct-Apr, closed 2 weeks mid-Jan & when rainfall threatens flooding; Ⓜ Alma-Marceau or RER Pont de l'Alma

Raw sewage runs beneath your feet along 480m of subterranean tunnels at this, yep, working-sewer museum. Exhibits demonstrate the development of Paris' waste-water disposal system, as well as its resident rats (an estimated one in the sewers for every Parisian above ground).

MUSÉE D'ORSAY

☎ 01 40 49 48 14; www.musee-orsay.fr; 62 rue de Lille, 7e; all-day ticket €8/5.50, entry after 4.15pm Tue, Wed & Fri-Sun & after 6pm Thu €5.50; ⏱ 9.30am-6pm Tue, Wed & Fri-Sun, to 9.45pm Thu; Ⓜ Solférino or RER Musée d'Orsay; ♿

Many of the d'Orsay's impressionist, postimpressionist and art nouveau works by some of the mid- to late 19th and early 20th century's foremost artists immortalise Paris. While here, take time out in its sumptuous restaurant and café

MEET THE LOCALS

To see Paris through local eyes, the new, nonprofit **Paris Greeter** (www.parisgreeter.org) service offers free two- to three-hour city tours. A volunteer 'greeter' meets you at your accommodation; tours can accommodate up to six people (children and adults). If there's a part of the city you particularly want to see you can suggest an itinerary; otherwise let your guide show you their favourite spots around Paris. You only need to pay for your fares — and your guide's — if your trip involves public transport. Register your request online at least one week prior to your visit.

(p46). A €12 combination ticket includes entry to the Musée Rodin (right). See also p12.

MUSÉE DU QUAI BRANLY
☎ 01 56 61 70 00; www.quaibranly.fr;
37 quai Branly, 7e; admission €8.50/6,
temporary exhibitions additional €7/5,
combined entry for all exhibitions €10/7;
🕒 11am-7pm Tue, Wed & Sun, to 9pm
Thu-Sat; Ⓜ Alma-Marceau or Bir
Hakeim; ♿
Raked ramps lead through this urban-industrial building to darkened, mesh-encased rooms, which form a sharp contrast to the ancient art and artefacts from Africa, Oceania, Asia and the Americas displayed here. Audioguides cost an additional €5 per person and €2 per additional guide for visitors travelling together. The on-site café (p46) and restaurant, Les Ombres (p46), both have ringside Eiffel tower views.

MUSÉE RODIN
☎ 01 44 18 61 10; www.musee-rodin
.fr; 77 rue de Varenne, 7e; permanent
or temporary exhibition plus garden

Musée Rodin

€6/4, both exhibitions plus garden €9/7, 1st Sun of the month free, garden only €1; ⏰ 9.30am-5.45pm, garden to 6.45pm Tue-Sun Apr-Sep, 9.30am-4.45pm, garden to 5pm Tue-Sun Oct-Mar; Ⓜ Varenne; ♿

This museum's tranquil, rose-clambered garden is home to Rodin's bronze sculptures including *The Thinker* and *Balzac*. Along with the marble monument to love, *The Kiss*, the 18th-century mansion's interior proves that Rodin's talents weren't limited to sculpture alone, with sketches, paintings and engravings, and works by his student/model/muse, Camille Claudel, also on display.

🏃 DO

🏃 ÉCOLE LE CORDON BLEU
Cooking Course

☎ 01 53 68 22 50; www.cordonbleu.edu; 8 rue Léon Delhomme, 15e; Ⓜ Vaugirard or Convention

To really impress your dinner party guests, sign up for a course at this 1895-established culinary school. In addition to its renowned professional training programs, it runs one-day themed workshops (€160) such as baked goods and two- and four-day courses (€299/869) on classic and modern sauces, bread and pastry making,

View from beneath the Eiffel Tower looking out to Parc du Champ de Mars

and also offers wine-tasting and wine-pairing classes.

🛍 SHOP

Most of the quarter's museums sell high-quality souvenirs (French for 'memories'), such as art books, postcards, prints, and scarves imprinted with classic works of art.

🍴 EAT

🍴 L'ARPÈGE
Gastronomic €€€
☎ 01 47 05 09 06; www.alain-passard .com in French; 84 rue de Varenne, 7e; ⏰ lunch & dinner Mon-Fri; Ⓜ Varenne
L'Arpège's warm, intimate dining room belies its *haute cuisine,* which gives its flashier rivals a run for their money. Chef Alain Passard excels in seafood, such as truffle-infused lobster, and inspired desserts like his signature tomatoes stuffed with a veritable orchard of a dozen dried and fresh fruits and served with aniseed ice cream. Book at least two weeks ahead.

🍴 LE JULES VERNE
Gastronomic €€€
☎ 01 45 55 61 44; www.restaurants -toureiffel.com; Champ de Mars, 7e; ⏰ lunch & dinner by reservation; Ⓜ Champ de Mars–Tour Eiffel or Bir Hakeim

> ### PANORAMIC PICNIC
> The expansive **Parc du Champ de Mars** (⏰ 24hr) lawns sprawling at the base of the Eiffel Tower are as scenic a picnic spot as you'll find in Paris. Buy a signature sourdough loaf from **Poilâne** (p46), and pick up fresh sandwich fillings, pastries and wine along the 7e's **rue Cler** (⏰ 7am or 8am-7pm or 7.30pm Tue-Sat, 8am-noon Sun), which buzzes with local shoppers, especially on weekends.

Alain Ducasse and chef Pascal Féraud have recently elevated the cuisine at Le Jules Verne – on the Eiffel Tower's 2nd level, accessed by private lift – on par with its incomparable setting (advance bookings essential). The less rarefied **Altitude 95** (☎ 01 45 55 20 04) on the 1st level serves moderately priced lunch and dinner daily, along with Seine views from its bay windows. Cheaper still, you can picnic on the lawns beneath the tower (see above).

🍴 LES DEUX ABEILLES
Salon de Thé €
☎ 01 45 55 64 04; 189 rue de l'Université, 7e; ⏰ 9am-7pm Mon-Sat; Ⓜ Alma-Marceau or Bir Hakeim
The faded floral wallpaper and even the somewhat stuffy service make this tearoom a charmingly old-fashioned stop for authentic

baked treats such as fluffy quiche, Madeline cakes and *clafoutis aux cerises* (cherry flan).

🍴 LES OMBRES
Gastronomic   €€€

☎ 01 47 53 68 00; www.lesombres
-restaurant.com; 27 quai Branly, 7e;
🕐 lunch & dinner; Ⓜ Alma-Marceau or
Bir Hakeim

Paris not only gained a new museum in the Musée du Quai Branly, it also gained this steel-and-glass-roofed 5th-floor restaurant. Named 'the shadows' for the patterns cast by the Eiffel Tower's ironwork and its own roof webbing, the dramatic views are complemented by Arno Busquet's creations such as ewe cheese ravioli with mango and sweet tomato sauce, or slow-cooked, caramelised pork belly.

POILÂNE *Bakery*   €

☎ 01 45 79 11 49; www.poilane.fr;
49 blvd de Grenelle, 15e; 🕐 7.15am-
8.15pm Tue-Sun; Ⓜ Dupleix

Poilâne's handcrafted, rounded sourdough loaves, made with stone-milled flour and Guérande sea salt and fired in a wood stove, are a hefty 1.9kg but you can buy just a half- or quarter-loaf. This is the second of Poilâne's two Paris *boulangeries* (bakeries); its inaugural shop is in the 6e (p162).

🍸 DRINK

🍸 CAFÉ BRANLY
Café, Salon de Thé

☎ 01 56 61 70 00; www.quaibranly
.fr; 27 quai Branly; 🕐 lunch noon-3pm,
tearoom 3pm until museum closing;
Ⓜ Alma-Marceau or Bir Hakeim

In the shadow of the Eiffel Tower, the Musée du Quai Branly's café sits amid reflecting pools and gardens. Light meals like a *tartine Parisienne* (open sandwich of Parisian ham, Emmental cheese, tomatoes and mustard-butter) offer an inexpensive alternative to dining in style upstairs at Les Ombres (opposite).

AS TIME GOES BY

Within the **Musée d'Orsay** (p42), time literally ticks by before your eyes at the **Café des Hauteurs** (🕐 10am-5pm Tue, Wed & Fri-Sun, 10.30am-9pm Thu), which looks out over Paris through the former station's glass clockface. The café's rooftop terrace also has panoramic views. Views of the clock itself extend from the museum's mezzanine.

Time has scarcely changed the **Restaurant Musée d'Orsay** (🕐 lunch Tue-Sun, dinner Thu, restaurant tearoom 3.30-5.30pm Tue, Wed & Fri-Sun), the museum's — and formerly the train station's — chandeliered restaurant. It serves well-priced lunch *menus* (adult/child €16.50/7.60), as well as dinner *menus* on Thursdays (€42).

⭐ PLAY

This stately quarter doesn't rock after dark, but night owls will find plenty of options nearby just north of the river (see p66) and east in Montparnasse (p164).

⭐ **LA PAGODE** *Cinema*
☎ 01 45 55 48 48; 57bis rue de Babylone;
🕙 vary; Ⓜ St-François Xavier
This 19th-century Japanese pagoda was converted into a cinema in the 1930s and remains the most atmospheric spot in Paris to catch arthouse and classic films.

>ARC DE TRIOMPHE, CHAMPS-ÉLYSÉES & GRANDS BOULEVARDS

Pomp and grandeur reign in the Arc de Triomphe, Champs-Élysées and Grands Boulevards quarter. This is where Baron Haussmann famously reshaped the Parisian cityscape. Haussmann's commanding reformation revolves around the Arc de Triomphe, from which 12 avenues radiate like spokes of a wheel. Of them, the most celebrated (and the scene of Paris' major celebrations) is the Champs-Élysées, which forms part of the *Axe Historique*. Nowadays, this 'Grand Axis' stretches from La Défense through the vast place de la Concorde and beyond. Nearby, nine grand boulevards, flanked by fashionable department stores, stand on the site of the old city ramparts.

The quarter's splendour extends to its dining scene, with some of France's finest *haute cuisine* chefs established here; its couture scene, with the likes of Chanel, Dior, Lacroix and Yves Saint Laurent in residence; and cultural venues, including the Palais Garnier opera house and the Palais de Tokyo's contemporary art installations.

ARC DE TRIOMPHE, CHAMPS-ÉLYSÉES & GRANDS BOULEVARDS

⊙ SEE

Arc de Triomphe	1	B3
Av des Champs-Élysées	2	D3
Belle Époque Toilets	3	F3
Cinéaqua	4	B5
Cité de l'Architecture et du Patrimoine	5	B5
Église de la Madeleine	6	F3
Galerie-Musée Baccarat	7	B4
Galeries du Panthéon Bouddhique du Japon et de la Chine	8	B4
Jardins du Trocadéro	9	B5
Maison de Balzac	10	A6
Musée d'Art Moderne de la Ville de Paris	11	C4
Musée de la Marine	12	A5
Musée de l'Homme	13	A5
Musée du Parfum	14	G3
Musée du Vin	15	A6
Musée Galliera de la Mode de la Ville de Paris	16	C4
Musée Guimet des Arts Asiatiques	17	B4
Musée Jacquemart-André	18	D2
Palais de Chaillot	19	B5
Palais de Tokyo	20	C4
Parc de Monceau	21	D2
Place de la Concorde	22	E4
Place de la Madeleine	23	F4
Place Vendôme	24	F4
Théâtre-Musée des Capucines	25	F3

🏃 DO

Les Coulisses du Chef Cours de Cuisine Olivier Berté	26	H4

🏠 SHOP

Boutique Maille	27	F4
Chanel	28	D4
Chloé	29	D4
Chloé	30	E3
Christian Dior	31	D4
Christian Lacroix	32	E3
Commes des Garçons	33	E3
Drugstore Publicis	34	C3
Eres	35	F3
Fauchon	36	F3
Flower Market	37	F3
Fromagerie Alléosse	38	C2
Galerie Vivienne	39	H4
Galeries Lafayette	40	G3
Givenchy	41	C4
Guerlain	42	D3
Hermès	43	F4
Jean-Paul Gaultier	44	C3
La Maison de la Truffe	45	F3
La Maison du Miel	46	F3
Lancel	47	C3
Lanvin	48	F4
Le Printemps	49	F3
Legrand Filles & Fils	50	H4
Louis Vuitton	51	C3
Passage des Panoramas	52	H3
Passage Jouffroy	53	H3
Passage Verdeau	54	H3
Virgin Megastore	55	D3
Yves Saint Laurent	56	E4

🍴 EAT

Alain Ducasse au Plaza Athénée	57	C4
Aux Lyonnais	58	H3
Guy Savoy	59	B2
Koba	60	G3
Le Bistrot du Sommelier	61	E3
Le Cristal Room	(see 7)	
Le J'Go	62	H3
Le Roi du Pot au Feu	63	F3
Maison Prunier	64	B3
Musée du Vin Restaurant	(see 15)	

🍸 DRINK

Bar Hemingway	65	F4
Harry's New York Bar	66	G4
Hédiard	67	F3
Ladurée	68	C3

★ PLAY

Au Limonaire	69	H3
Crazy Horse	70	C4
Le Baron	71	C4
Le Lido	72	C3
Le Queen	73	C3
L'Olympia	74	F3
Palais Garnier	75	G3
Social Club	76	H4

Please see over for map

QUARTERS

👁 SEE

🄾 ARC DE TRIOMPHE

☎ 01 55 37 73 77; www.monuments
-nationaux.fr; place Charles de Gaulle,
8e; viewing platform €9/6.50; ⏰ 10am-
11pm Apr-Sep, to 10.30pm Oct-Mar;
Ⓜ Charles de Gaulle-Étoile

If anything rivals the tower as the
symbol of Paris, it's this magnificent 1836-built monument to
Napoleon's 1805 victory at Austerlitz, which stands a proud 50m in
the centre of the Étoile (star), the
world's largest roundabout. Don't
attempt to cross the road if you
value your life – staircases lead

ARC DE TRIOMPHE, CHAMPS-ÉLYSÉES & GRANDS BOULEVARDS

WORTH THE TRIP – LA DÉFENSE

The futuristic glass-and-chrome skyline of the La Défense business district makes you half
expect a spaceship to dock on its vast concrete concourses.

La Défense rises just northwest of the *Périphérique* (ring road), and is best visited on a
weekday (excluding August) as its streets are eerily deserted outside office hours.

The area is named not for military connections but for an 1883 sculpture here commemo-
rating the defence of Paris during the Franco-Prussian War of 1870–71. Construction of its
highrises began in the 1950s. Today there are over 100 skyscrapers, mostly office buildings,
but this number is rapidly rising. New additions include three towers scraping 300m (no
height limits here!): US architect Thom Mayne's Tour Phare, French architects Denis Valode
and Jean Pistre's Gererali Tower (both due for completion by 2013), and Jean Nouvel's 71-
storey **Tour Signal** (p141), due for completion in 2015, which in addition to office space will
incorporate a hotel and shops in a push to turn La Défense into a 24-hour 'minicity'. These
three upcoming towers will each be over a third taller than those currently at La Défense and
just 23m shorter than the Eiffel Tower.

The dramatic gateway to the area is the 110m-high white Carrara marble and grey granite
Grande Arche (☎ 01 49 07 27 27; www.grandearche.com in French; 1 parvis de la Défense;
admission €9/7.50; ⏰ 10am-8pm Apr-Sep, to 7pm Oct-Mar; Ⓜ La Défense Grande Arche),
designed by Danish architect Johan-Otto von Sprekelsen and inaugurated on 14 July 1989.
A glass lift takes you to a gallery and a rooftop with views stretching along the Grand Axis.
Adjacent to the arch is a contemporary 'art garden', **Le Parvis**, with sculptures and murals,
including works by Miró and César.

Fascinating drawings, architectural plans and scale models, including projects that were
never built, are displayed at the **Musée de La Défense** (☎ 01 47 74 84 24; www.ladefense
.fr; 15 place de la Défense; admission free; ⏰ 9am-5.15pm Mon-Fri; Ⓜ La Défense Grande
Arche). At the same premises, the **Espace Info-Défense** information office (same hours) has
maps outlining walking tours through this very un-Parisian part of Paris.

For more on Paris' contemporary architecture, see p183.

beneath the traffic-choked boulevards to pedestrian tunnels (not linked to metro tunnels) that bring you out beneath the intricately carved triumphal arch. Climbing another 284 steps brings you to the top of the arch for swooping views down the Champs-Élysées.

AV DES CHAMPS-ÉLYSÉES

M Charles de Gaulle–Étoile, George V, Franklin D Roosevelt or Champs-Élysées Clemenceau
No trip to Paris is complete without strolling this elegant, tree-shaded avenue lined with luxury shops. Named for the Elysian Fields ('heaven' in Greek mythology), the Champs-Élysées is the final stretch of the Tour de France (p27), and is where Paris turns out for both organised and impromptu celebrations.

CINÉAQUA

☎ 01 40 69 23 23; www.cineaqua.com; 2 av des Nations Unies, 16e; admission €19.50/15.50; ☼ 10am-8pm, final entry 6pm Thu, 7pm rest of week; M Trocadéro; &
'Ciné' refers to the cinema screens and animation studio at this state-of-the-art, kid-friendly attraction adjoining the Jardins du Trocadéro (p54), but the main draw is the 'aqua'. Over 500 aquatic species, including some foreboding sharks, glide through this new

The illuminated Arc de Triomphe at dusk

aquarium. One of its huge tanks forms the backdrop to the onsite Japanese café-restaurant, Ozu. Regular concerts and events are posted on the website.

ÉGLISE DE LA MADELEINE

☎ 01 44 51 69 00; www.eglise -lamadeleine.com in French; place de la Madeleine, 8e; ☼ 9.30am-7pm; M Madeleine
Styled like an austere Greek temple, with 52 Corinthian columns, the interior of the Church of St Mary Magdalene is much more ornate, decorated with gilt, marble and frescoes. The colossal organ

above the main entrance on the southern side is played during Sunday Mass.

GALERIE MUSÉE BACCARAT

☎ 01 40 22 11 00; www.baccarat.com; 11 place des États-Unis, 16e; admission €5/3.50; ☉ 10am-6.30pm Mon & Wed-Sat; M Boissière or Iéna; ☒

Showcasing services designed for illustrious dining tables over the centuries, this crystal museum occupies striking rococo-style premises in the ritzy 16e. Its glittering gastronomic restaurant, Le Cristal Room, opens for lunch and dinner Monday to Saturday; book *way* ahead on ☎ 01 40 22 11 10.

JARDINS DU TROCADÉRO

M Trocadéro; ☒

By night, dramatic floodlighting illuminates these fountained gardens adjacent to the Palais de Chaillot (p56).

MAISON DE BALZAC

☎ 01 55 74 41 80; www.balzac.paris.fr in French; 47 rue Raynouard, 16e; admission free, temporary exhibitions €4/3; ☉ 10am-6pm Tue-Sun; M Passy or Kennedy Radio France

Nonliterary junkies can cross this one off their lists, but Balzac fans will be fascinated by the prolific French novelist's little cottage (rented between 1840 and 1847 in

Crystal chandeliers adorn the main hall at Galerie Musée Baccarat

his housekeeper's name to avoid his creditors) where he wrote for 18-hour days, fuelled by 'torrents' of coffee.

 MUSÉE D'ART MODERNE DE LA VILLE DE PARIS

☎ 01 53 67 40 00; www.mam.paris.fr in French; 11 av du Président Wilson, 16e; admission €5/2.50, temporary exhibits adult €5-9, concession €2.50-5.50; ⏱ 10am-6pm Tue, Wed & Fri-Sun, to 10pm Thu; Ⓜ Iéna; ♿

Housed in the Electricity Pavilion from the 1937 Exposition Universelle (World Fair), the city's Modern Art Museum spans virtually every major artistic movement of the 20th and nascent 21st centuries – fauvism, cubism, dadaism, surrealism, the School of Paris, expressionism, abstractionism and so on – by artists including Matisse, Picasso, Braque, Soutine, Modigliani and Chagall.

MUSÉE DU PARFUM

☎ 01 47 42 04 56; www.fragonard.com; 9 rue Scribe, 2e; admission free; ⏱ 9am-6pm Mon-Sat, to 5pm Sun; Ⓜ Opéra

The secrets of perfume-making are revealed at this museum run by Grasse-based *parfumerie* Fragonard in a beautiful 1860 townhouse designed by a protégé of Garnier. Its essences are sold mainly to factories, so you're unlikely to recognise the scents, but you can, of course,

Musée du Parfum

buy them here cheaply. Just south, at 39 blvd des Capucines, 2e, its 1900-built annexe, the **Théâtre-Musée des Capucines** (admission free; ⏱ 9am-6pm Mon-Sat), concentrates on the bottling process and bottles, including Bohemian crystal.

MUSÉE DU VIN

☎ 01 45 25 63 26; www.museeduvin paris.com; rue des Eaux, 5 square Charles Dickens, 16e; admission €8.90/7.50, restaurant diners free, audioguide €2; 10am-6pm Tue-Sun; Ⓜ Passy

Paris' Wine Museum not only contains displays of ancient viticultural equipment but also offers wine courses (some in English; €45 for two hours); tastings (from €14); and has an excellent restaurant serving lunch from Tuesday to Saturday by reservation (two-course *menus* from €25).

MUSÉE GALLIERA DE LA MODE DE LA VILLE DE PARIS

☎ 01 56 52 86 00; www.galliera.paris.fr; 10 av Pierre 1er de Serbie, 16e; admission €7/5.50; ⏱ 10am-6pm Tue-Sun during temporary exhibitions; Ⓜ Iéna
This Italianate villa and its luxuriant gardens are a fitting backdrop for Paris' Fashion Museum. Call ahead as it's only open when it's staging a temporary exhibition.

MUSÉE GUIMET DES ARTS ASIATIQUES

☎ 01 56 52 53 00; www.museeguimet .fr; 6 place d'Iéna, 16e; permanent exhibits €6.50/4.50, temporary exhibits €7/5, combined permanent & temporary exhibits €8.50/6; ⏱ Musée Guimet des Arts Asiatiques 10am-6pm Wed-Mon, Japanese gardens 1-5pm Wed-Mon; Ⓜ Iéna; ♿
France's leading Museum of Asian Art incorporates sculptures, paintings and *objets d'art* from Afghanistan, India, Nepal, Pakistan, Tibet, Cambodia, China, Japan and Korea. Buddhist art is displayed at the nearby annexe **Galeries du Panthéon Bouddhique du Japon et de la Chine** (Buddhist Pantheon Galleries of Japan & China; 19 av Iéna; admission free; ⏱ 10am-

6pm Wed-Mon). Afterwards, zen out in the Galeries' Japanese gardens.

MUSÉE JACQUEMART-ANDRÉ

☎ 01 45 62 11 59; www.musee-jacque mart-andre.com; 158 blvd Haussmann, 8e; admission €10/7.30; ⏱ museum 10am-6pm, tearoom 11.45am-5.45pm; Ⓜ Miromesnil
Works by Rembrandt, Van Dyck, Bernini, Botticelli and Donatello, among other masterpieces collected by Édouard André and his portraitist wife Nélie Jacquemart, are intimately displayed in this exquisite mid-19th-century residence. A double-helix marble staircase dominates its winter garden, which houses tropical plants. Be sure to at least peek at the frescoed tearoom.

PALAIS DE CHAILLOT

place du Trocadéro et du 11 November, 16; Ⓜ Trocadéro; ♿
The terrace separating the eastern and western wings of the Palais de Chaillot offers a stunning panorama of the river, the Eiffel Tower and the Jardins du Trocadéro (p54). The western wing incorporates the **Musée de l'Homme** (Museum of Mankind; ☎ 01 44 05 72 72; www.mnhn .fr; admission €7/5; ⏱ 9.45am-5.15pm Mon & Wed-Fri, 10am-6.30pm Sat & Sun), with some interesting ethnographical exhibits; and the **Musée de la Marine**

WORTH THE TRIP – MUSÉE MARMOTTAN

Paris' abundance of art means that the **Musée Marmottan** (☎ 01 44 96 50 33; www .marmottan.com; 2 rue Louis Boilly, 16e; admission €9/5.50; ⏰ 11am-9pm Tue, to 6pm Wed-Sun; Ⓜ La Muette; ♿), secluded in the Duke of Valmy's former hunting lodge, two blocks east of the **Bois de Boulogne** (p59), remains a little-visited gem. The Marmottan houses the world's largest collection of Claude Monet's works, including his *Impression: Sunrise*, which gave rise to the name of the impressionist movement. On the upper levels are numerous works by the impressionist master, along with paintings by Gauguin, Sisley, Pissarro, Renoir, Degas and Manet. Downstairs are paintings from Monet's spectacular *Waterlilies* series.

(Maritime Museum; ☎ 01 53 65 69 69; www .musee-marine.fr; admission €6.50/4.50; ⏰ 10am-6pm Wed-Mon), with an amazing collection of model ships. French architecture and heritage intertwine over three floors of the Palais' eastern wing at the **Cité de l'Architecture et du Patrimoine** (☎ 01 58 51 52 00; www.citechaillot.fr in French; admission €8/5; ⏰ 11am-7pm Mon, Wed & Fri-Sun, to 9pm Thu). Contemporary architecture buffs should head to the 2nd-floor Galerie d'Architecture Moderne & Contemporaine (Gallery of Modern and Contemporary Architecture).

◉ PALAIS DE TOKYO

☎ 01 47 23 38 86; www.palaisdetokyo .com; 13 av du Président Wilson, 16e; admission €6/4.50; ⏰ noon-midnight Tue-Sun; Ⓜ Iéna; ♿
The Tokyo Palace, created for the 1937 Exposition Universelle and now a contemporary art space, has no permanent collection.

Instead its shell-like interior of polished concrete and steel is the stark backdrop for rotating, often interactive art installations. There's a great €15 deal on admission plus a *plat du jour* and coffee at the café, which is something of an art installation itself, with bright lime- and fuchsia-coloured furnishings and oversized elliptical light fittings. DJs often hit the decks at night.

◉ PARC DE MONCEAU

blvd de Courcelles; ⏰ sunrise-sunset; Ⓜ Monceau
These 18th-century English-style gardens contain follies that include fluted Corinthian columns, winding walking paths and a rotunda. They were a favourite with Marcel Proust when he lived nearby, and they are frequented by fashionable Parisians today, especially on lovely Sunday afternoons.

⊙ PLACE DE LA CONCORDE

Ⓜ Concorde; ♿

Paris spreads around you, with views of the Eiffel Tower, the Seine and along the Champs-Élysées, when you stand in the city's largest square, laid out in 1775. Its 3300-year-old pink granite obelisk was a gift from Egypt in 1831.

⊙ PLACE VENDÔME

Ⓜ Tuileries or Opéra; ♿

In 1796 Napoleon married Josephine in building No 3 of this octagonal 'square'. Its colonnades now shelter boutiques as well as the drop-dead-posh Hôtel Ritz. The square's 43.5m bronze-and-stone column commemorates Napoleon's battle at Austerlitz, with bas-reliefs illustrating his subsequent victories, and a crowning statue depicting the great (little) leader as a Roman emperor.

🏃 DO

🏃 LES COULISSES DU CHEF COURS DE CUISINE OLIVIER BERTÉ *Cooking Course*

☎ 01 40 26 14 00; www.coursdecuisine paris.com; 2nd fl, 7 rue Paul Lelong, 2e; **Ⓜ Bourse**

The cookery instruction offered by Les Coulisses du Chef Cours de Cuisine Olivier Berté is ideal for getting a handle on the basics. Three-hour lessons (€100) take place at 10.30am from Wednesday to Saturday, with an additional class from 6pm to 9pm on Friday. Courses cater for kids over 12 (€30). Advance bookings essential.

Detail of bas-reliefs on a column at Place Vendôme

WORTH THE TRIP – BOIS DE BOULOGNE

Located on Paris' western edge, the rambling woods of Bois de Boulogne encompass charming château gardens, sports venues, and playgrounds for children and children at heart.

Midsummer days are idyllic for boating on Lac Inférieur, the largest of the woods' lakes and ponds. **Row boats** (🕙 10am-6pm mid-Mar–mid-Oct; Ⓜ Av Henri Martin) cost around €10 per hour.

Irises, roses and waterlilies splash colour across the lush **Parc de Bagatelle** (🕙 9.30am-5pm to 8pm depending on the season) in the woods' northwestern corner, surrounding the 1775-built **Château de Bagatelle** (☎ 01 40 67 97 00; route de Sèvres à Neuilly, 16e; admission €3/1.50; 🕙 9am-6pm Apr-Sep, to 5pm Oct-Mar), while plants, flowers and trees mentioned in Shakespearean plays flourish in the poetic Jardin Shakespeare.

Every Parisian kid is familiar with the **Jardin d'Acclimatation** (☎ 01 40 67 90 82; www.jardindacclimatation.fr in French; av du Mahatma Gandhi; admission €2.70/1.35; 🕙 10am-7pm May-Sep, to 6pm Oct-Apr; Ⓜ Les Sablons), an amusement park filled with rides and entertainment for tots. A little narrow-gauge train (€2.70 return) runs to the park from Porte Maillot.

At the woods' southern end, the Stade Roland Garros is home to the French Open tennis tournament as well as its museum, the **Tenniseum-Musée de Roland Garros** (☎ 01 47 43 48 48; www.rolandgarros.com; 2 av Gordon Bennett, 16e; admission €7.50/4, with stadium tour €15/10; 🕙 10am-6pm Wed & Fri-Sun; Ⓜ Porte d'Auteuil). The museum has several hundred hours of footage, including player interviews. Book ahead for stadium tours; English-language tours usually depart at 11am and 3pm. Nearby are two horse-racing tracks: the Hippodrome de Longchamp for flat races and the Hippodrome d'Auteuil for steeplechases.

The 845-hectare woods are ideal to discover by bike. **Paris Cycles** (☎ 01 47 47 76 50; per hr €5; 🕙 10am-7pm mid-Apr–mid-Oct) rents wheels from opposite the Porte Sablons entrance to the Jardin d'Acclimatation, and from the northern end of Lac Inférieur (Ⓜ Av Foch).

(Note that after dark – and occasionally during the day in more remote corners – the Bois de Boulogne is a favourite with prostitutes of all persuasions.)

🛍 SHOP

🏷 **BOUTIQUE MAILLE** *Food*

☎ 01 40 15 06 00; www.maille.com; 6 place de la Madeleine, 8e; 🕙 10am-7pm Mon-Sat; Ⓜ Madeleine

In a tucked-away corner of place de la Madeleine, Maille special-ises in mustard. You can buy it premade, or have an astonishing 30 different varieties prepared to complement various cuisines. It also sells high-quality vinegars.

ARC DE TRIOMPHE, CHAMPS-ÉLYSÉES & GRANDS BOULEVARDS

TRY BEFORE YOU BUY

French clothing *tailles* (sizes) vary not only from overseas, but elsewhere in Europe. For example, a women's dress size 8 in the UK (size 6 in the US) is a 36 in France, but a 34 in Germany or Spain, and a 40 in Italy. Some French labels use the simpler T1, T2 (small, medium) etc, but to be sure, head to a *cabine d'essayage* (fitting room).

Shoes are more standardised: a UK women's size 5 (7½ in the US), for instance, is a 38 Europe-wide.

The website www.onlineconversion.com/clothing has men's and women's shoe and clothing conversions for multiple countries.

CHLOÉ *Fashion*
☎ 01 47 23 00 08; www.chloe.com
in French; 44 av Montaigne, 8e;
🕙 10.30am-7pm Mon-Sat; Ⓜ George V
Bold prints, bohemian layers and uneven hemlines have given street cred to this 1956-established Paris-ian label. There's another boutique at 54 rue du Faubourg St-Honoré, 8e, which keeps the same hours.

Decadent treats entice passers-by at Fauchon

DRUGSTORE PUBLICIS
Department Store
☎ 01 44 43 79 00; www.publicisdrug
store.com; 131 av des Champs-Élysées;
Ⓜ Charles de Gaulle–Étoile
An institution since 1958, this revamped former haunt of Serge Gainsbourg (see p152) and Cath-erine Deneuve now incorporates a glassed-in, wi-fied brasserie and bar, *épicerie*, pharmacy and news-agent (all open from 8am to 2am); and a wine *cave* (cellar), cigar bar and beauty salon (all open from 11am to 11.30pm).

ERES *Fashion*
☎ 01 47 42 28 82; www.eres.fr; 2 rue
Tronchet, 8e; 🕙 10am-7pm Mon-Sat;
Ⓜ Madeleine
Before you and your suntan oil hit Paris Plages (p27), shimmy

into a swimsuit from this sleek beachwear boutique. In addition to shapely one-pieces and bikinis (with tops and bottoms sold separately), Eres also does its own line of lingerie.

☐ FAUCHON *Food & Drink*

☎ 01 47 42 60 11; www.fauchon.fr in French; 26-30 place de la Madeleine, 8e; ⏰ 8.30am-7pm Mon-Sat; Ⓜ Madeleine
Many a lavish Parisian dinner party has been catered for by this famous pair of glossy black-and-fuchsia-pink shops. Beautifully wrapped delicacies include pâté de foie gras and jams.

☐ FROMAGERIE ALLÉOSSE *Food & Drink*

☎ 01 46 22 50 45; www.alleosse.com; 13 rue Poncelet, 17e; ⏰ 9am-1pm & 4-7pm Tue-Thu, 9am-1pm & 3.30-7pm Fri & Sat, 9am-1pm Sun; Ⓜ Ternes
The only *fromagerie* in Paris with its own underground cellars, cheeses here are appropriately sectioned into five main categories: *fromage*

de chèvre (goat's cheese), *fromage à pâte persillée* (veined or blue cheese), *fromage à pâte molle* (soft cheese), *fromage à pâte demi-dure* (semihard cheese), and *fromage à pâte dure* (hard cheese).

☐ GALERIES LAFAYETTE *Department Store*

☎ 01 42 82 34 56; www.galeries lafayette.com; 40 blvd Haussmann, 9e; ⏰ 9.30am-7.30pm Mon-Wed, Fri & Sat, to 9pm Thu, gourmet food section to 8.30pm Mon-Wed, Fri & Sat, 9pm Thu; Ⓜ Auber or Chaussée d'Antin
Beneath a stained-glass dome, this opulent department store stocks innumerable fashion labels and stages free catwalk shows at 3pm Friday (bookings ☎ 01 42 82 30 25). Stunning views of the city unfold from the rooftop café. Its homewares store, Lafayette Maison, is at 35 blvd Haussmann.

☐ GUERLAIN *Perfume, Spa*

☎ boutique 01 45 62 52 57, spa bookings 01 45 62 11 21; www.guerlain.com;

PLACE DE LA MADELEINE

Tantalising fine-food shops garland the **Église de la Madeleine** (p53) on and around place de la Madeleine.

The grand staircase on the church's southern side offers spectacular views of place de la Concorde's obelisk and the Invalides' gold dome. To the east, the colourful **flower market** (⏰ 8am-7.30pm Tue-Sun) has been trading here since 1832. Below ground in the adjacent **public toilets** (⏰ 10am-noon & 1-6.15pm) exquisite **belle époque tiling** can be seen, for the cost of loose change.

QUARTERS

ARC DE TRIOMPHE, CHAMPS-ÉLYSÉES & GRANDS BOULEVARDS

68 av des Champs-Élysées, 8e; ⏰ boutique 10.30am-8pm Mon-Sat, 3-7pm Sun, spa 9am-7pm Mon-Wed, to 8pm Thu-Sat; Ⓜ Franklin D Roosevelt

At this 1912 *parfumerie* you can shop for scents including the namesake of the shop's address, the gold-and-pink-packaged Champs-Élysées, or take a decadent beauty treatment at the glistening toffee-tiled spa.

🏠 LA MAISON DE LA TRUFFE
Food & Drink

☎ 01 42 65 53 22; 19 place de la Madeleine, 8e; ⏰ shop 9am-10pm Mon-Sat, restaurant noon-10.30pm Mon-Sat; Ⓜ Madeleine

You can buy pricey 'black diamond' truffles (which can be cooked) and even pricier elusive white truffles (always eaten raw) at this boutique or taste them in pastas, eggs and other dishes at the on-site restaurant. It also sells

sandwiches such as brie or foie gras, laced with truffles, to take away from around €8 to €12.

🏠 LA MAISON DU MIEL
Food & Drink

☎ 01 47 42 26 70; www.maisondumiel .com; 24 rue Vignon, 9e; ⏰ 9.30am-7pm Mon-Sat; Ⓜ Madeleine

More than 50 varieties of honey produced throughout France and the world gleam on the shelves of this 1898-established, family-run 'honey house'.

🏠 LANCEL *Accessories*

☎ 01 56 89 15 70; www.lancel.com; 127 av des Champs-Élysées; ⏰ 10.30am-8pm Mon-Sat; Ⓜ Charles de Gaulle–Étoile

With its metallic-silver handbags dangling from the ceiling and open racks of luscious totes, this handbag purveyor is stealing thunder from its neighbour Louis Vuitton.

CITIES IN MINIATURE

Paris' covered passages first appeared in the 1820s, numbering 150 by the mid-19th century. Walter Benjamin's *The Arcades Project*, written between 1927 and 1940, uses these exquisite 'cities in miniature' to critique Parisian life, including cafés, collecting, commodity fetishism, fashion, window displays, advertising, architecture, photography and progress.

In today's remaining 18 passages, you'll find jewellery, fashion, homewares, memorabilia – even dolls' houses. Among the most beautiful:

Galerie Vivienne (6 rue Vivienne to 4 rue des Petits Champs, 2e)
Passage des Panoramas (off rue Vivienne, 2e)
Passage du Grand Cerf (Map pp70-1; 145 rue St-Denis to 10 rue Dussoubs, 2e)
Passage Jouffroy & Passage Verdeau (10-12 blvd Montmartre, 9e)

GOLDEN TRIANGLE

The well-heeled **Triangle d'Or** (Golden Triangle; M George V, Franklin D Roosevelt or Alma Marceau) is home to historic *haute couture* flagships including the following:

Chanel (40-42 av Montaigne, 8e)
Christian Dior (30 av Montaigne, 8e)
Christian Lacroix (73 rue Faubourg St-Honoré, 8e)
Commes des Garçons (54 rue du Faubourg St-Honoré, 8e)
Givenchy (3 av Georges V, 8e)
Hermès (24 rue du Faubourg St-Honoré, 8e)
Jean-Paul Gaultier (44 av George V, 8e)
Lanvin (22 rue du Faubourg St Honoré, 8e)
Louis Vuitton (101 av des Champs-Élysées, 8e)
Yves Saint Laurent (38 rue du Faubourg St-Honoré, 8e)

🏠 LE PRINTEMPS
Department Store

☎ 01 42 82 50 00; www.printemps.com;
64 blvd Haussmann, 9e; ⏲ 9.35am-
7pm Mon-Wed, Fri & Sat, to 10pm Thu;
M Havre Caumartin

One of Paris' most resplendent
grands magasins (department
stores), Le Printemps' fashion,
accessories and homewares span
three neighbouring buildings,
including its original building
topped by a stained-glass, 7th-
floor art nouveau cupola.

🏠 LEGRAND FILLES & FILS
Wine

☎ 01 42 60 07 12; www.caves-legrand
.com in French; 1 rue de la Banque, 2e;
⏲ 11am-7pm Mon, 10am-7.30pm Tue-
Fri, 10am-7pm Sat; M Pyramides

Opening onto Galerie Vivienne
(opposite), this wondrous

wine and wine-accoutrement
emporium (Paris' oldest) has a
fully equipped *espace dégusta-
tion* (tasting area) where it holds
regular bilingual presentations,
usually on Tuesday evenings (from
€80; reserve ahead). Anytime, stop
by for wines by the glass with
charcuterie and cheese.

Streetwise prêt-à-porter at Le Printemps

🎵 VIRGIN MEGASTORE *Music*
☎ 01 49 53 50 00; www.virginmega.fr in French; 52-60 av des Champs-Élysées, 8e; ⏱ 10am-midnight Mon-Sat, noon-midnight Sun; Ⓜ Franklin D Roosevelt
The music retailer itself needs no introduction, but this is one of Virgin's handiest branches for buying event tickets – see p211.

🍴 EAT
This part of Paris has some of the city's finest dining but there are plenty of affordable options too.

🍴 ALAIN DUCASSE AU PLAZA ATHÉNÉE
Gastronomic   €€€
☎ 01 53 67 65 00; www.alainducasse.com; Hôtel Plaza Athénée, 25 av de Montaigne, 8e; ⏱ lunch Thu & Fri, dinner Mon-Fri, closed mid-Jul–mid-Aug & mid-Dec–end Dec; Ⓜ Alma Marceau
Seated beneath 10,000 crystal shards glittering from the ceiling's chandeliers, dine on triple Michelin-starred fare like Iranian caviar with langoustines while sipping vintages from the 47-page wine list.

🍴 AUX LYONNAIS
Lyonais   €€
☎ 01 42 96 65 04; www.alainducasse.fr; 32 rue St-Marc, 2e; ⏱ lunch Tue-Fri, dinner Tue-Sat; Ⓜ Richelieu Drouot

Beneath Alain Ducasse's ever-expanding umbrella, this beautiful art nouveau venue turns out Lyonais cuisine focussing on frogs' legs, free-range poultry and pork. You'll still need to book, but you could eat here for the best part of a week for the cost of one meal at Ducasse's Plaza Athénée digs (left).

🍴 GUY SAVOY
Gastronomic   €€€
☎ 01 43 80 40 61; www.guysavoy.com; 18 rue Troyon, 17e; ⏱ lunch Tue-Fri, dinner Tue-Sat; Ⓜ Charles de Gaulle–Étoile
Famed for his artichoke soup served with layered brioche of black truffles and wild mushrooms, Guy Savoy's innovations also include poached foie gras in red cabbage jus, followed by a melt-in-your-mouth chocolate cake layered with praline and chicory cream, or Tahitian vanilla-laced rhubarb with Begonia flowers.

🍴 KOBA *Japanese*   €€
☎ 01 47 42 16 58; 7 rue de la Michodière, 2e; ⏱ lunch Mon-Sat, dinner daily; Ⓜ Quartre Septembre
Shiny Jetsons-style sushi places are popping up all over Paris lately, but this down-to-earth place filled with the aromas of sizzling *yakizakana* (grilled fish of the day) has been rolling out outstanding sushi and sashimi for years.

🍴 LE BISTROT DU SOMMELIER
Gastronomic €€€

☎ 01 42 65 24 85; www.bistrotdusomme
lier.com; 97 blvd Haussmann, 8e; 🕑 lunch
& dinner Mon-Fri; Ⓜ St-Augustin

If you like *haute cuisine* with your
wine (rather than the other way
around), this brainchild of star
sommelier Philippe Faure-Brac
offers superb degustation menus
with pre-paired wines. On Fridays,
take advantage of the three-course
tasting lunch with wine for €45
and five-course dinner with wine
for €70 (reservations essential).

🍴 LE J'GO
Southwestern France €€

☎ 01 40 22 09 09; 4 rue Drouot, 9e;
lunch & dinner Mon-Sat; Ⓜ Richelieu
Drouot

Fronted by a tomato-red façade,
the rugby-player-founded Le J'Go
serves enormous dishes to share,
such as roast leg of lamb or a
whole side of pork, plus Basque
tapas in its downstairs bar.

🍴 LE ROI DU POT AU FEU
French €€

☎ 01 47 42 37 10; 34 rue Vignon, 9e;
🕑 lunch & dinner Mon-Sat; Ⓜ Havre
Caumartin

True to its name, this homey
1930s bistro dishes up wonderful
hotpots, with the herb-infused
stock served as an entrée, and the
beef and root vegetables as the

main, as well as classic desserts
like crème caramel. There are no
bookings; just turn up.

🍴 MAISON PRUNIER
Gastronomic €€€

☎ 01 44 17 35 85; www.prunier.com in
French; 16 av Victor Hugo, 16e; 🕑 lunch
& dinner Mon-Sat; Ⓜ Charles de
Gaulle–Étoile

A 1925 art deco treasure, the highlight of this erstwhile restaurant is
Prunier's own brand of caviar (also
sold at its on-site boutique), along
with seafood and vodkas.

🍸 DRINK

🍸 BAR HEMINGWAY *Bar*

☎ 01 43 16 30 30; www.ritzparis.com;
Hôtel Ritz Paris, 15 place Vendôme,
1er; 🕑 6.30pm-2am; Ⓜ Concorde or
Madeleine

Legend has it that Hemingway
himself, wielding a machine gun,
helped liberate this timber-
panelled, leather-upholstered
bar during WWII. Today the Ritz's
showpiece is awash with photos
taken by Papa and has the best
martinis in town. Dress to impress.

🍸 HARRY'S NEW YORK BAR
Bar

☎ 01 42 61 71 14; www.harrys-bar.fr; 5
rue Daunou, 2e; 🕑 10am-4am, piano bar
10pm-2am Mon-Fri, to 3am Sat; Ⓜ Opéra

ARC DE TRIOMPHE, CHAMPS-ÉLYSÉES & GRANDS BOULEVARDS

The larger-than-life presences of Hemingway and F Scott Fitzgerald linger at this mahogany-panelled beauty of a bar. Harry's great gift to the world was, allegedly, the Bloody Mary, which was invented here in 1921 following the advent of canned tomato juice. (Incidentally, Harry's also invented the Blue Lagoon in 1960, but we'll forgive it for that.) The basement piano bar knocks out Sinatra-style tunes.

☆ **HÉDIARD** *Salon de Thé*
☎ 01 43 12 88 88; www.hediard.fr; 21 place de la Madeleine, 8e; ☽ tea-room 3-6pm Mon-Sat, restaurant breakfast, lunch & dinner Mon-Sat; Ⓜ Madeleine
Since 1880 this gourmet emporium has sold gourmet teas and luxury goods here at its original location. The upstairs tearoom-restaurant serves sumptuous brunches: try for a window seat overlooking place de la Madeleine.

☆ **LADURÉE** *Salon de Thé*
☎ 01 40 75 08 75; www.laduree.fr; 75 av des Champs-Élysées, 8e; ☽ tearoom/restaurant 7.30am-12.30am, shop 7.30am-11pm Mon-Fri, 8.30am-midnight Sat, 8.30am-10pm Sun; Ⓜ George V
Graced by a pistachio-coloured, gilded portico, Ladurée's house-speciality macaroons, in flavours like rose-and-citron, can be taken away or nibbled in the tearoom.

⭐ PLAY

☆ **AU LIMONAIRE** *Chansons*
☎ 01 45 23 33 33; http://limonaire .free.fr; 18 cité Bergère; admission free; ☽ 6pm-midnight Tue-Sun; Ⓜ Grands Boulevards
Traditional *chansons* enthral audiences at this perfect little Parisian wine bar, which is tucked away from the glitz and glamour of the quarter's big-name venues.

☆ **CRAZY HORSE** *Cabaret*
☎ 01 47 23 32 32; www.lecrazyhorse paris.com; 12 av George V, 8e; Ⓜ Alma Marceau
Paris' most risqué cabaret raised eyebrows when it appeared in Woody Allen's 1965 film, *What's New Pussycat?*.

☆ **LE BARON** *Club*
☎ 01 47 20 04 01; www.clublebaron .com; 6 av Marceau, 8e; ☽ vary; Ⓜ Alma Marceau
Ensconced in a former brothel, this hipper-than-thou club, frequented by an endless list of celebs, is renowned for its formidable door policy. Try to look as famous as possible.

☆ **LE LIDO** *Cabaret*
☎ 01 40 76 56 10; www.lido.fr; 116bis av des Champs-Élysées, 8e; Ⓜ George V
In 1946, a newly liberated Paris embraced the opening of this

sparkling cabaret venue on the Champs-Élysées, and the lavish sets, towering feather head-dresses, sequinned gowns and synchronised dancing still dazzle the crowds today.

⭐ LE QUEEN *Gay & Lesbian*
☎ 01 45 63 16 87; www.queen.fr; 102 av des Champs-Élysées, 8e; admission €15-20; ⌚ 11pm-6am; Ⓜ George V

These days this doyen of a club is as popular with a straight crowd as it is with its namesake clientele but Monday's disco nights are still prime dancing queen territory.

⭐ L'OLYMPIA *Live Music*
☎ 08 92 68 33 68; www.olympiahall .com; 28 blvd des Capucines, 9e; tickets from €35; Ⓜ Opéra

Opened in 1888 by the founder of the Moulin Rouge, this hallowed concert hall's past performers include Hallyday, Hendrix and Piaf, as well as Jeff Buckley, who considered his 'Live at the Olympia' his best-ever gig. The website lists upcoming performances.

⭐ PALAIS GARNIER *Opera House*
☎ 08 92 89 90 90, tours 08 25 05 44 05; www.operadeparis.fr; place de l'Opéra, 9e; tours €12/10, museum €8/5; ⌚ English-language tours 11.30am & 2.30pm daily Jul & Aug, 11.30am & 2.30pm Wed, Sat & Sun Sep-Jun, museum 10am-6pm Jul & Aug, to 5pm Sep-Jun; Ⓜ Opéra

The fabled 'phantom of the opera' (p202) lurked in this grand opera house – one of only two designed by Charles Garnier (the other is in Toulon). A performance here is unforgettable – see p211 for ticket booking agencies (but buy carefully: some seats have limited or no visibility). Otherwise, you can take a guided tour; or visit the attached museum, with three centuries' worth of costumes, backdrops, scores and other memorabilia, which includes a self-guided behind-the-scenes peek provided there's no matinee or rehearsal taking place (in which case the cut-off is 1pm).

⭐ SOCIAL CLUB *Club*
☎ 01 40 28 05 55; www.myspace.com /parissocialclub; 142 rue Montmartre, 2e; admission free-€20; ⌚ 11pm-3am Wed & Sun, to 6am Thu-Sat; Ⓜ Grands Boulevards

Spread over three subterranean rooms, the former Triptyque has a new name but remains a magnet for clubbers with electro, hip-hop and funk, and occasional live acts.

>LOUVRE & LES HALLES

Carving its way through the city, Paris' Grand Axis passes through the Tuileries Gardens and the Arc de Triomphe du Carrousel before reaching IM Pei's glass pyramid at the world's largest museum, the Louvre. Many smaller museums and galleries cluster around this art lovers' Holy Grail.

Shoppers crowd along rue de Rivoli, which has beautiful cloisters along its western end, and congregate within Les Halles – the underground mall that supplanted the city's ancient marketplace. The original markets' spirit lives on in Les Halles' lively backstreets, such as rue Montorgueil.

The bright blue and red Centre Pompidou attracts art aficionados with its amazing hoard of modern art. Outside, place Georges Pompidou is a hub for buskers, and the adjacent place Igor Stravinsky's mechanical fountains are a riot of skeletons, dragons and outlandish creations.

LOUVRE & LES HALLES

⊙ SEE

Arc de Triomphe du Carrousel	1	C4
Centre Pompidou	2	H5
Jardin des Tuileries	3	B4
Jardin du Palais Royal	4	E3
Jeu de Paume	5	A3
Musée de la Mode et du Textile	(see 7)	
Musée de la Publicité	(see 7)	
Musée de l'Orangerie	6	A4
Musée des Arts Décoratifs	7	C4
Musée Nationale d'Art Moderne (MNAM)	(see 2)	
Musée du Louvre	8	D5
Tour St-Jacques	9	G6

🛍 SHOP

A Simon	10	F3
agnès b Children's Shop	11	F4
agnès b Men's Shop	12	F4
agnès b Women's Shop	13	F4
Antoine	14	D3
Astier de Villatte	15	D4
Carrousel du Louvre	16	D4
Colette	17	C3
E Dehillerin	18	F3
Forum des Halles	19	G4
Galerie Véro Dodat	20	E4
Galignani	21	B3
Kenzo	22	F5
Librairie Gourmande	23	F3
Maroquinerie Saint-Honoré	24	C3
Mora	25	F4
Passage du Grand Cerf	26	G3

🍽 EAT

Au Pied de Cochon	27	F4
Au Rocher de Cancale	28	G3
Café Marly	29	D4
Comptoir de la Gastronomie	30	F4
Georges	(see 2)	
Le Grand Véfour	31	E3
L'Escargot	32	G4
Stohrer	33	G3

🍸 DRINK

Angélina	34	B3
Café La Fusée	35	H4
Kong	36	F5
Le Conchon à l'Oreille	37	F3
Le Tambour	38	F3

⭐ PLAY

Comédie Française Salle Richelieu	39	D4
Comédie Française Studio Théâtre	40	D4
Forum des Images	(see 19)	
Le Baiser Salé	41	G5
Le Duc des Lombards	42	G5
Le Grand Rex	43	G1
Rex Club	(see 43)	
Sunset & Sunside	44	G5

Please see over for map

 SEE

Rising above rue de Rivoli just north of place du Châtelet is the 52m flamboyant gothic belltower Tour St-Jacques. Constructed in 1523, it's undergoing extensive renovations which are due to wrap up in 2010.

◉ ARC DE TRIOMPHE DU CARROUSEL
place du Carrousel, 1er; Ⓜ Palais Royal–Musée du Louvre; ♿
Although smaller than Paris' most famous Arc de Triomphe, this 1805 triumphal arch, located in the Jardin du Carrousel at the east-ern end of the Tuileries, is more ornate. Its eight pink marble pillars are each topped with a statue of a soldier in Napoleon's army.

◉ CENTRE POMPIDOU
☎ 01 44 78 12 33; www.centrepompidou
.fr; place Georges Pompidou, 4e; library noon-10pm Mon & Wed-Fri, 11am-10pm Sat & Sun; Ⓜ Rambuteau; ♿
The building that houses Paris' premier cultural centre is so iconic that you could spend hours looking at it without ever going inside. Architects Renzo Piano and Richard Rogers' bold design – with plumbing, pipes and air vents forming part of

Vivid sculptures reside in the mechanical fountain at place Igor Stravinsky, Centre Pompidou

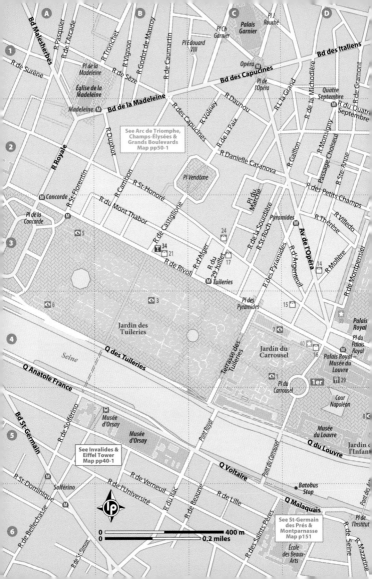

the external façade – caused a *scandale* when the centre opened in 1977. Especially when viewed from a distance, such as from Sacré-Cœur, the centre's primary-coloured, boxlike form amid a sea of muted-grey Parisian rooftops makes it look like a child's Meccano set abandoned on someone's very elegant living room rug. Cultural offerings include temporary exhibition spaces, the Bibliothèque Publique d'Information (BPI; public library), cinemas and entertainment venues, as well as the Musée National d'Art Moderne (MNAM; opposite). Although just six storeys high, Paris' low-rise cityscape means panoramic views extend from the centre's roof (reached by external escalators enclosed in tubes), and its restaurant, Georges (p79).

JARDIN DES TUILERIES

☎ 01 40 20 90 43; 🕐 7am-11pm Jun-Aug, 7am-9pm Apr, May & Sep, 7.30am-7.30pm Oct-Mar; Ⓜ Tuileries or Concorde; ♿

Bisected by the Axe Historique, these 28-hectare formal gardens are where Parisians paraded their finery in the 17th century. Now a Unesco World Heritage Site, the paths, ponds and merry-go-round are as enchanting as ever for a stroll. A funfair sets up here in midsummer.

JARDIN DU PALAIS ROYAL

place du Palais Royal, 1er; 🕐 7.30am-10pm Apr & May, 7am-11pm Jun-Aug, 7am-9.30pm Sep, 7.30am-8.30pm Oct-Mar; Ⓜ Palais Royal–Musée du Louvre; ♿

Flanked by colonnaded arcades (p74), this park is just north of the Palais Royal, where a young Louis XIV once resided (and which now houses government buildings). The black-and-white striped columns at its southern end created by sculptor Daniel Buren in 1986 prompted a public outcry that interrupted construction; installation wasn't completed until 1995.

JEU DE PAUME

☎ 01 44 77 80 07; www.jeudepaume.org; 1 place de la Concorde; admission €6/3, combined ticket with Jeu de Paume – Site Sully €8/4; 🕐 10am-6pm Wed-Mon; Ⓜ Concorde

In the northwestern corner of the Jardin des Tuileries, this former royal tennis court is now France's national photography centre, and features rotating exhibitions of images. A second site is located in the Hôtel de Sully (see p114).

MUSÉE DE L'ORANGERIE

☎ 01 42 97 49 21; www.musee-orangerie .fr; Jardin des Tuileries, 1er; admission €7.50/5.50, audioguide €5/3; 🕐 12.30-7pm Wed, Thu & Sat-Mon, 12.30-9pm Fri; Ⓜ Concorde; ♿

Monet's prized cycle of eight enormous *Waterlilies* (below) occupies the upper level of this light-filled museum. The lower level houses the astonishing collections of Jean Walter and Paul Guillaume, which include additional works by Monet and many by Sisley, Renoir, Cézanne, Gauguin, Picasso, Matisse and Modigliani, as well as Derain's *Arlequin & Pierrot*.

◎ MUSÉE DU LOUVRE

☎ 01 40 20 53 17; www.louvre.fr; place du Louvre, 1er; permanent collections/permanent collections & temporary exhibits €9/13, after 6pm Wed & Fri €6/11; ◷ 9am-6pm Mon, Thu, Sat & Sun, to 10pm Wed & Fri; Ⓜ Palais Royal–Musée du Louvre; ♿

The Louvre's star attraction, Da Vinci's *La Joconde* (*Mona Lisa; p74*), resides behind a wooden railing and bulletproof glass in the glass-roofed Salle des Etats

on the 1st floor. The rest of the rambling palace houses priceless art dating from antiquity to the 19th century. Mona aside, *pièces de résistance* include the crown jewels of Louis XV, the *Venus de Milo* and Michelangelo's *The Dying Slave*, and a trove of Oriental, Egyptian, Greek and Roman treasures. For the lowdown on navigating this national vault, see p18. Dedicated Louvre-goers can purchase extensive guides (up to 475 pages long!) at the museum's bookshop.

◎ MUSÉE NATIONAL D'ART MODERNE (MNAM)

☎ 01 44 78 12 33; www.centrepompidou.fr; place Georges Pompidou, 4e; admission €10/8; ◷ 11am-9pm Wed-Mon; Ⓜ Rambuteau; ♿

Within the groundbreaking 1970s Centre Pompidou (p69), the National Museum of Modern Art

QUARTERS

LOUVRE & LES HALLES

WALL FLOWERS

Recent renovations of the **Musée de l'Orangerie** (opposite) hit a wall (literally) when workers encountered a stone fortification built by Charles IX to enclose his palace and the Jardin des Tuileries, where the museum (originally the palace's greenhouse and its only remaining structure) is located.

Monet's *Nymphéas (Waterlilies)*, which he conceived specifically for this building, wrap around two skylit oval rooms. From the rooms' elliptical benches, the pink, violet and wintergreen lilies appear to float on the canvas.

An unforeseen bonus: part of the rediscovered wall is also displayed.

More of Monet's lilies can be seen at the **Musée Marmottan** (p57) and the **Musée d'Orsay** (p42). The real-life lilies float in the ponds of Monet's former home in **Giverny** (p168).

BEHIND THE WORLD-FAMOUS SMILE

Canadian scientists recently used infrared technology to peer through paint layers of Da Vinci's *Mona Lisa*, confirming her identity as mother-of-five Lisa Gherardini, wife of Florentine merchant Francesco de Giocondo (hence the alternative name *La Joconde*, meaning de Giocondo). They also discovered her dress was covered in a transparent gauze veil typically worn in early-16th-century Italy by pregnant or new mothers; it's surmised that the work was painted to commemorate the birth of her second son, around 1503, when she was aged about 24.

picks up more or less where the Musée d'Orsay leaves off, housing the national collection of art from 1905 on (some 50,000 pieces) including works by the surrealists and cubists, a fabulous Matisse collection, pop art and contemporary creations.

◉ OTHER PALAIS DU LOUVRE MUSEUMS

☎ 01 44 55 57 50; www.lesartsdecoratifs .fr; 107 rue de Rivoli, 1er; admission for all 3 museums €8/6.50; ⏰ 11am-6pm Tue, Wed & Fri, to 9pm Thu, 10am-6pm Sat & Sun; Ⓜ Palais Royal–Musée du Louvre; ♿

Not content with being the largest museum in the world, the Louvre shelters three additional museums in its Rohan Wing: the **Musée des Arts Décoratifs**, featuring furniture, ceramics and glassware; the **Musée de la Publicité**, displaying advertising including posters dating from the 13th century; and the **Musée de la Mode et du Textile**, showcasing couture and fabrics.

🛍 SHOP

Fashion basics and sporting goods can be found along the eastern end of rue de Rivoli's chain stores, while the backstreets house quirkier boutiques. The arcades bordering the Jardin du Palais Royal (p72) house shops selling everything from old smoking pipes, silverware, music boxes, retro toys (including French childhood favourites such as Barbar the Elephant and Barbapapa) to Marc Jacobs' designerwear and accessories.

🛍 AGNÈS B *Fashion*

☎ 01 45 08 56 56; www.agnesb.com; 6 rue du Jour, 1er; ⏰ 10am-7pm Mon-Fri, to 7.30pm Sat; Ⓜ Les Halles

Parisian label-turned–global empire agnès b is synonymous with durable basics in muted colours, such as well-cut jackets, body-hugging shirts and snap-fastened cardigans, plus quirky items such as artist-designed humanitarian

T-shirts. As well as the women's shop, there is also a men's shop (3 rue du Jour, 1er), and a children's shop (2 rue du Jour, 1er) located nearby.

🏠 ANTOINE *Accessories*
☎ 01 42 96 01 80; www.antoine1745 .com; 10 av de l'Opéra; 🕑 10.30am-1pm & 2-6.30pm Mon-Sat; Ⓜ Palais Royal–Musée du Louvre or Pyramides
Founded in 1785 under Louis XV's royal decree, M and Mme Antoine rented out the first-ever 'public umbrellas'. The shop now sells dozens of umbrellas and parasols as well as new and antique walking canes.

🏠 ASTIER DE VILLATTE *Homewares*
☎ 01 42 60 74 13; www.astierdevillatte .com; 173 rue St-Honoré, 1er; 11am-7.30pm Mon-Sat; Ⓜ Palais Royal–Musée du Louvre
This beautiful, old-fashioned shop is the only retail outlet of Parisian manufacturer of ceramic tableware settings and decorations Astier de Villatte, which sells to order worldwide.

🏠 CARROUSEL DU LOUVRE *Shopping Centre*
☎ 01 43 16 47 10; www.carrouseldulouvre .com; 99 rue de Rivoli, 1er; 🕑 10am-8pm; Ⓜ Palais Royal–Musée du Louvre

---

THE ART OF TRAVEL

Metro stations increasingly incorporate artistic themes (usually in certain sections only), including the following:

Abbesses Hector Guimard's finest glass-canopied, twin wrought-iron lamp posts illuminating the dark-green-on-lemon-yellow *Metropolitain* sign.

Arts et Métiers Jules Verne–inspired copper panelling.

Bastille Revolution-era newspaper-engraving frescoes.

Cluny–La Sorbonne Academia.

Concorde Lettered tiles spell out the Déclaration des Droits de l'Homme et du Citoyen (Declaration of the Rights of Man and of the Citizen).

Franklin D Roosevelt History of the metro.

Louvre-Rivoli Statues and bas-reliefs.

Palais Royal–Musée du Louvre Contemporary twist on Guimard's entrances incorporating 800 colourful glass balls.

Parmentier Agricultural crops.

Pont Neuf Medals and coins.

All of Guimard's remaining art nouveau entrances are listed at www.parisinconnu.com (in French).

IM Pei's inverted glass pyramid is the focal point of this underground shopping centre's upmarket shops and restaurants.

COLETTE
Fashion, Accessories

☎ 01 55 35 33 90; www.colette.fr; 213 rue St-Honoré, 1er; ⏱ 11am-7pm Mon-Sat; Ⓜ Tuileries

The thumping music reverberating from this uberhip concept shop means you'll probably hear it before you spot its discreet signage. Streetwear and hi-tech gadgets that change according to the zeitgeist fill the ground floor. Upstairs are serious party frocks and menswear, plus cosmetics and collectors' items like Claude Closky pencils misspelling Paris' name (but with the correct phonetic pronunciation: Parii, Parih and so on). The blue-and-white basement 'water bar' serves dozens of varieties of water as well as champagne.

FORUM DES HALLES
Shopping Mall

☎ 01 44 76 96 56; rues Berger & Rambuteau, 1er; ⏱ 10am-7.30pm Mon-Sat; Ⓜ Les Halles

It seemed like a good idea at the time: move Paris' wholesale markets (and disease-breeding rats)

Check the fashion forecasts at Colette

FUTURE FORUM

Ever since Paris' old markets were forsaken for the banal **Forum des Halles** (opposite), Parisians have been up in arms. Four decades later, a facelift is in the works, with completion due by 2012. Polls showed Parisians preferred finalist Jean Nouvel's adventurous 'suspended gardens'. The green light, however, went to architects Patrick Berger and Jacques Anziutti's less radical rainforest-inspired giant glass canopy and landscape designer David Mangin's opened-up gardens (finally eradicating the '70s arbours). This simpler design only gives the mall a light renovation in stages. Hence business should continue more-or-less as usual, with minimal disruption to city's largest metro/RER hub.

outside the city, and replace them with a street-level park and underground mall. Today, the park attracts illicit 'vendors', while below, artificially lit, could-be-anywhere corridors of chain stores (including a vast Fnac) wrap around a sunken courtyard. But improvements are imminent – see above. For a glimpse of the old markets, pop into Le Conchon à l'Oreille (p82).

GALERIE VÉRO DODAT
Arcade

19 rue Jean-Jacques Rousseau to 2 rue du Bouloi, 1er; ☺ **vary;** Ⓜ **Louvre Rivoli**
Browse for bric-a-brac, antique dolls and curios in this covered passage.

KENZO *Fashion, Perfume*

☎ **01 73 04 20 03; www.kenzo.com; 1 rue du Pont Neuf, 1er;** ☺ **11.30am-7.30pm Mon, 11am-7.30pm Tue-Sat;** Ⓜ **Pont Neuf**
While landmark La Samaritaine next door undergoes renovations until c 2011, Kenzo flies the flag for

fashion on this high-profile strip. Designer Antonio Marras keeps the label at the cutting edge, as does the building's Philippe Starck–designed bar, Kong (p80).

LIBRAIRIE GOURMANDE
Books

☎ **01 43 54 37 27; www.librairie-gourmande.fr in French; 90 rue Montmartre, 2e;** ☺ **10am-7pm Mon-Sat;** Ⓜ **Sentier or Étienne Marcel**
The city's leading food bookshop recently relocated from its long-time home on the Left Bank to Paris' 'culinary quarter' near the famous kitchenware shops (p78). All the classic texts are here, along with new recipe collections.

MAROQUINERIE SAINT-HONORÉ *Accessories*

☎ **01 42 60 03 28; 334 rue St-Honoré; 10.30am-6.30pm Mon-Sat;** Ⓜ **Tuileries**
Behind this boutique's black-enamelled antique façade (which bears the name B Biberon & Fils in

GADGETS GALORE

Street stalls and early-opening bistros might be the most prominent legacies of the old *halles* but in this quarter you'll also find a smorgasbord of cookware shops. Paris' professional chefs still stock up here on knives, whisks, pastry moulds, chopping blocks, pots, pans and more. Among the most venerable shops are the 1814-established **Mora** (☎ 01 45 08 19 24; www.mora.fr in French; 13 rue Montmartre, 1er; Ⓜ Les Halles), the 1884-established **A Simon** (☎ 01 42 33 71 65; 48 rue Montmartre, 2e; Ⓜ Étienne Marcel) and the 1820-established **E Dehillerin** (☎ 01 42 36 53 11; www.e-dehillerin.fr; 18 rue Coquillière, 1er; Ⓜ Les Halles).

gold letters), you'll find affordable handbags including coveted Frederic T designs.

🍴 EAT

A slew of inexpensive cafés of varying quality can be found in the maze of pedestrian streets ensnaring Les Halles. One of the most atmospheric spots for dining is along lively rue Montorgueil – see opposite. At the *haute* end of the spectrum is one of the world's most magnificent dining rooms, Le Grand Véfour (opposite).

🍴 AU PIED DE COCHON
French   €€

☎ 01 40 13 77 00; www.pieddecochon
.com; 6 rue Coquillère, 1er; 🕑 24hr;
Ⓜ Les Halles

The former *halles* (markets; described by novelist Emile Zola as the 'belly of Paris') may have shifted out of the centre long ago, but this enduring brasserie spe-

cialising in pigs' trotters and onion soup still opens around the clock, just as it did when marketeers started and ended their day in its lamplit interior.

🍴 AU ROCHER DE CANCALE
Seafood   €€

☎ 01 42 33 50 29; www.aurocherdecan
cale.fr in French; 78 rue Montorgueil, 2e;
🕑 8am-2am Mon-Sat, 8am-11pm Sun;
Ⓜ Les Halles or Étienne Marcel

Rue Montorgueil was once the old *halles*' oyster market and this 1846-founded, timberlined restaurant is its legacy. Virtually unchanged since the markets' days, its salads are great value, as are its oysters from Cancale, Brittany's foremost oyster port.

🍴 CAFÉ MARLY *French*   €€

☎ 01 46 26 06 60; rue de Rivoli, 1er;
🕑 8am-2am; Ⓜ Palais Royal-Musée
du Louvre

The glittering views of IM Pei's glass pyramid, and of the French movers, shakers and stars who frequent this café, do their best to distract from Marly's sumptuous pastas.

🍴 COMPTOIR DE LA GASTRONOMIE *Gastronomic* €€

☎ 01 42 33 31 32; www.comptoir-gas tronomie.com; 34 rue Montmartre, 1er; 🕑 épicerie 6am-11pm Mon-Sat, to 7pm Sun, restaurant 11am-11pm Mon-Sat, to 7pm Sun; Ⓜ Les Halles

Here since 1894, this gorgeous art nouveau establishment has an elegant dining room where dishes are constructed around delicacies such as foie gras, truffles and caviar. The adjoining *épicerie* (specialist grocer) stocks a scrumptious array of gourmet goods.

🍴 GEORGES *International* €€€

☎ 01 44 78 47 99; www.centrepompi dou.fr; 6th fl, Centre Pompidou, place Georges Pompidou, 4e; 🕑 lunch & dinner Wed-Mon; Ⓜ Rambuteau

Encased in aluminium sheeting with modular white seats, the Centre Pompidou's hyperindustrial dining room has stunning views over Paris' rooftops and the Eiffel Tower. The chic menu includes a popular avocado-and-crab salad. Curiously, vintage years aren't indicated on the wine list.

🍴 LE GRAND VÉFOUR *Gastronomic* €€€

☎ 01 42 96 56 27; www.grand-vefour .com in French; 17 rue de Beaujolais, 1er; 🕑 lunch Mon-Fri, dinner Mon-Thu, closed 3rd week of Apr & Aug & last week of Dec; Ⓜ Pyramides

Chef Guy Martin preserves the reputation of this 1784-established splendour, replete with gilt-edged mirrors and chandeliers, whose past guests include Napoleon. A sommelier pairs Martin's opuses – such as chicken and foie gras with ginger-infused tofu – with France's finest wines.

RUE MONTORGUEIL

Running north from Les Halles, this pedestrianised strip (G4) was once a splinter of the historic *halles* (markets). Rue Montorgueil crosses rue Étienne-Marcel (showcasing up-and-coming fashions, especially edgy streetwear designers), before changing names to rue Petite Carreaux (look out for horse-meat butcher J Davin at No 9) further north. It continues north through the Sentier garment-making quarter, where bolts of fabric and bowed clothing-racks are wheeled through the streets.

By day (except Monday), grocers and speciality shops set up trellis-table stalls on the cobblestones, while both day and night, drinkers and diners spill from its bars, cafés and restaurants.

ℍ L'ESCARGOT French €€€
☎ 01 42 36 83 51; www.escargot-montorgueil.com; 38 rue Montorgueil, 1er; 🕑 lunch Sun-Fri, dinner daily, closed August; Ⓜ Les Halles

A giant gold snail adorns the forest-green façade of this heritage-listed monument. Snails also feature on the menu, along with frogs' legs, Chateaubriand steak served with Béarnaise sauce, veal sweetbreads, and whisky-flambéed Breton lobster. Try to grab a seat at the intimate loggia, perched above the entrance like a private box at the theatre. Past guests range from Proust to Bogie and Bacall.

ℍ STOHRER
Patisserie, Tratieur €
☎ 01 42 33 38 20; www.stohrer.fr; 51 rue Montorgueil, 2e; 🕑 7.30am-8.30pm, closed 1st 2 weeks Aug; Ⓜ Étienne Marcel or Sentier

Opened during the reign of Louis XV in 1730, this beautiful patisserie's pastel murals were added in 1864 by Paul Baudry, who also decorated the Garnier Opèra's Grand Foyer. All of the cakes, pastries, ice cream and savoury delicacies are made on the premises, including specialities invented here such as *baba rhum* (rum-drenched brioche) and *puit d'amour* (cream-filled, caramel-topped puff pastry).

🍸 DRINK

🍸 ANGÉLINA Salon de Thé
☎ 01 42 60 82 00; 226 rue de Rivoli, 1er; 🕑 9am-5pm; Ⓜ Tuileries

Beneath the rue de Rivoli's cloisters, this 1903 belle époque tearoom is so renowned for its decadent African hot chocolate (served with a pot of whipped cream) that queues regularly stretch out the door. Kids are welcomed by accommodating staff, as are those *toute seule* (on your own), who might want to bring a book from Galignani, France's first-ever English-language bookstore (also stocking French literature), at neighbouring 224 rue de Rivoli.

🍸 CAFÉ LA FUSÉE Café
☎ 01 42 76 93 99; 168 rue Saint-Martin, 3e; 11am-2am; Ⓜ Rambuteau

Close to the Centre Pompidou but away from the crowds, this hip café, strung with coloured lights, is a lively and laid-back local hangout. Along the same stretch of rue St-Martin you'll find other funky spots to eat, drink or hunt for obscure vinyl records.

🍸 KONG Bar
☎ 01 40 39 09 00; 1 rue du Pont Neuf, 1er; 🕑 10.30am-2am Sun-Thu, to 3am Fri & Sat; Ⓜ Pont Neuf

Late nights at this Philippe Starck–designed riot of iridescent

Clotilde Dusoulier
Food Writer

Background? I learned by watching my mother cook; good food was so 'normal' to me that initially I trained as a software engineer. But after starting my blog (http://chocolateandzucchini.com) to record and share my own recipes, I was offered a contract to write a cookbook (*Chocolate & Zucchini*, 2007), then a restaurant/food shopping book (*Clotilde's Edible Adventures in Paris*, 2008). **Why 'chocolate and zucchini'?** It's both sides of my culinary personality: sweets/baking and fresh/natural/healthy. **Signature recipe?** Chocolate and zucchini cake. **Which came first?** The name, then the cake! But finely grated zucchini adds moisture without adding butter, giving it a fluffy texture. **Best place for…picnic ingredients?** Marché des Batignolles (p91), and rue des Martyrs (Map p85, C5)**…dinner with friends?** Le J'Go (p65)**…a romantic meal?** L'Ourcine (p148)**…kitchenware supplies?** The shops around rues Montmartre/Étienne Marcel (p78). **Favourite aspect of Parisian life?** Exploring – there's always something new to discover.

champagne-coloured vinyl booths, Japanese cartoon cutouts and garden gnome stools see Paris' glam young set guzzling Dom Pérignon and shaking their designer-clad booty on the tables. But the best time to visit this bar-restaurant-club on the top two floors of the Kenzo building is at sunset, when you have incredible views of the river.

☑ LE CONCHON À L'OREILLE
Bistro, Bar
☎ 01 42 36 07 56; 15 rue Montmartre, 1er; 10am-midnight Tue-Sat; Ⓜ Étienne Marcel, Sentier or Les Halles

A Parisian jewel, this heritage-listed hole-in-the-wall retains 1890-laid tiles depicting vivid market scenes of the old *halles*, and a handful of railway-carriage-style slatted wooden seats. There's a small but wonderful menu of inexpensive traditional bistro fare served at lunch and

dinner, or you can just stop in for a drink.

☑ LE TAMBOUR *Bistro, Bar*
☎ 01 42 33 06 90; 41 rue Montmartre, 2e; noon-6am Tue-Sat, 6pm-6am Sun & Mon; Ⓜ Étienne Marcel or Sentier

Insomniacs head to this local landmark for its rowdy, good-natured atmosphere and filling, inexpensive French fare (including legendary desserts such as its *tarte tatin* – traditional upside-down caramelised-apple tart) served until 3.30am. But what makes this place truly magical is its salvaged décor, such as an old Stalingrad metro map and Parisian street furniture. Proprietor/local icon André Camboulas (who previously worked at the old *halles* with his father, a butcher) says of the decorations that 'life brings them to us…people give us thousands of things, but everything must find

JAZZ IN THE CITY

Jazz clubs swing on rue des Lombards.
Le Baiser Salé (The Salty Kiss; ☎ 01 42 33 37 71; www.lebaisersale.com in French; 58 rue des Lombards, 1er; admission free–€20; 5pm-6am; Ⓜ Châtelet) Unearths trad, Afro- and fusion-jazz talent, and hosts pop-rock and *chansons*.
Le Duc des Lombards (☎ 01 42 33 22 88; www.ducdeslombards.com in French; 42 rue des Lombards, 1er; admission free–€20; 9pm-4am; Ⓜ Châtelet) Revamped venue with an inexpensive restaurant on-site.
Sunset & Sunside (☎ 01 40 26 46 60; www.sunset-sunside.com; 60 rue des Lombards, 1er; admission free–€25; 8pm-4am Mon-Sat; Ⓜ Châtelet) World music–oriented electric and fusion downstairs at Sunset, acoustic upstairs at Sunside.

the right place in the room – like a shrine. It's a temple to know the soul of Paris'.

⭐ PLAY

⭐ COMÉDIE FRANÇAISE
Theatre

☎ 08 25 10 16 80; www.comedie-fran caise.fr in French; place Colette, 1er; tickets €11-37; ⏱ box office 11am-6pm; Ⓜ Palais Royal–Musée du Louvre

Founded in 1680, France's oldest theatre stages works by playwrights such as Molière, Racine and Beaumarchais. The 'French Comedy' encompasses the main **Comédie Française Salle Richelieu** (place Colette, 1er), just west of the Palais Royal, as well as the **Comédie Française Studio Théâtre** (99 rue de Rivoli, 1er), and the Théâtre du Vieux Colombier (see p164). If you're under 27, you can purchase unsold seats one hour before curtain time for €10 to €12 at the main box office.

⭐ FORUM DES IMAGES
Cinema

☎ 01 44 76 63 00; www.forumdesim ages.net in French; 1 Grande Galerie, Porte St-Eustache, Forum des Halles, 1er; ⏱ vary; Ⓜ Les Halles

Following extensive renovations (due to be completed by the time you're reading this), this archive centre devoted to Paris on film will feature a new library and research centre with newsreels, documentaries and advertising. Also here are cinemas showing films set in Paris and various art-house screenings and festivals, as well as a mainstream multiplex.

⭐ LE GRAND REX *Cinema*

☎ 01 45 08 93 58; www.legrandrex .com; 1 blvd Poissonnière, 2e; tour only €9.80/8, tour & film €14.80/13; tours every 5min Wed-Sun, daily during school holidays; Ⓜ Bonne Nouvelle

In addition to screenings, this 1932 art deco icon runs hugely entertaining 45-minute behind-the-scenes tours (English soundtracks available). Tracked by a sensor slung around your neck, you're directed up in the lift behind the giant screen, and put on a soundstage and in a recording studio (you get to see and hear yourself on playback), with whizz-bang special effects along the way. A winner with kids (and adults too).

⭐ REX CLUB *Club*

☎ 01 42 36 10 96; www.rexclub.com in French; 5 blvd Poissonnière, 2e; admission free-€15; 11.30pm-6am Wed-Sat; Ⓜ Bonne Nouvelle

Attached to Le Grand Rex (above), Paris' premier house and techno venue has a phenomenal sound system tested to the limits by some of the world's hottest DJs.

>MONTMARTRE

In the 1960s' bittersweet hit (and perennial busker favourite) *La Bohème*, French crooner Charles Aznavour laments a bohemian Montmartre whose days are numbered. Almost half a century later, much of modern-day Montmartre *is* overrun with tourists. Yet its slinking streets, steep staircases lined with crooked ivy-clad buildings and pocket-sized parks retain a fairytale charm.

Crowned by the Roman-Byzantine basilica, Sacré-Cœur, Montmartre is the city's steepest quarter (*mont* means hill – the martyr was St Denis, beheaded here about AD 250). Its lofty views, gnarled wine-producing vines and village squares lured painters from the 19th century on. Picasso, Pissarro, Toulouse-Lautrec and Van Gogh were among those who set up their easels here; and, though the rents no longer support bohemian budgets, Montmartre is still frequented by artists and their palettes today.

Hedonists revel in Montmartre's southern neighbours, Pigalle and Clichy, home to cabarets including the Moulin Rouge, bawdy bars and neonlit strip clubs.

MONTMARTRE

◎ SEE
Basilique du
  Sacré Cœur 1 C4
Cimetiére de
  Montmartre 2 B3
Dalí Espace
  Montmartre 3 C4
Musée de l'Érotisme....... 4 B4
Musée de Montmartre ... 5 C3
Place du Tertre 6 C4

🏠 SHOP
Marché aux Puces
  de St-Ouen 7 C1
Rebecca Rils.................... 8 B4
Tati................................. 9 D4
Zut!.............................. 10 C4

🍴 EAT
À la Cloche d'Or 11 B4
Arnaud Delmontel
  (18e) 12 B3
Arnaud Delmontel
  (9e) 13 C5
Aux Négociants 14 D3
Charlot, Roi des
  Coquillages................ 15 B4
Chez Marie.................... 16 C4
Chez Toinette 17 C4
La Maison Rose............. 18 C3
Le Relais Gascon 19 C4
Marché des
  Batignolles................ 20 A4
Ripaille......................... 21 A4
Rue des
  Martyrs...................... 22 C5

🍸 DRINK
Café Le Refuge 23 C3
La Fourmi 24 C4
Les Deux Moulins 25 B4

⭐ PLAY
Académie
  de Billard 26 B4
Au Lapin Agile.............. 27 C3
Chez Louisette....... (see 7)
Cinéma des
  Cinéastes.................. 28 A4
Folies-Bergère.............. 29 D6
La Cigale 30 C4
Le Divan du Monde 31 C4
L'Élysée-Montmartre ... 32 C4
Moulin Rouge............... 33 B4

SEE

Montmartre's backstreets make for an enchanting stroll, especially early morning or midweek when the tourists are few – see opposite.

BASILIQUE DU SACRÉ-CŒUR
☎ 01 53 41 89 00; www.sacre-coeur -montmartre.com; Parvis du Sacré-Cœur, 18e; basilica free, dome €5; basilica 6am-10.30pm, dome 9am-7pm Apr-Sep, to 6pm Oct-Mar; Anvers, or funicular

Sacré-Cœur is a high point of any Parisian itinerary (see p22), but keep one eye on the mesmerising views and the other on your belongings as the base of the basilica attracts pickpockets and touts. Metro tickets and travel passes can be used on the RATP-operated funicular railway, which also has ticket booths at the upper and lower stations.

CIMETIÈRE DE MONTMARTRE
☎ 01 53 42 36 30; conservation office 20 av Rachel, 18e; admission free; 8am-6pm Mon-Fri, 8.30am-6pm Sat, 9am-6pm Sun mid-Mar–early Nov, 8am-5.30pm Mon-Fri, 8.30am-5.30pm Sat, 9am-5.30pm Sun early Nov–mid-Mar; Place de Clichy

Famous graves in this cobbled cemetery, established in 1798,

Drink in breathtaking vistas of Paris from the Basilique du Sacré-Cœur

MEANDERING MONTMARTRE

From the Abbesses metro station (p75), wend your way north past café-clad rue des Trois Frères to the **Dalí Espace Montmartre** (below), a homage to just one of the legendary **painters** (p88) who set up their easels on **place du Tertre** (below). Further north, the **Musée de Montmartre** (below) transports you to the bygone windmill-filled village. Montmartre's two surviving windmills, Moulin de la Galette and Moulin Radet, are just west of rue Girardon.

On your way down from **Sacré-Cœur** (opposite) you can cut through the terraced gardens to square Willette and continue east to the colourful Château Rouge area, overflowing with North African market stalls, shops and bars.

include writers Emile Zola, Alexandre Dumas and Stendhal (Marie-Henri Beyle), composer Jacques Offenbach, artist Edgar Degas, film director François Truffaut and dancer Vaslav Nijinsky. Pick up a free map from the conservation office.

◉ DALÍ ESPACE MONTMARTRE

☎ 01 42 64 40 10; www.daliparis.com; 11 rue Poulbot, 18e; admission €10/7; 🕙 10am-6pm; Ⓜ Abbesses

Catalan surrealist Dalí's illustrations, sculptures, engravings and furniture, such as his 'lips' sofa, are displayed against the black-painted walls of this dramatic museum.

◉ MUSÉE DE L'ÉROTISME

☎ 01 42 58 28 73; www.musee-erotisme .com; 72 blvd de Clichy, 18e; admission €8/6; 🕙 10am-2am; Ⓜ Blanche

Exhibits at this museum are surprisingly artistic and represent the history of erotica from around the

world, incorporating 5000-plus statues, paintings, black-and-white 1920s silent porn and mind-boggling toys. If you're inspired, the Rebecca Rils sex supermarket (p88) is next door.

◉ MUSÉE DE MONTMARTRE

☎ 01 49 25 89 37; www.museedemont martre.fr in French; 12-14 rue Cortot, 18e; admission €7/5.50; 🕙 10am-6pm Tue-Sun; Ⓜ Lamarck Caulaincourt

Housed in Montmartre's oldest building, a 17th-century garden-set manor, the quarter's history comes to life through a series of paintings and documents.

◉ PLACE DU TERTRE

The main square of the original village before it was incorporated into Paris proper, place du Tertre has drawn countless painters in its time. Now, particularly at weekends and in summer, it's almost a caricature of its former self, with portraitists clamouring to sketch tourists' likenesses giving it the feel of a theme park. Still, the buskers and crowds create something of a carnival atmosphere, and some of the portraitists are surprisingly good.

🛍 SHOP

🏠 MARCHÉ AUX PUCES DE ST-OUEN *Market*

www.les-puces.com; rue des Rosiers, av Michelet, rue Voltaire, rue Paul Bert & rue Jean-Henri Fabre, 18e; ⏱ **9.30am-6pm Sat-Mon;** Ⓜ **Porte de Clignancourt**
Europe's largest flea market has over 2500 stalls spread across 10 speciality 'villages'. Among them you'll find quality antique dealers such as French clock specialist Liberty's (www.libertys.com), and some great vintage clothing and jewellery. The market is at its best

on Sunday; Mondays can be very quiet. While here, don't miss lunch at the legendary Chez Louisette (p92). See p14 for more on Paris' markets.

🏠 REBECCA RILS *Sex Shop*

76-78 blvd de Clichy; ⏱ **11am-2am;** Ⓜ **Blanche**
Next door to the Musée de L'Érotisme (p87) you can wheel a shopping trolley through the aisles of toys, B&D gear and DVDs and outfits at this bright, modern sex supermarket, and try on outfits in fitting rooms with red velour chaise longues.

🏠 TATI *Department Store*

☎ **01 55 29 50 00; www.tati.fr; 4 blvd de Rochechouart, 18e;** ⏱ **10am-7pm Mon-Fri, 9.15am-7pm Sat;** Ⓜ **Barbès Rochechouart**

TOP 10 MONTMARTRE ARTISTS

These are just some of the seminal artists who have lived in Montmartre over the years. Works by all these masters are on display in Paris' museums and galleries.

Edouard Manet (born 1832, died 1883)
Edgar Degas (1834–1917)
Pierre-August Renoir (1841–1919)
Vincent van Gogh (1853–90)
Henri de Toulouse-Lautrec (1864–1901)
Raoul Dufy (1877–1953)
Pablo Picasso (1881–1973)
Maurice Utrillo (1883–1955)
Amedeo Modigliani (1884–1920)
Salvador Dalí (1904–89)

This rough-and-tumble, frill-free department store is every fashionable Parisian's guilty secret – where customers fight for bargains (and there are some great ones stuffed in the clothes bins and piled on tables) – but never admit it.

ZUT! *Antiques*
☎ 01 42 59 69 68; www.antiquites -industrielles.com; 9 rue Ravignan, 18e; 🕑 11am-1pm & 4-7pm Wed-Sat, 11am-1pm Sun, & by appointment; Ⓜ Abbesses

If you're looking for a conversation piece to dominate your lounge room – a turn-of-the-20th-century railway clock or other oversized industrial object – Zut's proprietor, Frédéric Daniel, can help you track it down. Even if you're not, it's worth sticking your head around the doorway to see some resplendent relics of Paris' past.

🍴 EAT

Montmartre has more than its fair share of tourist traps. As a rule, places with English-language menus out front are more likely to have a bad price-to-quality ratio, but non-French speakers shouldn't be deterred as more authentic options (usually just off main drags) often have English menus inside.

French doll, Marché aux Puces de St-Ouen

🍴 À LA CLOCHE D'OR
French €€
☎ 01 48 74 48 88; 3 rue Mansart, 9e; 🕑 lunch & dinner to 4am; Ⓜ Blanche or Pigalle

Once owned by the family of actress Jeanne Moreau, the 'Golden Bell' has vaudeville charm with photos of stars, an open fire in winter, and a timeless steak tartare.

ARNAUD DELMONTEL
Bakery €
☎ 01 48 78 29 33; www.arnaud-delmontel .com in French; 39 rue des Martyrs, 9e; 🕑 7am-8.30pm Wed-Mon; Ⓜ St-Georges

Winning the city's 'best baguette in Paris' competition comes as no surprise to Arnaud Delmontel's loyal customers. There's also an 18e branch (57 rue Damrémont; 🕑 7am-8.30pm Tue-Sat, to 2.30pm Sun; Ⓜ Lamarck Caulaincourt). For more on bread, see p90.

DAILY BREAD

Some 80% of Parisians eat bread with *every* meal, hence the aromas wafting from Paris' *boulangeries* (bakeries) throughout the day. The shape of a baguette (literally 'stick' or 'wand') evolved when Napoleon Bonaparte ordered army bakers to create loaves for soldiers to stuff down their trouser legs on the march. Common variations:

Baguette – definitive long, thin crusty loaf around 5cm to 6cm wide, 3cm to 4cm high and up to 1m long; 250g.

Baguette Tradition *('une tradi')* – the 70cm-long artisan baguette distinguished by pointy tips and coarse, handcrafted surface; 250g to 300g.

Bâtard – shorter and wider than a standard baguette; 250g.

Ficelle – thinner and crunchier than a standard baguette; 200g.

Flûte – similar length to a standard baguette but thicker; 400g.

Pain – the generic word for 'bread', *pain* also refers specifically to a wider, softer loaf with a chewier crust than a standard baguette; 400g.

ⓘ AUX NÉGOCIANTS French €
☎ 01 46 06 15 11; 27 rue Lambert, 18e; ⓘ lunch & dinner Mon-Fri; Ⓜ Château Rouge

The Montmartre known and loved by Charles Aznavour is alive and well at this jovial, locally patronised wine bar serving rib-sticking classics such as bœuf bourguignon.

ⓘ CHARLOT, ROI DES COQUILLAGES Seafood €€€
☎ 01 53 20 48 00; www.charlot-paris .com in French; 12 place de Clichy, 9e; ⓘ lunch & dinner to midnight Sun-Wed, to 1am Thu-Sat; Ⓜ Place de Clichy

Renowned for its good-value seafood platters, the art deco 'King of Shellfish' also does delicious grilled sardines and bouillabaisse to make any Marseillais homesick.

ⓘ CHEZ MARIE French €
☎ 01 42 62 06 26; 27 rue Gabrielle, 18e; ⓘ lunch & dinner; Ⓜ Abbesses

Decoupaged with old theatre and advertising posters, this little place away from the tourist crowds isn't the venue for a blow-out gourmet meal. But if you're after simple French standards such as onion soup followed by thigh of duck or well-cooked fish, with strong house wines, it's a treat. Hours can vary.

ⓘ CHEZ TOINETTE French €€
☎ 01 42 54 44 36; 20 rue Germain Pilon, 18e; ⓘ dinner Tue-Sat; Ⓜ Abbesses

Game, including partridge, doe and roebuck, figures strongly among the dishes chalked on the blackboard of this authentic bistro, along with the house speciality, duck fillet with sage and honey.

🍴 LA MAISON ROSE French €€
☎ 01 42 57 66 75; 2 rue de l'Abreuvoir, 18e; 🕑 lunch & dinner daily Mar-Oct, lunch Thu-Mon, dinner Mon & Thu-Sat Nov-Feb; Ⓜ Lamarck Caulaincourt
Perched on the hillside just far enough north of place du Tertre to evade the coach-loads of tourists, this rose-pink cottage was rendered in lithographs by Utrillo. Reasonably priced bistro fare is dished up in the cosy rooms and on the tiny terrace in fine weather.

🍴 LE RELAIS GASCON
Brasserie €€
☎ 01 42 58 58 22; lerelaisgascon@ yahoo.fr; 6 rue des Abbesses, 18e; 🕑 10.30am-2am; Ⓜ Abbesses
Climbing the wooden staircase to this narrow townhouse's 1st-floor dining room rewards with rooftop views of Montmartre. The solidly French menu includes seafood and meat dishes, but the reason locals back the communal tables here is to tuck into one of Gascon's gargantuan salads, served in giant bowls with thin-sliced fried potatoes sautéed in garlic.

🍴 MARCHÉ DES BATIGNOLLES
Market
blvd des Batignolles btwn rue des Batignolles & rue Puteaux, 8e & 17e; 🕑 9am-2pm Sat; Ⓜ Place de Clichy or Rome

Saturday mornings see this *marché biologique* (organic market) busy with shoppers stocking up for the week.

🍴 RIPAILLE French €€
☎ 01 45 22 03 03; 69 rue des Dames, 17e; 🕑 lunch Mon-Fri, dinner Mon-Sat; Ⓜ Rome
Forget the fast-food joints around blvd de Clichy and head a few blocks south to owner/chef Philippe Fauré's arty, tangerine-toned dining room. Expertly prepared dishes such as St-Jacques scallops and salmon risotto are served on brightly coloured china along with well-chosen wines.

🍸 DRINK
There's no shortage of great little cafés in this area, and again, the backstreets are your best bet for finding genuine local haunts. For more action, Pigalle and place de Clichy have a plethora of places to drink.

🍸 CAFÉ LE REFUGE Café
☎ 01 42 55 27 58; 72 rue Lamarck, 18e; 🕑 7.15am-midnight Mon-Sat, 9am-8pm Sun; Ⓜ Lamarck Caulaincourt
Perfect for a sundowner on the terrace, this *café du quartier* (local café) has fantastic interior vintage tiling, a gleaming timber bar and *sympa* (cool) staff.

♈ LA FOURMI *Bar*
☎ 01 42 64 70 35; 74 rue des Martyrs, 18e; 8am-2am Mon-Thu, to 4am Fri & Sat, 10am-2am Sun; Ⓜ Pigalle

Spread over two levels and wrapping around a zinc bar, this Pigalle stalwart has a dynamic energy both day and night, and is a great spot to pick up leaflets and flyers on club and DJ nights.

♈ LES DEUX MOULINS *Café*
☎ 01 42 54 90 50; 15 rue Lepic, 18e; 7am-2am Mon-Sat, 8am-2am Sun; Ⓜ Blanche; ♿

The 'Two Windmills', where Amélie (p203) waitressed, remains, bless it, a down-to-earth local for lingering over the newspapers, chatting with regulars, or just sitting by the big picture windows and watching Montmartre go by.

★ PLAY

Paris' main red-light district (albeit a tame one) stretches from Clichy to Pigalle, keeping this quarter lively after dark. Around place de Clichy you'll find multiplex cinemas, as well as late-night dining spots.

★ ACADÉMIE DE BILLARD
Pool Hall
☎ 01 48 78 32 85; www.academie-billard .com; 84 rue de Clichy, 18e; pool per hr from €5; 11am-6am; Ⓜ Place de Clichy

Beneath stained-glass ceilings, this old-fashioned pool hall lit by antique lamps is staffed by bow tie–wearing waiters, who deliver your drinks while you snooker your opponents. Players must be over 18; bring photo ID.

★ AU LAPIN AGILE *Cabaret*
☎ 01 46 06 85 87; www.au-lapin-agile .com; 22 rue des Saules, 18e; tickets €24/17, no concession Sat; 9pm-2am Tue-Sun; Ⓜ Lamarck Caulaincourt

Opened when Montmartre was still a bucolic village outside Paris proper, this intimate 60-seat venue has scarcely changed since. Its name (the 'Agile Rabbit') comes from *Le Lapin à Gill*, a mural of a rabbit jumping out of a cooking pot by caricaturist André Gill, on the façade above the entrance. The cabaret's comanager and performer Frédéric Thomas (opposite) describes the format as 'like a tested recipe, and we improvise within that frame'. Around eight or 10 of its team of about 20 artists perform during its four-hour shows, which kick off at 9.30pm.

★ CHEZ LOUISETTE *Chansons*
☎ 01 40 12 10 14; Marché aux Puces de St-Ouen; noon-6pm Sat-Mon; Ⓜ Porte de Clignancourt

Inside Paris' biggest flea market, this time-warp of a restaurant is a priceless spot to catch old-time

⭐ **Frédéric Thomas**
Comanager/Cabaret Performer, Au Lapin Agile

Cabaret's history? It was started by the local mayor in 1869. Altogether it's been in my family for over 100 years: my step-great-grandfather Frédé bought it in 1903 and Picasso/the Cubists hung out here and made it the centre of artistic life. Aristide Bruant (the red-scarf-clad *chansonnier* in Toulouse-Lautrec's poster) saved it from demolition in 1913 and sold it affordably to Frédé's son. There's a 'human charge' of the past; memory is alive every time we do a show. **Did you consider doing anything else?** No, I didn't want to miss out on history. **Choice of performers?** *Chansonniers* in the broad sense – comedians, musicians, poets, singers who express the core of humanity through original and traditional compositions. We keep the tradition of no censorship, free expression. **Best thing about performing yourself?** When you're totally inside the expression, completely swimming in it. **Favourite aspect of Parisian life?** The cultural gatherings.

MONTMARTRE

HAT TIP

For *chanson* venues that don't charge an entry fee or cover charge, such as restaurants like **Chez Louisette** (p92), performers typically pass around the hat at the end of a set. You're not obliged to tip, but it's the way that these artists – many of them very talented – earn a crust, and tipping helps keep this Parisian tradition alive. Don't spend all your money at once, though – over the course of *chansons*, there are often several different performers with a short interval between them, each with their own hat.

chanteurs and *chanteuses* accompanied by accordion players swaying with gusto. The food (hearty French) is great and the wine flows, invariably inspiring you to dance between the tightly packed tables.

⭐ **CINÉMA DES CINÉASTES** *Cinema*
☎ 01 53 42 40 20; www.cinema-des -cineastes.fr; 7 av de Clichy, 17e; tickets €8.70/6.80; Ⓜ Place de Clichy
Avant-garde flicks are shown on the three screens of this cinema, whose founders include *Betty Blue* director Jean-Jacques Beneix. There are thematic screenings, documentaries and talks, and a fabulous 1st-floor wine bar.

⭐ **FOLIES-BERGÈRE** *Cabaret*
☎ 08 92 68 16 50; www.foliesbergere .com in French; 32 rue Richer, 9e; most tickets around €30-40; Ⓜ Cadet
If the walls could talk. This is the legendary club where Charlie Chaplin, WC Fields and Stan Laurel

appeared on stage together one night in 1911, and where Josephine Baker – accompanied by her diamond-collared pet cheetah and wearing only stilettos and a skirt made from bananas – bewitched audience members including Hemingway. Lately its various concerts are predominately solo performers.

⭐ **LA CIGALE** *Live Music*
☎ 01 49 25 89 99; www.lacigale.fr; 120 blvd de Rochechouart, 18e; tickets from €25; Ⓜ Anvers or Pigalle
A heritage-listed monument, this 1887 music hall overhauled by Philippe Starck presents edgy rock, jazz and roots (Primal Scream, Ani Di Franco et al).

⭐ **LE DIVAN DU MONDE** *Club*
☎ 01 42 52 02 46; www.divandumonde .com in French; 75 rue des Martyrs, 18e; admission free-€20; 7pm-3am Tue-Thu, to 6am Fri & Sat; Ⓜ Pigalle
Anything from rock parties to big-name DJs and obscure acts goes at this Pigalle party spot.

⭐ L'ÉLYSÉE-MONTMARTRE
Live Music, Club

☎ 01 44 92 45 47; www.elyseemont
martre.com; 72 blvd de Rochechouart,
18e; tickets from €15; Ⓜ Anvers
In the heart of party-hard Pigalle,
this old-style music hall hosts
indie artists such as The Melvins,
Billy Paul and Anthony B. Doors
open for concerts at 6.30pm; club
events crank up from 11.30pm on
Fridays and Saturdays.

⭐ MOULIN ROUGE *Cabaret*
☎ 01 53 09 82 82; www.moulinrouge.fr;
82 blvd de Clichy, 18e; Ⓜ Blanche
Immortalised in the posters of
Toulouse-Lautrec and later on
screen by Baz Luhrmann's 2001
film starring Nicole Kidman and
Ewan McGregor, the Moulin
Rouge twinkles beneath a 1925
replica of its original red windmill.
Yes, it's rife with bus-tour crowds.

But from the first bars of opening
music to the last high kick it's a
whirl of fantastical costumes, sets,
choreography and champagne.

The iconic windmill of the Moulin Rouge

WORTH THE TRIP – STADE DE FRANCE
Football and/or rugby fans can take a pilgrimage to France's national stadium, the **Stade de France** (☎ 08 92 70 09 00; www.stadefrance.com; rue Francis de Pressensé, ZAC du Cornillon Nord, 93216 St-Denis la Plaine; tours €12/8; ☒ tours on the hour in French 10am–5pm, in English 10.30am & 2.30pm; Ⓜ St-Denis-Porte de Paris; ♿), located just north of the ring road in St-Denis. Built for the 1998 football World Cup, which France hosted and ultimately won here before 80,000 elated spectators, this immense, futuristic structure also hosted 2007 rugby World Cup fixtures, and mounts a variety of sporting events, as well as major concerts.

Guided tours lasting one hour are the only way to see the stadium (bar attending a match or event), but are well worth it, taking you into the dressing rooms, the edges of the pitch, and into the presidential stand, providing there's not an event taking place.

>BELLEVILLE & SURROUNDS

Today's Belleville may be remembered with the same sentimentality as Montmartre's heyday. This long-impoverished district is where song-stress Édith Piaf was allegedly born in the gutter in 1915. Later Belleville became home to thousands of immigrants, mainly from Northern Africa and China. Like Montmartre, Belleville sits on a hill, and an influx of artists established ateliers and collectives here and in neighbouring Ménilmontant. And like Montmartre before it, Belleville is becoming *branché* (trendy), with hip bars, restaurants and clubs – and rising rents that threaten to drive artists out. For now, its eclectic streets and diverse ethnic mix still offer an authentic, off-the-tourist-track experience.

West of Belleville is Canal St-Martin, criss-crossed with iron footbridges and lined with *bobo*-chic cafés and boutiques. Eastwards, you'll find Cimetière du Père Lachaise's maze of cobbled lanes where 'residents' include Belleville's Édith Piaf.

BELLEVILLE & SURROUNDS

👁 SEE
Cimetière du Père Lachaise	1	F5
Cité des Sciences et de l'Industrie	2	E1
Édith Piaf plaque	3	E4
Maison de l'Air	4	E4
Musée Édith Piaf	5	E5
Parc de Belleville	6	E4
Parc de la Villette	7	F1
Parc des Buttes Chaumont	8	E3

🏃 DO
Cuisine Fraîch' Attitude	9	B3
O-Château	10	D4

🛍 SHOP
Antoine et Lili	11	C4
Frivoli	12	C4

Marché aux Puces de Montreuil	13	H6
Seven Seventies	14	C4
Stella Cadente	15	C4

🍴 EAT
Au Village	16	D5
Bistro Indien	17	B4
Hôtel du Nord	18	C4
Krishna Bhavan	19	C2
Le Chansonnier	20	C3
Le Chateaubriand	21	D4
Le Krung Thep	22	E4
Le Look	23	B3
Le Villaret	24	D5
Marché Belleville	25	E4
Marché St-Quentin	26	C3

🍸 DRINK
Café Bonnie	27	C3
Café Charbon	28	E5

Café Chéri(e)	29	D4
Chez Prune	30	C4
L'Atmosphere	31	C3
Le Petit Château d'Eau	32	C4
L'Île Enchantée	33	D3

⭐ PLAY
La Flèche d'Or	34	G6
La Java	35	D4
Le Nouveau Casino	36	E5
Le Vieux Belleville	37	E4
New Morning	38	C4
Philharmonie de Paris Site	39	F1
Point Éphémère	40	D3

Please see over for map

◎ SEE

◎ CIMETIÈRE DU PÈRE LACHAISE

☎ Conservation office 01 55 25 82 10; 16 rue du Repos, 20e; www.pere-lachaise.com; main entrance blvd de Ménilmontant; admission free; ⏱ 8am-6pm Mon-Fri, 8.30am-6pm Sat, 9am-6pm Sun mid-Mar–early Nov, 8am-5.30pm Mon-Fri, 8.30am-5.30pm Sat, 9am-5.30pm Sun early Nov–mid-Mar; Ⓜ Philippe Auguste, Gambetta or Père Lachaise; ♿

Alongside the famous names buried here and their tombs' time-honoured traditions (see below), one particularly haunting set of graves in the world's most visited cemetery is that of the last Communard insurgents. Cornered by government forces, survivors were lined up against the Mur des Fédérés (Federalists' Wall) and systematically shot, then buried where they fell. See also p20.

◎ CITÉ DES SCIENCES ET DE L'INDUSTRIE

☎ 01 40 05 80 00; www.cite-sciences.fr; 30 av Corentin Cariou; admission per individual attraction free-€10.50, combination tickets available; ⏱ 10am-6pm Tue-Sat, to 7pm Sun; Ⓜ Porte de la Villette; ♿

Hi-tech exhibits abound at the enormous City of Science and Industry, situated in the Parc de la Villette (p101). Some attractions are free, while others, such as the iconic silver sphere Géode, screening 180-degree films, the science-based Explora, and the Cité des Enfants ('Children's City'; lots of robots) incur fees. Handy *Keys to the Cité* maps (free) are available from the main entrance.

◎ MAISON DE L'AIR

☎ 01 43 28 47 63; Parc de Belleville; admission €3.35; ⏱ 1.30-5.30pm Mon-Fri, to 6.30pm Sun Apr-Sep, 1.30-5pm Mon-Fri, to 5.30pm Sun Oct-Mar; Ⓜ Pyrénées

TOMB TRADITIONS

Long-standing traditions at **Père Lachaise** (above) include leaving love letters on Abélard and Héloïse's crypt, red roses on Édith Piaf's grave, and lipstick kisses on Oscar Wilde's naked-winged-angel tomb. And would-be mothers stroke 19th-century journalist Victor Noir's amply proportioned bronze effigy hoping to conceive. But the most venerated tomb belongs to the Doors' Jim Morrison, who died in Paris in 1971. Prior to complaints from Morrison's family, 'traditions' included fans drinking, taking drugs and having sex atop his grave. There's now a permanent security guard and code-of-conduct leaflet – making you wonder if Morrison isn't finding the new arrangements rather lame.

The concrete-bound 'Museum of Air', which is located in Parc de Belleville (right), has environmental exhibits.

MUSÉE ÉDITH PIAF

☎ 01 43 55 52 72; 5 rue Crespin du Gast, 11e; by appt 1-6pm Mon-Wed, 10am-noon Thu; M Ménilmontant

You need to reserve ahead but it's worth it to visit this small museum cluttered with memorabilia, recordings and video footage of legendary Parisian chanteuse Édith 'Non, je ne regrette rien' Piaf. Born Édith Gassion, the diminutive (142cm) singer was nicknamed la Môme Piaf (the Lit-tle Sparrow) by nightclub-owner Louis Leplée, who launched her immortal career. Although she was reportedly born on the steps of 72 rue de Belleville, 20e, marked by a plaque, her birth certificate at the museum gives her birthplace as the Tenon hospital.

PARC DE BELLEVILLE

sunrise to sunset; M Couronnes

One of the best panoramas of Paris unfolds alongside the teensy vineyard at the top of this little-known park, which is terraced down the slopes over 4.5 hectares. Early mornings see locals from the

Boxing gloves and portraits of Édith Piaf and the love of her life, Marcel Cerdan, at Musée Édith Piaf

OPEN DOORS

More than 240 Belleville artists open their studios each May during the **Portes Ouvertes des Ateliers d'artistes de Belleville** (Open Studio Doors of the Artists of Belleville; www.ateliers-artistes-belleville.org in French). Nearby, the **Portes Ouvertes des Ateliers du Père Lachaise Associés** (www.apla.fr in French) sees its own artists open their doors in May. Neighbouring Ménilmontant runs **Portes Ouvertes des Ateliers de Ménilmontant** (www.ateliersdemenilmontant.org in French) each September with around 130 artists taking part. It's often possible to visit the areas' ateliers outside these events by contacting them directly.

Details of all three 'open doors' programs are also available at www.parisinfo.com.

nearby Chinese community practising t'ai chi on the upper lawns.

PARC DE LA VILLETTE
☎ 01 04 03 75 75; www.villette.com; admission free; ⏱ 6am-1am; Ⓜ Porte de la Villette or Porte de Pantin; ♿

At this 35-hectare pavilion-filled 'park of the future' you can wander between 10 themed gardens/playgrounds including the Jardin des Îles (Garden of Islands), Jardin des Bambous (Bamboo Gardens), Jardin des Miroirs (Mirror Gardens) and Jardin du Dragon (Dragon Garden). Situated at the northern end is the Cité des Sciences et de l'Industrie (p97). Also here as of 2012 will be the Philharmonie de Paris (p189).

PARC DES BUTTES CHAUMONT
rue Manin & rue Botzaris, 19e; ⏱ 7.30am-11pm May-Sep, to 9pm Oct-Apr; Ⓜ Buttes Chaumont or Botzaris

A far cry from its former life as a rubbish tip and quarry for Baron Haussmann's nineteenth-century overhaul of the city (see p183), these 25 forested hectares conceal grottoes, artificial waterfalls and a temple-topped island reached by footbridges.

🏃 DO

ÇA SE VISITE! BELLEVILLE WALKING TOURS *Walking Tour*
☎ 01 48 06 27 41; www.ca-se-visite.fr; walks €12/9

This local initiative arranges two- to 2½-hour 'urban discovery tours' through Belleville. Residents lead small groups (up to 15 people) through their streets, introducing you to artists and craftspeople and teaching you about the area's history. French-language tour schedules are posted on the website; contact the organisation about English-language tours.

BELLEVILLE & SURROUNDS

✈ CUISINE FRAÎCH' ATTITUDE
Cooking Course

www.cuisinefraichattitude.com in French; 60 rue du Faubourg Poissonnière, 10e; Ⓜ Poissonnière

Fresh fruit and veg are the focus of the lunchtime lessons offered by well-known chefs at this cookery school. Courses start from €12 – book well ahead.

✈ O-CHÂTEAU
Wine-tasting Course

☎ 01 44 73 97 80; www.o-chateau.com; 100 rue de la Folie Méricourt, 11e; Ⓜ Goncourt

Olivier Magny's wine loft is a laid-back spot to learn about France's favourite liquid. Lessons start from €20 for an hour-long introduction to a €50 two-hour tasting of seven wines. The fun-loving Magny also runs hour-long champagne-tasting Seine cruises (€40), as well as wine-and-cheese lunches (€65) and wine-paired dinners (€129). All are in English. Venues for some classes vary – check when you book.

🛍 SHOP

Canal St-Martin (p21) harbours offbeat designer and vintage boutiques, particularly on the northern stretch of rue Beaure-paire (C4), and along the quays. Many shops here open on Sunday afternoons; most shut on Mondays.

Local artists sell works direct from their ateliers – see p101.

🏠 ANTOINE ET LILI
Fashion, Homewares

☎ 01 40 37 41 55; www.antoineetlili.com; 95 quai de Valmy, 10e; ⏰ 10.30am-7pm Mon, to 7.30pm Tue-Fri, 10am-8pm Sat, 12.30-7.30pm Sun; Ⓜ République or Gare de l'Est

Flower-children of the new millennium flock to this urban-grunge-meets-tribal boutique, occupying a clutch of banana-, lime- and pomegranate-coloured buildings, with lurid raspberry interiors. Along with offbeat clothing (for adults and kids) by Antoine and Lili's designers, you can pick up earthy homewares such as Nepalese votive candles, or, on Thursdays from 3.30pm to 6.30pm, have your tarot cards read (☎ reservations 06 64 50 07 22; readings from €30). There's a handful of other branches in Paris, including one in the Marais (p119).

🏠 FRIVOLI *Fashion*

☎ 01 42 38 21 20; 26 rue Beaurepaire, 10e; ⏰ 11am-7pm Tue-Fri, 2-7pm Sat & Sun; Ⓜ Jacques Bonsergent

Flip through colour-coded racks of cast-offs at this fabulous vintage boutique.

🏠 MARCHÉ AUX PUCES DE MONTREUIL *Market*
av du Professeur André Lemière, 20e; 🕐 **8am-7.30pm Sat-Mon;** Ⓜ **Porte de Montreuil**
This 19th-century flea market has great vintage clothes and designer cast-offs, as well as antique jewellery, linen and crockery.

🏠 SEVEN SEVENTIES
Fashion, Accessories
☎ **01 42 02 07 88; 29 rue Beaurepaire, 10e;** 🕐 **11.30am-7.30pm Tue-Fri, 12.30-7.30pm Sat, 1-7pm Sun;** Ⓜ **Jacques Bonsergent**
Cheap '70s vintage fashion and accessories like braided belts, beaded knitwear and retro sunglasses are laid out in this disco-decorated boutique.

🏠 STELLA CADENTE
Fashion
☎ **01 42 09 66 60; 93 quai de Valmy, 10e;** 🕐 **11am-7.30pm;** Ⓜ **République or Gare de l'Est**
Stella Cadente's artistic designs include floaty layered chiffon dresses inspired by Monet's waterlilies, along with fitted bodices and stiffened petticoats.

🍴 EAT

Belleville and its surrounds offer a kaleidoscope of inexpensive restaurants. Unlike many other parts of Paris, there's often no need to book ahead. Wander around and you'll find many of Paris' mondial communities (p186) here, including African, Thai, Korean, Japanese, Chinese, Indian and dozens of others, with plenty of traditional French bistros in between.

🍴 AU VILLAGE *Senegalese* €€
☎ **01 43 57 18 95; 86 av Parmentier, 11e;** 🕐 **dinner to midnight Mon-Thu, to 1am Fri-Sun;** Ⓜ **Parmentier**
Fried plantain bananas with red sauce and semolina-and-cream-cheese salad for dessert are among the delicious dishes at this lively African restaurant.

🍴 HÔTEL DU NORD
French €€
☎ **01 40 40 78 78; www.hoteldunord .org; 102 quai de Jemmapes, 10e; lunch & dinner;** Ⓜ **Jacques Bonsergent or Gare de l'Est**
Yes, this is the setting for Marcel Carnés 1938 film of the same name. Although the film (about a Romeo-and-Juliet-style suicide pact) was shot in a studio, author Eugène Dabit, whose stories formed the basis of the film, lived here when the hotel was run by his parents. It's now a book-lined restaurant, that serves up contemporary fare like duck with caramelised potatoes, crab ravioli with avocado, and a gourmet cheeseburger with fries,

followed by desserts such as a lemon-scented crème brûlée, or rose-and-hibiscus sorbet. The bar stays open until 2am.

🍴 KRISHNA BHAVAN Indian €

☎ 01 42 05 78 43; www.krishna-bhavan .eresto.net in French; 24 rue Cail, 10e; lunch & dinner; Ⓜ Garde du Nord or La Chapelle; Ⓥ

With so many Indian restaurants along rue Cail it's easy to bypass this outstanding little place with tangerine tablecloths and iridescent religious icons adorning the walls. The all-vegetarian southern Indian menu includes *thaali* platters laden with spicy curries and basmati rice, and a crispy *masala dosa* crêpe stuffed with potatoes and onions. For more Indian options in this part of Paris, see below.

🍴 LE CHANSONNIER French €€

☎ 01 42 09 40 88; www.lechansonnier .com in French; 14 rue Eugène-Varlin, 10e; ⏲ lunch Mon-Fri, dinner Mon-Sat; Ⓜ Château Landon

Behind a claret-coloured façade, Le Chansonnier's antique zinc bar and moulded cornices have a quintessential Parisian charm. Classic French bistro fare includes a traditional *mijoté* pot of rabbit with green olives, with a decent kids' menu too.

🍴 LE CHATEAUBRIAND Bistro €€

☎ 01 43 57 45 95; 129 av Parmentier, 11e; lunch Tue-Fri, dinner Tue-Sat, closed 3 weeks Aug; Ⓜ Goncourt

In a simple but elegantly tiled art deco dining room with bare timber tables, Basque chef Iñaki Aizpitarte's tapas and no-choice, five-course tasting menu at dinner (chalked on the oversize blackboard up the back) have been wowing foodies since he opened here a couple of years ago, and it remains one of Paris' hottest addresses.

PASSAGE BRADY

Unlike many of Paris' ornate arcades, the dilapidated **Passage Brady** (46 rue du Faubourg St-Denis & 33 blvd de Strasbourg; C4) isn't aesthetically beautiful. But aromatically, it's just as tantalising, crammed wall-to-wall with Indian, Pakistani and Bangladeshi cafés and grocery stores. You can get a fantastic lunch for under €10, and dinner for only slightly more. Neighbouring **Bistro Indien** (☎ 01 53 34 63 08; 42 rue Faubourg St-Denis, 10e; Ⓜ Château d'Eau or Strasbourg St-Denis) has terrific tandoori-oven naan and enormous set *menus*.
Curry fiends should also trawl rue Cail (above).
Indeaparis (www.indeaparis.com in French) lists every Indian restaurant in Paris.

🍴 LE KRUNG THEP *Thai* €

☎ 01 43 66 83 74; 93 rue Julien Lacroix, 20e; 🕑 lunch Sat & Sun, dinner daily; Ⓜ Pyrénées

This aromatic restaurant cluttered with kitsch decor serves green curries, chicken steamed in banana leaves and vegetarian dishes galore, which are up there with those you'll find in Le Krung Thep's namesake Bangkok.

🍴 LE LOOK *Café* €

☎ 09 50 10 20 31; 17 rue Martel, 10e; 9am-7pm Mon-Wed, 9am-2am Thu & Fri; Ⓜ Château d'Eau

Geometric blue, green and purple vinyl banquettes run the length of one wall of this groovy little sandwich bar. Serving fresh juices and *tartines* (open-faced sandwiches) at breakfast, gourmet salads and sandwiches at lunch and Belgian beers (including potent Duvel) for *apéros*, it's also a burgeoning creative hub.

🍴 LE VILLARET *French* €€€

☎ 01 43 57 89 76; 13 rue Ternaux, 11e; 🕑 lunch Mon-Fri, dinner Mon-Sat; Ⓜ Parmentier or Oberkampf

In-the-know Parisians come from all over the city to this buzzing bistro for its daily-changing *menus* featuring French classics, such as succulent leg of lamb and crispy roast chicken, accompanied by a strong wine list.

Painting at Le Chansonnier restaurant

🍴 MARCHÉ BELLEVILLE
Market

blvd de Belleville btwn rue Jean-Pierre Timbaud & rue du Faubourg du Temple, 11e & 20e; 🕑 7am-2.30pm Tue & Fri; Ⓜ Belleville or Couronnes

Belleville's diverse community comes together at this vibrant market, which has African, Middle Eastern and Asian stalls piled high with fruit, vegetables, spices, condiments and delicacies. Local artists also sell their works here.

🍴 MARCHÉ ST-QUENTIN *Market*

85 blvd de Magenta, 10e; ⏱ **8am-1pm & 3.30-7.30pm Tue-Sat, 8am-1pm Sun;** Ⓜ **Gare de l'Est**
Since 1866, this iron-and-glass-roofed covered market has sold a vast array of foodstuffs; these days the offerings are often very gourmet.

🍸 DRINK

Rue Oberkampf (E5) is the area's main drag for edgy bars. Cafés line Canal St-Martin (C3), and there are more throughout Belleville proper, many unchanged in decades. Others have had a recent facelift in line with the area's new gritty-chic status, but this is still a world away from the touristy parts of Paris.

🍸 CAFÉ BONNIE *Café*

☎ **01 40 35 54 51; www.cafebonnie .com in French; 9 rue des Récollets, 10e; 10.30am-2am Mon-Sat, to midnight Sun;** Ⓜ **Château Landon or Jacques Bonsergent**
Pink-feather light fittings flutter from the ceiling of this retro-kitsch place filled with pictures of divas from Audrey Hepburn to Disney's Snow White. Its various DJs and concerts are posted on its website.

🍸 CAFÉ CHARBON *Café*

☎ **01 43 57 55 13; 109 rue Oberkampf, 11e;** ⏱ **9am-2am Sun-Thu, to 4am Fri & Sat;** Ⓜ **Parmentier**
The distressed *belle époque* Café Charbon was the first of rue Oberkampf's hip cafés and puts on a standout Sunday brunch. The performance venue, Le Nouveau Casino, is next door (p109).

🍸 CAFÉ CHÉRI(E) *Bar*

☎ **01 42 02 02 05; 44 blvd de la Villette, 19e;** ⏱ **8am-2am;** Ⓜ **Belleville**
Electro beats, a redlit bar and rum punches make this a perennially happenin' spot to kick the night off, especially in summer out on the terrace.

🍸 CHEZ PRUNE *Café*

☎ **01 42 41 30 47; 71 quai de Valmy, 10e;** ⏱ **8am-2am Mon-Sat, 10am-2am Sun;** Ⓜ **Jacques Bonsergent or République**
Flowing onto a canalside terrace, the original Parisian *bobo* hangout retains its original mosaic-tiled interior, views over the bridges from its wrought-iron tables, and lively, unpretentious vibe.

🍸 L'ATMOSPHERE *Café*

☎ **01 40 38 09 21; 49 rue Lucien-Sampaix, 10e;** ⏱ **9.30am-1.45am Mon-Sat, 9.30am-midnight Sun;** Ⓜ **Château Landon or Jacques Bonsergent**
One of our favourites in this part of town (not least for the well-

priced drinks), this timber-and-tile café on the kink of Canal St-Martin's western bank has an arty, spirited ambience day and night.

▼ LE PETIT CHÂTEAU D'EAU
Café

☎ 01 42 08 72 81; 34 rue du Château d'Eau; 9am-2am Mon-Fri; Ⓜ Jacques Bonsergent or Château d'Eau

Part of the magic of Paris is stumbling across unchanged-in-decades neighbourhood cafés where locals chat with staff over the stainless-steel-topped timber bar. Lined with cracked lemon-and-lime tiles, oversized mirrors, and time-worn maroon-leather booths, Le Petit Château d'Eau is a classic example, and serves some of the best – and cheapest! – coffee in Paris. ('Château d'Eau', incidentally, refers to the water reservoir at the end of the street where Paris' fire brigade fills up.)

▼ L'ÎLE ENCHANTÉE *Bar, Café*

☎ 01 42 01 67 99; www.myspace
.com/ileenchantee; 65 blvd de la Villette, 19e; 8am-2am Mon-Fri, 6pm-2am Sat & Sun; Ⓜ Colonel Fabien

Pre-clubbers loosen up over drinks at this cool Belleville spot, especially on Thursday to Saturday nights (Friday to Saturday nights in summer), when well-known Parisian DJs spin electro and house. By day, its light-flooded interior, framed by floor-to-ceiling windows, is a laid-back place for a meal.

☆ PLAY

☆ LA FLÈCHE D'OR *Club*

☎ 01 44 64 01 02; www.flechedor.fr in French; 102bis rue de Bagnolet, 20e; admission free; 8pm-2am Mon-Thu, to 6am Fri & Sat, noon-2am Sun; Ⓜ Alexandre Dumas or Gambetta

An abandoned railway station has been transformed into the alternative 'Golden Arrow' club with emerging DJs and live music acts, especially reggae and rock.

☆ LA JAVA *Live Music*

☎ 01 42 02 20 52; 105 rue du Faubourg du Temple, 10e; tickets €5-24; ⏱ 7.30pm-3am Tue-Thu, 11pm-6am Fri & Sat; Ⓜ Goncourt

Belleville's Édith Piaf got her first break in this dance hall. These

COFFEE TALK
Un café A single shot of espresso.
Un café allonge An espresso lengthened with hot water (usually, but not always, served separately).
Un café au lait A coffee with milk.
Un café crème A shot of espresso lengthened with steamed milk (closest thing to a *caffè latte*).
Un double A double shot of espresso.
Une noisette A shot of espresso with a spot of milk.

Benoît Rousseau
Artistic Director – Music, Point Éphemère

Job? Booking and organising DJs, concerts, parties and musician residencies. **Your take on Paris' nightlife scene?** It's complicated to have interesting nightlife here – police and residents/neighbours have a lot of power. There are clubs with shitty music but I can count the clubs with good music on one hand: Social Club (p67), Rex (p83), La Flèche d'Or (p107), Nouveau Casino (opposite), and here (opposite). **Booking philosophy?** I'm always listening to music…talking to artists…sometimes I hear a demo and 'wow'! I don't book every night, because I think first of artistic quality, not money. **Best performers you've broken here?** DJ Brodinski (young Parisian DJ now playing worldwide), who's really talented; and Turzi (French psychedelic rock band now on the same record label as Air). **Favourite aspect of Parisian life?** Walking across the city after a club before the metro's running, with the sun rising through the streets.

days it features world music concerts, and DJs spinning salsa beats.

⭐ LE NOUVEAU CASINO
Live Music

☎ 01 43 57 57 40; www.nouveaucasino
.net in French; 109 rue Oberkampf, 11e;
admission club €5-10, concerts €15-22;
🕑 vary; Ⓜ Parmentier

Intimate concerts, top DJs. Electro, pop, deep house, and rock all feature at this performance venue annexed to Café Charbon (p106).

⭐ LE VIEUX BELLEVILLE
Chansons

☎ 01 44 62 92 66; 12 rue des Envierges, 20e; 🕑 performances from 8.30pm Tue, Thu & Fri; Ⓜ Pyrénées

Perched at the top of the Parc de Belleville, this old-fashioned bistro is an atmospheric and not even slightly touristy venue for *chansons* performances featuring accordions and an organ grinder. It's a favourite with locals of all ages, though, so booking ahead is advised. 'The Old Belleville' also serves classic bistro fare (lunch Tuesday to Saturday, dinner Thursday to Saturday).

⭐ NEW MORNING *Jazz*

☎ 01 45 23 51 41; www.newmorning
.com; 7-9 rue des Petites Écuries, 10e;

tickets from €15; 🕑 8pm-2am most days; Ⓜ Château d'Eau

The excellent acoustics at this former printing press makes New Morning a superb place to catch the headlining jazz acts, as well as a diverse range of music including blues, rock, funk, salsa, Brazilian and Afro-Cuban styles.

⭐ POINT ÉPHEMÈRE
Club, Cultural Centre

☎ 01 40 34 02 48; www.pointephemere
.org in French; 200 quai de Valmy, 10e;
admission free-€14; 🕑 bar noon-2am,
restaurant lunch & dinner, concerts/club
events vary; Ⓜ Louis Blanc or Jaurès

Located within a converted warehouse, this 'centre for dynamic artists' has an arty student campus vibe, in part due to the resident artists and musicians who are working at its on-site studios. In addition to no-holds-barred art exhibitions, chilled bar and cheap café-restaurant, there are usually three or four bands and/or DJ sets per week and one nightclub event per week. You might even catch occasional 'surprise' gigs by bands such as Sonic Youth, who contacted music director Benoît Rousseau (opposite) to do a warm-up show just two hours before hitting its stage.

>MARAIS & BASTILLE

Hip bars, clothing and homewares boutiques, restaurants, and the city's thriving gay and Jewish communities all squeeze cheek-by-jowl into this vibrant patch.

Paris' *marais* (marsh) was cleared in the 12th century, with grand aristocratic mansions built here from the 16th century onwards. Haussmann's reformations largely bypassed the area, leaving its tangle of laneways intact. After falling from grace, the Marais underwent a revitalisation in the 1960s that hasn't stopped since and remains a see-and-be-seen spot for a *soirée* (evening out) on the town.

The adjoining Bastille was a flashpoint for the French Revolution and is still the focal point of Paris' not-infrequent political protests. This long-time grassroots district now continues to boom alongside its intertwined neighbour as a pumping party hub.

Above the Bastille, the raised Promenade Plantée walkway provides a peaceful retreat from the urban action. The nearby Bercy area (p146) is part of the latest renaissance of Paris' east.

MARAIS & BASTILLE

⊙ SEE

Guimard Synagogue 1 D3
Hôtel de Sully 2 D4
Hôtel de Ville 3 B3
Jeu de Paume -
  Site Sully ....(see 2)
Maison de Victor Hugo... 4 E4
Maison Européenne
  de la Photographie 5 C3
Musée Carnavalet 6 D3
Musée Cognacq-Jay....... 7 D3
Musée d'Art et d'
  Histoire du Judaïsme.. 8 C2
Musée des Arts
  et Métiers 9 C1
Musée Picasso 10 D2
Pavillon de l'Arsenal ... 11 D5
Place de la Bastille 12 E4
Place des Vosges 13 D3
Pletzel 14 C3
Promenade Plantée 15 F5

⌂ SHOP

Antoine et Lili................ 16 C3
Bazar de l'Hôtel
  de Ville (BHV)........... 17 C3
Boutique
  Paris-Musées............. 18 D3

Le Mots à la Bouche 19 C3
L'Habilleur.................... 20 D2
Marché aux
  Puces d'Aligre........... 21 F5
Nomades 22 E4
Red Wheelbarrow
  Bookstore................. 23 D4
Shine 24 D2
Un Chien dans
  le Marais.................. 25 C3
Viaduc des Arts 26 F5
Village St-Paul............. 27 D4

⑪ EAT

Bazar de l'Hôtel de Ville
  (BHV) Cáfétéria ......(see 17)
Brasserie Bofinger........ 28 E4
Chez Marianne 29 C3
Crêperie Bretonne......... 30 G4
Grand Appétit............... 31 E4
La Boutique Jeune........ 32 C3
L'As de Felafel............. 33 C3
Le Clown Bar 34 E1
Le Coude Fou 35 C3
Le Loir dans
  la Théière................ 36 D3
Le Petit Bofinger.......... 37 E4
Le Train Bleu............... 38 F6

Marché aux
  Enfants Rouges 39 D1
Marché Bastille 40 E4
Marché Beauvau ....(see 21)
Pozzetto 41 C3

▼ DRINK

3W Kafé......................... 42 C3
Andy Wahloo................. 43 C1
Café Baroc 44 C3
Café des Phares 45 C3
Curieux Spaghetti Bar.. 46 B2
Le Baron Rouge 47 F5
Le Cox.......................... 48 C3
Le Progrès.................... 49 D2
Le Pure Café................. 50 G4
Le Quetzal 51 C3
Le Viaduc Café...........(see 26)
Mariage Frères 52 C3
Open Café 53 C3

★ PLAY

Barrio Latino 54 F4
Le Balajo 55 E4
Opéra Bastille.............. 56 E4

Please see over for map

Courtyard and garden, Musée Carnavalet

👁 SEE

👁 HÔTEL DE SULLY

☎ 01 47 03 12 52; www.jeudepaume
.org; 62 rue St-Antoine, 4e; admission
€5/2.50, combined ticket with Jeu de
Paume – Site Concorde €8/4; 🕙 noon-
7pm Tue-Fri, 10am-7pm Sat & Sun;
Ⓜ St-Paul; ♿

Housed in a 17th-century mansion,
the Jeu de Paume – Site Sully is an
annexe of the national photography centre (p72), and focuses
on monograph and thematic
photography exhibitions. In the
same building, framed by two
Renaissance courtyards, is the
headquarters of the Monuments
Nationaux (www.monum.fr), which
has reams of info about France's
national monuments.

👁 HÔTEL DE VILLE

☎ 01 42 76 40 40; www.paris.fr; place
de l'Hôtel de Ville, 4e; exhibitions free;
🕙 10am-7pm Mon-Sat; Ⓜ Hôtel de
Ville; ♿

Paris' beautiful neo-Renaissance
town hall, completed in 1882,
is adorned with 108 statues of
illustrious Parisians. Temporary
exhibitions are held here, usually
with a Paris theme, such as the
photography of Robert Doisneau
(who snapped his world-famous
Kiss at the Hôtel de Ville here in
1950). A winter ice-skating rink
sets up outside – see p28.

MAISON DE VICTOR HUGO

☎ 01 42 72 10 16; www.musee-hugo
.paris.fr; 6 place des Vosges; admission
free; 🕙 10am-6pm Tue-Sun; Ⓜ St-Paul
or Bastille

One of the symmetrical houses
on the place des Vosges (p116) is
this former home of Victor Hugo.
The museum offers an evoca-
tive insight to the writer's life,
featuring drawings, portraits, and
furnishings preserved just as they
were when he wrote much of *Les
Misérables* here. Temporary exhibitions occasionally cost extra.

MAISON EUROPÉENNE DE LA PHOTOGRAPHIE

☎ 01 44 78 75 00; www.mep-fr.org in
French; 5-7 rue de Fourcy, 4e; admission
€6/3; 🕙 11am-8pm Wed-Sun; Ⓜ St-
Paul or Pont Marie; ♿

Exhibition prints, the printed
page and films from the 1950s on
feature in this light-filled photography museum housed in an early-
18th-century Marais mansion.
Documentaries and short films
screen most weekend afternoons,
while regular temporary exhibitions spotlight major French and
international photographers.

MUSÉE CARNAVALET

☎ 01 44 59 58 58; www.carnavalet.paris
.fr in French; 23 rue de Sévigné, 3e;
permanent exhibitions free, temporary
exhibitions extra; 🕙 10am-6pm Tue-
Sun; Ⓜ St-Paul or Chemin Vert

Housed in a pair of sumptuous
private mansions dating from the
16th and 17th centuries, Paris' history museum weaves together the
city's story from the Gallo-Roman
period through the French Revolution to its art nouveau epoch.
Among the 140 rooms, don't miss
Marcel Proust's corklined bedroom
transplanted from his former home
on blvd Haussmann.

MUSÉE COGNACQ-JAY

☎ 01 40 27 07 21; www.cognacq-jay
.paris.fr in French; 8 rue Elzévir, 3e;
admission free; 🕙 10am-6pm Tue-Sun;
Ⓜ St-Paul or Chemin Vert

PLETZL

The area around the Marais' rue des Rosiers and rue des Écouffes was traditionally known
as the Pletzl, home to a poor but vibrant Jewish community. These days, stylish boutiques
neighbour Jewish bookshops, *cacher* (kosher) pizza joints, butchers, delis, and takeaway-
felafel windows.

The Pletzl's **Guimard synagogue** (10 rue Pavée, 4e) was designed in 1913 by art nouveau architect Hector Guimard (he of the city's famous metro entrances; p75). The interior
is closed to the public.

QUARTERS

MARAIS & BASTILLE

PLACE DES VOSGES

The stone cloisters of this 1612-built ensemble of mansions resonate with busking violinists and cellists, who provide an atmospheric soundtrack for sipping tea in one of several elegant cafés or browsing the arcaded galleries and antique shops. Victor Hugo's former **residence-turned-museum** (p115) is at No 6, while today's most famous resident is Japanese designer Issey Miyake, whose Paris' headquarters are at No 3.

In the centre you'll see au pairs playing with their charges in the little gated park.

The oil paintings, pastels, sculpture, *objets d'art,* jewellery, porcelain and 18th-century furniture amassed by the founder of La Samaritaine department store are a great excuse to see inside the beautiful Hôtel de Donon, the private mansion in which it's housed.

☉ MUSÉE D'ART ET D'HISTOIRE DU JUDAÏSME

☎ 01 53 01 86 60; www.mahj.org; 71 rue du Temple, 3e; admission €6.80/4.50; ☾ 11am-6pm Mon-Fri, 10am-6pm Sun; Ⓜ Rambuteau; ☒
Documents from the Dreyfus Affair, famously championed by Parisian novelist Emile Zola in his open letter to the government, *J'accuse…!* (*I Accuse…!,* 1898), are the highlights of this comprehensive Jewish Art and History Museum tracing Jewish communities throughout Europe from the Middle Ages to today. The 17th-century mansion is also an impressive showcase for works by Chagall and Modigliani.

☉ MUSÉE DES ARTS ET MÉTIERS

☎ 01 53 01 82 00; www.arts-et-metiers
.net; 60 rue Réaumur, 3e; permanent exhibits €6.50/4.50, temporary exhibits €3/2, permanent & temporary exhibits €7.50/5.50, audioguide €2.50; ☾ 10am-6pm Tue, Wed & Fri-Sun, to 9.30pm Thu; Ⓜ Arts et Métiers; ☒
Foucault's original pendulum, used in 1855 to prove the world turns on its axis, is among the 80,000 instruments, machines and working models displayed at Europe's oldest science and technology museum. On the 1st floor, communications devices including early computers and TVs are a reminder of just how much has changed in the past few decades alone.

☉ MUSÉE PICASSO

☎ 01 42 71 25 21; www.musee-picasso
.fr in French; 5 rue de Thorigny, 3e; admission €6.50/4.50; ☾ 9.30am-6pm Wed-Mon Apr-Sep, to 5.30pm Wed-Mon Oct-Mar; Ⓜ St-Sébastien Froissart, St-Paul or Chemin Vert; ☒

Small enough to feel intimate yet large enough to trace Picasso's life through his evolving body of work (some 3500 pieces), this 17th-century mansion is an extraordinary insight into one of the world's most celebrated artists. Also on display is Picasso's personal art collection, including prized works by Braque, Cézanne, Matisse and Degas.

PAVILLON DE L'ARSENAL

☎ 01 42 76 33 97; www.pavillon-arsenal .com; 21 blvd Morland, 4e; admission free; 🕑 10.30am-6.30pm Tue-Sat, 11am-7pm Sun; M Sully Morland; 🕭 Scale models of Paris from different eras are the focal point of the city's town-planning and architectural centre, housed in glass-and-iron-roofed art nouveau premises. A comprehensive history of Paris' built environment from its beginnings through to the present day is laid out on the ground floor, as well as models of upcoming buildings. Upstairs, temporary exhibitions encompass various themes such as eco-architecture.

PLACE DE LA BASTILLE

M Bastille
Nothing remains of the former prison that was mobbed on 14 July 1789, igniting the French Revolution, but you can't miss the 52m green-bronze column topped by a gilded, winged Liberty. Revolutionaries from the uprising of 1830 are buried beneath. Now a skirmishly busy roundabout, this is still Paris' most symbolic destination for traffic-stopping protest marches.

PROMENADE PLANTÉE

www.promenade-plantee.org in French; 12e; admission free; 🕑 8am-5.30pm to 9.30pm Mon-Fri, 9am-5.30pm to 9.30pm Sat & Sun depending on season; 🕭 This pioneering park, with its walking path, flowers and park benches extending above the rooflines, has led to similar projects in the US and UK. It was a romantic backdrop for one of the central scenes in the film *Before Sunset* (see p203), and is a highlight of any visit to Paris – see p19.

Musée Picasso

🏃 DO

🏃 PROMENADES GOURMANDES *Cooking Course*

☎ 01 48 04 56 84; www.promenades
gourmandes.com

Bilingual Parisian Paule Caillat offers a personalised perspective of her Marais *quartier's* food shops plus cooking classes in her home kitchen. Half-day classes, including a shopping trip in the markets and a cookery lesson, cost €250. Full-day classes, which tack on a gourmet walking tour, cost €360 (prices are cheaper if there are two or more of you); or you can just take the gourmet walking tour for €110. Paule also runs classes for creating natural cosmetics from organic ingredients (€250).

WORTH THE TRIP – BOIS DE VINCENNES

Blanketing 995 hectares of Paris' southeast, the **Bois de Vincennes** (blvd Poniatowski, 12e; Ⓜ Porte de Charenton or Porte Dorée; ♿) is best known for its giant annual funfair, the Foire du Trône (p25).

During the rest of the year, these sprawling woods merit a visit for the royal palace, the **Château de Vincennes** (☎ 01 48 08 31 20; www.chateau-vincennes.fr; av de Paris, 12e; grounds free; 🕑 10am-6pm May-Aug, to 5pm Sep-Apr, call for guided tour departure times; Ⓜ Château de Vincennes), complete with 14th-century **dungeons** (🕑 by guided tour only; tour €7.50/4.80). Adjacent to the chateau is the flower-filled **Parc Floral de Paris** (☎ 01 49 57 24 84; esplanade du Château de Vincennes, 12e; admission €3/1.50; 🕑 9.30am-5pm to 8pm depending on season; Ⓜ Château de Vincennes), with its fluttering Jardin des Papillons (Butterfly Garden).

If you go down to the woods, you'll also be in for a surprise in the form of the out-of-water **Aquarium Tropical** (☎ 01 53 59 58 60; www.histoire-immigration.fr in French; Palais de la Porte Dorée, 293 av Daumesnil, 12e; admission €5.70/4.20; 🕑 10am-5.15pm Tue-Fri, to 7pm Sat & Sun; Ⓜ Porte Dorée). A legacy of France's colonial past, the aquarium is housed in a 1931 pavilion from the Exposition Coloniale. Today it's a teaching facility as well as a venue for visitors to see multicoloured fish and marine life. The same building houses Paris' hard-hitting new immigration museum, the **Cité Nationale de l'Histoire de l'Immigration** (admission during exhibitions €5.50/3.50, non-exhibition periods €3/2; 🕑 same hr as aquarium), with multimedia exhibits confronting family separations, workers' dorm conditions and more. Combined tickets for the aquarium and museum cost €8.50 during exhibitions and €6 outside exhibition periods (no reductions).

In addition to sea creatures swimming in the aquarium, around 600 animals call the woods home over at **Paris Zoo** (Parc Zoologique de Paris; ☎ 01 44 75 20 10; www.mnhn .fr; 53 av de St-Maurice, 12e; admission €5/1.50; 🕑 9am-6pm Mon-Sat, to 6.30pm Sun Apr-Sep, to 5pm Mon-Sat, to 5.30pm Sun Oct-Mar; Ⓜ Porte Dorée).

⛸ ROLLERS & COQUILLAGES
Mass-skate

www.rollers-coquillages.org; admission free; ☯ **Sun 2.30-5.30pm, arrive 2pm;** Ⓜ **Bastille**

Suitable for all levels, this mass-skate (p129) sets off on 21km-or-so routes from Nomades (p120) skate shop.

🛍 SHOP

The Marais' miniature streets are like a jewellery box, spilling over with brightly coloured shops selling quirky, one-off items.

🛍 ANTOINE ET LILI
Fashion, Homewares

☎ **01 42 72 26 60; www.antoineetlili .com; 51 rue des Francs Bourgeois, 4e;** ☯ **10.30am-7pm Mon, to 7.30pm Tue-Fri, 10am-8pm Sat, 12.30-7.30pm Sun;** Ⓜ **St-Paul**

This is another candy-coloured branch of this offbeat boutique (see p102).

🛍 BAZAR DE L'HÔTEL DE VILLE (BHV) *Department Store*

☎ **01 42 74 90 00; www.bhv.fr in French; 14 rue du Temple, 4e;** ☯ **9.30am-7.30pm Mon, Tue, Thu & Fri, to 9pm Wed, to 8pm Sat;** Ⓜ **Hôtel de Ville**

Parisians renovating their apartments head to this recently renovated department store's basement hardware section for hammers, nails, drill bits and even DIY and decorating workshops (bookable via the website). You'll also find a wide range of clothes, accessories and stationery, and an upstairs cafeteria (p121).

🛍 BOUTIQUE PARIS-MUSÉES
Arts & Crafts

☎ **01 42 74 13 02; 29 rue des Francs Bourgeois, 4e;** ☯ **2-7pm Mon, 11am-1pm & 2-7pm Tue-Sat, noon-7.30pm Sun;** Ⓜ **Chemin Vert or St-Paul**

Innovative works by young, up-and-coming Parisian artists share shelf space with quality reproductions of paintings and sculptures on display at Paris' museums.

🛍 LE MOTS À LA BOUCHE
Books

☎ **01 42 78 88 30; www.motsbouche .com in French; 6 rue Ste-Croix de la Bretonnerie, 4e;** ☯ **11am-11pm Mon-Sat, 1-9pm Sun;** Ⓜ **Hôtel de Ville**

'On the Tip of the Tongue' is Paris' premier gay and lesbian bookshop, with reams of info about gay Parisian life. On the ground floor you'll find English-language books, including travel guides; things steam up when you go down (stairs).

🛍 L'HABILLEUR *Fashion*

☎ **01 48 87 77 12; 44 rue de Poitou, 3e;** ☯ **11am-8pm Mon-Sat;** Ⓜ **St-Sébastien Froissart**

Savvy Parisians grab last season's designer-wear at up to 70% off original prices at this haut Marais (below) menswear and womenswear boutique. Look out for labels like Paul & Joe, Patrick Cox, Dries van Noten and Helmut Lang.

🏛 MARCHÉ AUX PUCES D'ALIGRE *Market*
place d'Aligre, 12e; ⌚ 7.30am-1.30pm Tue-Sun; Ⓜ Ledru Rollin
Rummage through boxes and racks jammed with vintage fashions at Paris' most central flea market. The Marché Beauvau (p124) food market is next door.

🏛 NOMADES
Sports Equipment
☎ 01 44 54 07 44; www.nomadeshop .com in French; 37 blvd Bourdon, 4e; weekday/weekend blade hire per half-day from €5/6; ⌚ 11.30am-7.30pm Tue-Fri, 10am-7pm Sat, noon-6pm Sun; Ⓜ Bastille
The home of the Rollers & Coquillages mass-skate (p119), Nomades sells and rents inline skates and protective equipment.

🏛 RED WHEELBARROW BOOKSTORE *Books*
☎ 01 48 04 75 08; www.theredwheelbar row.com; 22 rue St-Paul, 4e; ⌚ 10am-7pm Mon-Sat, 2-6pm Sun; Ⓜ St-Paul
Brimming with quality English-language literature, this much-loved North American–run bookshop also has adorable kids' books and info on literary events.

🏛 SHINE *Fashion, Accessories*
☎ 01 48 05 80 10; 5 rue de Poitou, 3e; ⌚ 11am-7pm Mon-Sat, 2-5pm Sun; Ⓜ Filles du Calvaire
Since it opened its doors a few years ago, this innovative boutique stocking hand-picked pieces from the current crop of young designers, including Bijoux de Sophie jewellery, has inspired a wave of likeminded enterprises in the area – see below.

🏛 UN CHIEN DANS LE MARAIS *Fashion*
☎ 01 42 74 30 06; www.unchiendansle marais.com; 35bis rue du Roi de Sicile, 4e; ⌚ 11am-7pm; Ⓜ St-Paul

HAUT MARAIS
The northern Marais – aka haut Marais (high/upper Marais) or, occasionally, the anglo moniker NoMa – is rapidly becoming a hub of up-and-coming designers. Both men and women will find creative new fashions and quality vintage gear as well as accessories, homewares and art. Most of the action concentrates around rues de Poitou, de Saintonge, Vieille du Temple, Debelleyme and Charlot, 3e (Ⓜ St Sébastien Froissart or Filles du Calvaire), with new places popping up all the time – keep tabs via http://hautmarais.blogspot.com.

PAMPERED POOCHES

Coiffed, perfumed, and sporting the latest fashions, dogs are treated with adulation in Paris. They're welcomed in shops (even food shops, where shopkeepers might slip them some tasty morsel). They ride the metro (with their own ticket). They dine in restaurants (sometimes on special stools beneath the tables, and sometimes on laps). Dog psychologists dealing in 'image problems' command top dollar, as do day-spa-like grooming salons. And department stores and specialised boutiques keep them well dressed. But these days there's less evidence of Parisian pups on the pavements than there once was – see p199.

This little boutique stocks nothing but dog outfits in all sizes. You can pick out a design from the latest autumn/winter and spring/summer collections from casual T-shirts, hoodies, pants, skirts and dresses through to eveningwear and fancy-dress costumes, plus raingear, bathrobes and pyjamas.

🏛 VIADUC DES ARTS
Arts & Crafts

www.viaduc-des-arts.com; av Daumesnil, 12e; ⏱ vary; Ⓜ Bastille or Gare de Lyon

Located beneath the Promenade Plantée, in the brick arches of its 19th-century viaduct, traditional craftsmen and women carry out renovations and repairs of antiques, and create new items using traditional methods. The 51 artisans include furniture and tapestry restorers, interior designers, cabinet makers, violin- and flute-makers, embroiderers and jewellers.

🏛 VILLAGE ST-PAUL
Antiques, Arts & Crafts

www.parislemarais.com; rue St-Paul; 11am-7pm Thu-Mon; Ⓜ St-Paul

On the site of an ancient convent, this delightful 'village' brings together over 60 antiques dealers (18th-century through to art deco) and arts and crafts boutiques. Unusual gifts found here range from old postcards of Paris through to wacky new homewares inventions.

🍴 EAT

🍴 BAZAR DE L'HÔTEL DE VILLE (BHV) CAFÉTERIA
Cafétéria   €

14 rue du Temple, 4e; ⏱ 11.15am-6.30pm Mon, Tue & Thu-Sat, 11.15am-8.30pm Wed; Ⓜ Hôtel de Ville

Eye-level views of the statues adorning the Hôtel de Ville's roofline extend from this *cafétéria* on the 5th floor of the department store (p119). It's kid-friendly and wallet-friendly, with a carvery, and desserts such as parfaits.

🍴 BRASSERIE BOFINGER
Brasserie €€

☎ 01 42 72 87 82; www.bofingerparis
.com; 5-7 rue de la Bastille, 4e; 🕐 lunch & dinner to 12.30am; Ⓜ Bastille

To experience brasserie dining in all its art nouveau splendour, there's no better place in town. The historic Bofinger's food is first-rate, its service genuine, and a seat under its glass cupola sublime. Past diners span Mikhail Gorbachev to Madonna, but it's the little snippets of Parisian life around you that make a meal here unforgettable.

🍴 CHEZ MARIANNE *Jewish* €

☎ 01 42 72 18 86; 2 rue des Hospital-ières St-Gervais, 4e; 🕐 noon-midnight; Ⓜ St-Paul

There's often a wait for a table at Chez Marianne's black-and-white-tiled restaurant, but the phenom-enal mix-and-match platters, with choices including olives, hommus, aubergine and much more, are worth every minute. Otherwise you can pack a picnic from the deli to take to the place des Vosges (p116), or pick up felafel sandwich-es from the takeaway window.

🍴 CRÊPERIE BRETONNE
Breton, Crêperie €

☎ 01 43 55 62 29; 67 rue de Charonne, 12e; 🕐 lunch Mon-Fri, dinner Mon-Sat; Ⓜ Charonne

Authentic down to its buckwheat *galettes* and perfectly buttered sweet crêpes (with salted butter, of course), this place is filled with emotive photos of Brittany, and, joy of joys, serves brut Val de Rance cider. *Yec'hed mat* (cheers)!

Head to Chez Marianne for appetising platters or a takeaway feast

🍴 GRAND APPÉTIT
Vegetarian €

☎ 01 40 27 04 95; 9 rue de la Cerisaie, 4e; ⏰ lunch Mon-Fri, dinner Mon-Wed; Ⓜ Bastille or Sully Morland; Ⓥ

Just when you thought there were no vegan eateries in Paris, along comes this old-school-hippie place serving dishes made with organic cereals, raw and cooked vegetables and seaweed. There's a macrobiotic shop next door (open 9.30am to 7.30pm Monday to Thursday, to 4pm Friday).

🍴 LA BOUTIQUE JEUNE
Jewish €

☎ 01 42 72 78 91; www.laboutique jaune.com in French; 27 rue des Rosiers, 4e; ⏰ 10am-7pm Wed-Mon, closed mid-Jul–mid-Aug; Ⓜ St-Paul

Since 1946 this bright yellow–fronted *traiteur* has been purveying fantastic cakes, breads, *charcuterie*, and its famous 'Yiddish sandwich', filled with the flavours of Eastern Europe and served hot. There's a tiny sit-down area.

🍴 L'AS DE FELAFEL *Jewish* €

☎ 01 48 87 63 60; 34 rue des Rosiers, 4e; ⏰ noon-midnight Sun-Thu, to 5pm Fri; Ⓜ St-Paul

L'As de Felafel's flawlessly textured fried chickpea balls are better value to take away than to eat in. Be prepared to queue at the street-opening takeaway window midweek, when local workers make a beeline here on their lunch break.

🍴 LE CLOWN BAR *French* €€

☎ 01 43 55 87 35; 114 rue Amelot, 11e; ⏰ lunch & dinner to 1am Mon-Sat; Ⓜ Filles du Calvaire

If you've ever fantasised about running away with the circus, this bistro's frescoes and mosaics of clowns and circus memorabilia will make you feel like you already have. (The evil-themed clowns will scare the pants off kids and coulrophobes, though.) Traditional *menus* are good value.

🍴 LE COUDE FOU *French* €

☎ 01 42 77 15 16; www.lecoudefou .com; 12 rue du Bourg Tibourg, 4e; ⏰ lunch & dinner, bar until 2am; Ⓜ Hôtel de Ville

This cosy bistro, with classic tiled and muraled walls, is always buzzing with local customers, who come for the specialist wines as well as hearty traditional French fare.

🍴 LE PETIT BOFINGER
French €€

☎ 01 42 72 05 23; 6 rue de la Bastille, 4e; ⏰ lunch & dinner to 12.30am; Ⓜ Bastille

Considering the grandeur of Brasserie Bofinger (opposite), the prices are extremely reasonable.

Still, if you're on a budget, its splendidly tiled little brother across the street, Le Petit Bofinger, is a cheaper but atmospheric alternative, serving fresh market fare.

🍴 LE TRAIN BLEU French   €€€
☎ 01 44 75 76 76; www.le-train-bleu .com; 26 pl Louis Armand, Gare de Lyon, 12e; ☇ lunch & dinner; Ⓜ Gare de Lyon
Featured in Luc Besson's *La Femme Nikita* (1991), this railway station's heritage-listed, *belle époque* showpiece is a sumptuous place to dine on foie gras with pears and gingerbread, steak tartare with fries and cactus sorbet for dessert, followed by a pot of Blue Moon Ceylon tea. There's an excellent children's menu, and a bar for a

> **BRUNCHING IN PARIS**
> Sunday lunch is traditionally France's main meal of the week, but numerous bars and cafés now offer brunch, often starting at noon and usually stretching out to around 4pm, and costing roughly €15 to €30.
>   Our favourite spot to spend a languorous Sunday remains the *Alice in Wonderland*–named **Le Loir dans la Théière** (The Dormouse in the Teapot; ☎ 01 42 72 90 61; 3 rue des Rosiers, 4e; ☇ 9.30am-7pm), a wonderful old space filled with retro toys and comfy couches. Its farm-style wooden tables are laden at brunch, which is served here on both Saturday and Sunday.

digestif before boarding your train to the Côte d'Azur.

🍴 MARCHÉ AUX ENFANTS ROUGES Market
39 rue de Bretagne, 3e; ☇ **9am-2pm & 4-8pm Tue-Fri, 9am-8pm Sat, to 2pm Sun;** Ⓜ **Filles du Calvaire**
Named for a nearby 17th-century orphanage whose little residents were dressed in red, Paris' oldest covered market (built in 1615) sits behind an inconspicuous green gate. Many of its inexpensive dishes are ready-to-eat; alternatively, head to the far back corner to its whitewashed, bare-boarded wine bar, L'Estaminet.

🍴 MARCHÉ BASTILLE Market
blvd Richard Lenoir, 11e; ☇ **7am-2.30pm Thu, to 3pm Sun;** Ⓜ **Bastille or Richard Lenoir**
If you only get to one open-air market in Paris, this one – stretching between the Bastille and Richard Lenoir metro stations – is among the very best.

🍴 MARCHÉ BEAUVAU Market
place d'Aligre, 12e; ☇ **9am-1pm & 4-7.30pm Tue-Fri, 9am-1pm & 3.30-7.30pm Sat, 9am-1.30pm Sun;** Ⓜ **Ledru Rollin**
Adjacent to the place d'Aligre flea market (p120), this covered market sells Arab and North African food specialities such as couscous and sweet pastries.

Search for anything and everything, from delicious produce to old wares, at Marché Bastille

🍴 POZZETTO Ice Cream €
☎ 01 42 77 08 64; http://pozzetto.biz
in French; 39 rue du Roi de Sicile, 4e;
🕙 noon-11pm Mon-Thu, to 2am Fri-Sun;
Ⓜ St-Paul

Addiction warning. This gelato maker opened a couple of years ago when a group of friends from northern Italy couldn't find their favourite ice cream in Paris, and so imported the ingredients to create it here from scratch. Flavours (spatula'd, not scooped) include *gianduia* (hazelnut chocolate) and *fiordilatte* (milk). It also sells Piedmontese biscuits, and the staff pour quite possibly the best espresso this side of the border.

🍸 DRINK

For a plethora of drinking and nightlife options, head to the Pletzl area (p115) or the lively establishments ringing place de la Bastille. Rue de Bretagne (D1) is lined with great cafés, with more around place d'Aligre.

🍸 3W KAFÉ Gay & Lesbian
☎ 01 48 87 39 26; www.3w-kafe.com
in French; 8 rue des Écouffes, 4e;
🕙 5.30pm-2am; Ⓜ Hôtel de Ville

Men are welcome but rare at this sleek lesbian lounge in the Marais.

GETTING PHILOSOPHICAL

Grappling with concepts such as existentialism is required for Parisians to pass the *baccalauréat* (school certificate) – hence the popularity of *philocafés* (philosophy cafés), where wide-ranging, brain-teasing discussions like 'what is a fact?' take place. The original (and arguably best), the **Café des Phares** (below), was established by late philosopher and Sorbonne professor Marc Sautet (1947–98). Most *philocafé* sessions are in French, but there's a popular English-language version at the **Café de Flore** (p162) on the first Wednesday of every month from 7pm to 9pm. Entry's free but you need to buy a drink. To sign up, visit http://philosophy.meetup.com/274.

▼ ANDY WAHLOO *Bar*

☎ 01 42 71 20 38; 69 rue des Gravilliers, 3e; 🕑 5pm-2am Tue-Sat; Ⓜ Arts et Métiers

Although its name means 'I have nothing' in Arabic, this clubby bar's eye-popping, multicoloured Moroccan decor and ear-splitting music owe a greater debt to its almost-namesake, Andy Warhol.

▼ CAFÉ BAROC *Bar*

☎ 01 48 87 61 30; 37 rue du Roi de Sicile, 4e; 🕑 5pm-2am Tue-Sun; Ⓜ St-Paul

Baroc's old cinema seats are ideal for sipping beers with a twist of syrup in flavours such as lemon or peach. Normally a chilled little place, things get hyper when bar staff crank up fabulously camp '80s tunes. Downstairs there's a basement with vintage sofas. Hours can vary in midsummer.

▼ CAFÉ DES PHARES *Café*

☎ 01 42 72 04 70; 7 place de la Bastille, 4e; 🕑 7.30am-3am Sun-Thu, to 4am Fri

& Sat, philosophy debates 11am-1pm Sun; Ⓜ Bastille

Even if your French isn't up to following the convoluted philosophy exchanges at this *philocafé* (see above), it still offers a fascinating cultural insight; and is a convivial spot for a drink anytime.

▼ CURIEUX SPAGHETTI BAR *Bar*

☎ 01 42 72 75 97; www.curieuxspag.com; 14 rue St-Mérri, 4e; 🕑 noon-4am Thu-Sat, to 2am Sun-Wed; Ⓜ Rambuteau

This neon-pink-lit, loungey bar spins decent beats, and also serves spaghetti as part of a hip international menu, as well as test-tube shots of vodka in flavours like pina colada and bubble gum. Post-clubbers descend for Sunday brunch from noon (book ahead).

▼ LE BARON ROUGE *Wine Bar*

☎ 01 43 43 14 32; 1 rue Théophile Roussel, 12e; 10am-2pm & 5-10pm Mon-Thu,

10am-10pm Fri & Sat, 10am-3pm Sun; Ⓜ **Ledru Rollin**
Amid big wooden barrels and bottles lining its walls, this spirited wine bar serves superb wines by the glass. It takes on something of a party atmosphere on Sundays after the Marché aux Puces d'Aligre (p120) wraps up.

☿ LE COX *Gay & Lesbian*
☎ **01 42 72 08 00; www.cox.fr in French; 15 rue des Archives, 4e; noon-2am Mon-Fri, 1pm-2am Sat & Sun;** Ⓜ **Hôtel de Ville**
The name of Paris' gay bar-of-the-moment says it all. Happy hour (6pm to 9pm) is prime cruising time.

☿ LE PROGRÈS *Café*
☎ **01 42 72 01 44; 1 rue de Bretagne, 3e;** ⏱ **8am-10pm Mon-Sat;** Ⓜ **St-Sébastien Froissart or Filles du Calvaire**
This sunlit, art deco–tiled café is a favourite with Paris' current 'Lost Generation' of writers for its cheap bistro fare, strong coffee, and pitchers of wine.

☿ LE PURE CAFÉ *Café*
☎ **01 43 71 47 22; 14 rue Jean Macé, 11e;** ⏱ **7am-2am Mon-Fri, 8am-2am Sat, noon-midnight Sun;** Ⓜ **Charonne or Faidherbe Chaligny**
A classic Parisian haunt, this rustic, cherry-red corner café found its way onto the big screen in *Before Sunset* (p203). The kitchen turns

out well-crafted fare (sometimes with a fusion twist), but above all it's an unpretentious place for a coffee or glass of wine.

☿ LE QUETZAL *Gay & Lesbian*
☎ **01 48 87 99 07; 10 rue de la Verrerie, 4e;** ⏱ **5pm-5am;** Ⓜ **Hôtel de Ville**
A 30-something gay male crowd congregates at this house- and dance-spinning bar, which aptly sits opposite rue des Mauvais Garçons (Bad Boys' Street; named after the brigands who congregated here in 1540).

☿ LE VIADUC CAFÉ *Café*
☎ **01 44 74 70 70; 43 av Daumesnil, 12e;** ⏱ **9am-2am;** Ⓜ **Gare de Lyon**
Wedged into a glassed-in arch of the Viaduc des Arts (p121), this is a sophisticated place for a day or night-time tipple. Live jazz plays from noon to 4pm during Sunday brunch from mid-June to mid-September.

☿ MARIAGE FRÈRES
Salon de Thé
☎ **01 42 72 28 11; www.mariagefreres .com; 30 rue du Bourg Tibourg, 4e;** ⏱ **shop 10.30am-7.30pm, tearooms noon-7pm;** Ⓜ **Hôtel de Ville**
Established in 1854, Paris' first-ever tea shop sells over 500 varieties of tea from 35 countries, which you can sip in the genteel tearoom.

QUARTERS

MARAIS & BASTILLE

▼ OPEN CAFÉ *Gay & Lesbian*
☎ 01 42 72 26 18; www.opencafe.fr; 17 rue des Archives, 4e; ⏱ 11am-2am Sun-Thu, to 4am Fri & Sat; Ⓜ Hôtel de Ville
The wide, white-seated terrace at this long-established gay bar is a prime spot to survey the scene or strike up a conversation, with a predominately social rather than cruisey vibe.

⭐ PLAY

BARRIO LATINO *Salsa Bar*
☎ 01 55 78 84 75; 46-48 rue du Faubourg St-Antoine, 11e; ⏱ 11am-2am Sun-Thu, to 3am Fri & Sat; Ⓜ Bastille

You can salsa your socks off in this vast venue. The crowd is as mixed as a well-shaken cocktail: gay, straight, locals and visitors.

⭐ LE BALAJO *Club*
☎ 01 47 00 07 87; www.balajo.fr; 9 rue de Lappe, 11e; admission from €12; ⏱ 10pm-2am Tue & Thu, 9pm-2am Wed, 11pm-5am Fri & Sat, 3-7.30pm Sun; Ⓜ Bastille
Opened in 1936, Le Balajo still pulls in the crowds for a diverse range of offerings – from the ubiquitous salsa to rock, DJs and R&B. It evokes its past during its Sunday *musette* (accordion gig) from 3pm to 7pm, with old-time tea dancing.

Curved walls of gridded glass form the gleaming exterior of the Opéra Bastille

ON A ROLL

Paris is home to the world's largest inline mass-skate, **Pari-Roller** (p155), which regularly attracts over 10,000 bladers. Dubbed 'Friday Night Fever', routes incorporate cobblestones and downhill stretches, and are geared for experienced bladers only (for your safety and everyone else's).

Less feverish are the courses covered by **Rollers & Coquillages** (p119), though you'll still need basic proficiency (ie knowing how to brake!). These depart from **Nomades** (p120), which sells and rents gear.

Both of Paris' mass-skates are accompanied by yellow-jersey-clad volunteer marshals, along with police (some on inline skates), and ambulances. Wear bright clothes to make yourself visible to drivers and other skaters.

⭐ OPÉRA BASTILLE
Opera House

☎ 08 92 89 90 90; www.operadeparis
.fr in French; 2-6 place de la Bastille, 12e;
🕑 box office 10.30am-6.30pm Mon-Sat;
Ⓜ Bastille

Instigated by Mitterrand as the city's second opera house, this 1989-built monolith seats 3400 people. Bargain-priced opera seats are only available from the box office, as are €5 standing-only tickets (available 90 minutes prior to performances). Last-minute seats for those aged under 28 or over 60 are sold off cheaply 15 minutes before curtain-time.

>THE ISLANDS

Paris' geographic and historic heart is situated here in the Seine.

The city's watery beginnings took place on the Île de la Cité, the larger of the two inner-city islands. Today, all distances in France are measured from Kilometre Zéro, marked by a bronze star outside Notre Dame. The island is also home to the beautiful Ste-Chapelle; the Conciergerie, where Marie Antoinette was imprisoned; a colourful flower market; and some picturesque parks such as place Dauphine and square du Vert Galant.

To the east, the tranquil Île St-Louis is graced with elegant mansions that are among the city's most exclusive residential addresses, along with a handful of intimate hotels and exquisite boutiques. Buying a cone of the island's famous Berthillon ice cream and strolling the cobbled streets is a time-honoured ritual – see p17.

Connecting the two islands, the Pont St-Louis is an impossibly romantic spot at sunset.

THE ISLANDS

◉ SEE
Cathédrale de Notre
    Dame de Paris 1 E4
Conciergerie 2 C2
Pont Neuf 3 B1
Ste-Chapelle...................4 C2

◻ SHOP
Clair de Rêve...................5 G4
La Petite Scierie 6 G4

Librairie Ulysse...............7 G4
Marché aux Fleurs..........8 D2
Oliviers & Co 9 F4

◻ EAT
Amorino 10 G4
Brasserie de
    l'Île St-Louis 11 F4
Café le Flore
    en l'Île 12 F4

Maison Berthillon 13 G4
Sorza.............................14 G4

▼ DRINK
La Charlotte
    en L'Île 15 G4
Taverne Henri IV..........16 A1

Please see over for map

QUARTERS

THE ISLANDS

The magnificent gothic exterior of Cathédrale de Notre Dame de Paris illuminated at night

◉ SEE

◉ CATHÉDRALE DE NOTRE DAME DE PARIS

☎ 01 42 34 56 10; www.cathedralede
paris.com; place du Parvis Notre Dame,
4e; cathedral admission free, audioguide
€5, towers €7.50/4.80, treasury €3/2;
⏲ cathedral 7.45am-6.45pm, towers
10am-6.30pm Apr-Sep, to 7.30pm
Oct-Mar, treasury 9.30am-6pm Mon-Sat,
1-6pm Sun; Ⓜ Cité; ♿

Light streams through three rose
windows into the interior of Paris'
gargoyled cathedral. Climbing
the towers' 422 spiralling steps
(no wheelchair access) rewards
you with breathtaking panoramas
across Paris. The best views of the
cathedral's flying buttresses are
from square Jean XXIII around the
back. Free 90-minute guided tours
in English depart at 2pm Wednesday and Thursday and 2.30pm on
Saturday. See also below.

SAVED BY THE BOOK
Although the Gothic wonder that is the Cathédrale de Notre Dame de Paris (above) took
200 years to build – from 1163 to the early 14th century – severe damage during the
French Revolution saw it fall into ruin, and it was destined for demolition. Salvation came
with the widespread popularity of Victor Hugo's 1831 novel, The Hunchback of Notre Dame,
which sparked a petition to save it. Subsequently, architect Eugène Emmanuel Viollet-le-Duc
undertook extensive renovations between 1845 and 1864. Some 10 million visitors now cross
its threshold annually, making it the most visited site in Paris.

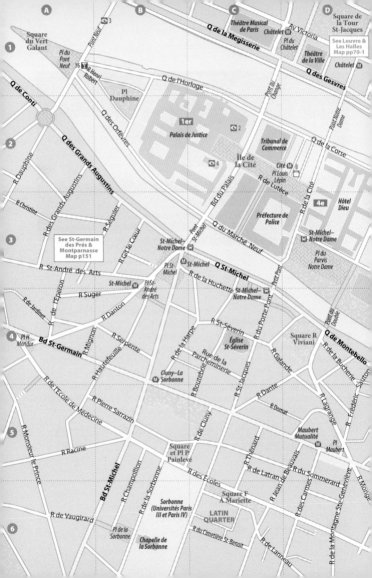

◎ CONCIERGERIE

☎ 01 53 40 60 97; www.monum.fr; 2 blvd du Palais, 1er; admission €8/6, combined ticket with Ste-Chapelle €11.50/9; ⏱ 9.30am-6pm Mar-Oct, 9am-5pm Nov-Feb; Ⓜ Cité

This cross-vaulted 14th-century palace was turned into a prison and torture chamber where 2780 *condamnés* (condemned) that had been brought before the Revolutionary Tribunal in the adjoining Palais de Justice – notably Marie Antoinette – were incarcerated before being sent to the guillotine.

◎ PONT NEUF

Ⓜ Pont Neuf

Paris' oldest and most famous bridge (ironically called 'new bridge') was inaugurated in 1607, linking the Île de la Cité with the Seine's left and right banks. Its semicircular benches, recessed into the sparkling white stone, are a picturesque spot to watch Paris' riverboats pass by.

◎ STE-CHAPELLE

☎ 01 53 40 60 97; www.monum.fr; 4 blvd du Palais, 1er; admission €6.50/4.50, combined ticket with Conciergerie €11.50/9; ⏱ 9.30am-6pm Mar-Oct, 9am-5pm Nov-Feb; Ⓜ Cité; ♿

The luminous stained-glass windows of this 'Holy Chapel', consecrated in 1248, are particularly ethereal as the backdrop for classical concerts by composers such as Vivaldi and Bach. Concert tickets generally cost €25 for adults, €16 for concessions, offsetting much of the entry price and allowing you to spend extended time in its glorious surroundings – check outside for posters.

🛍 SHOP

🏷 CLAIR DE RÊVE *Toys*

☎ 01 43 29 81 06; www.clairdereve.com; 35 rue St-Louis en l'Île, 4e; ⏱ 11am-1pm & 2-7pm Mon-Sat; Ⓜ Pont Marie

---

BOUQUINISTES

Lining both banks of the Seine through the centre of Paris, the open-air *bouquiniste* stalls selling secondhand, and often out-of-print, books, rare magazines, postcards and old advertising posters are a definitive Parisian sight. The name comes from *bouquiner*, meaning 'to read with appreciation'. At night, *bouquinistes'* dark-green metal stalls are folded down and locked like suitcases. Many open only from spring to autumn (and many shut in August), but even in the depths of winter, you'll still find somewhere to barter for antiquarian treasures.

SAY IT WITH FLOWERS

If you're inspired to buy someone flowers in this romantic city, beware of sending the wrong message. *Chrysanthèmes* (chrysanthemums) are strictly for cemeteries, *œillets* (carnations) supposedly bring bad luck, *roses jaunes* (yellow roses) imply adultery, and *roses rouges* (red roses) expressly signify passion. And flowers are presented in odd-numbered bunches (so not a dozen, but, due to superstition, never 13!).

Stringed marionettes bob from the ceiling of this endearing little shop. Papier-mâché and leather marionettes start at around €100; expect to pay around six times that for one made of porcelain. It also sells wind-up toys. See p153 for info on marionette shows in Paris.

LA PETITE SCIERIE
Food & Drink

☎ 01 55 42 14 88; www.lapetitescierie
.fr; 60 rue St-Louis en l'Île, 4e; 🕙 11am-
7pm Thu-Mon; Ⓜ Pont Marie

Strewn with stuffed ducks, this tiny shop specialises in foie gras (made by the family who run it), which you can taste in-store on chunks of baguette.

LIBRAIRIE ULYSSE *Books*

☎ 01 43 25 17 35; www.ulysse.fr in
French; 26 rue St-Louis en l'Île, 4e; 🕙 2-
8pm Tue-Fri; Ⓜ Pont Marie

You can barely move in between this shop's antiquarian and new travel guides, *National Geographic* back-editions and maps. Opened in 1971 by the intrepid Catherine Domaine, this was the world's first

travel bookshop. Ulysse's hours can be erratic, but knock on the door or telephone and Catherine will open up if she's around.

Exquisitely decorated rose window, Ste-Chapelle

🏠 MARCHÉ AUX FLEURS
Market

place Louis Lépin, 4e; ⏱ **8am-7.30pm Mon-Sat;** Ⓜ **Cité**
Blooms have been sold at this flower market since 1808, making it the oldest market of any kind in Paris. On Sunday, between 9am and 7pm, it transforms into a twittering **bird market**.

🛍 OLIVIERS & CO
Food & Drink

☎ **01 40 46 89 37; www.oliviersandco .com; 81 rue St-Louis en l'Île, 4e;** ⏱ **11am-2pm & 3-7.30pm Mon-Fri, 11am-7.30pm Sat & Sun;** Ⓜ **Pont Marie**
This olive oil shop was the first of what is now a worldwide chain; created by Olivier Baussan, who also founded natural cosmetic company L'Occitane (there's a L'Occitane boutique on this street at No 55). In addition to Baussan's native Provence, Oliviers & Co also stocks oils from Italy, Greece, Israel, Turkey and Portugal.

🍴 EAT

You'll find a smattering of bistros away from the tourist crowds around the Île de la Cité's place Dauphine (B1). The Île St-Louis' most famous foodstuff is Berthillon ice cream (p17),

but it's not the only *glacier* here. Some places sell various ice creams which people assume are Berthillon; check the sign. And gelato maker Amorino opened its inaugural shop (47 rue St-Louis en l'Île, 4e) on the Île St-Louis and now has outlets as far afield as Shanghai. (Though in our opinion Amorino's gelato isn't a lick on Pozzetto's, p125.)

🍴 BRASSERIE DE L'ÎLE ST-LOUIS *Brasserie*   €€

☎ **01 43 54 02 59; 55 quai de Bourbon, 4e;** ⏱ **6pm-1am Thu, noon-midnight Fri-Tue;** Ⓜ **Pont Marie**
Renowned for its Alsatian cuisine, with various dishes doused in Riesling, you might just as easily be in a Strasbourg *winstub* – were it not for the Seine views from the terrace.

🍴 CAFÉ LE FLORE EN L'ÎLE
Brasserie, Ice Cream   €€

☎ **01 43 29 88 27; 42 quai d'Orléans, 4e;** ⏱ **8am-1am;** Ⓜ **Pont Marie**
Beneath the green-and-gold awnings framing this beautiful gilded, timber-panelled tearoom, Le Flore en L'Île's takeaway window does a roaring trade in Berthillon ice cream. But, while brasserie fare is decent and service friendly, if you're just stopping by for a Berthillon cone, be aware that this place charges up to a euro more than other establishments

around the island, including Maison Berthillon's own premises (below).

🍴 MAISON BERTHILLON
Salon de Thé, Ice Cream €

☎ 01 43 54 31 61; www.berthillon -glacier.fr; 31 rue St-Louis en l'Île, 4e; ⏱ 10am-8pm Wed-Sun, closed mid-Jul–early Sep; Ⓜ Pont Marie

The producer of the island's legendary ice cream sells its wares here at its own premises, as well as through a number of other outlets that are sprinkled around the island (and elsewhere throughout Paris). Proof of just how much Parisians work to live, not vice versa (see p201), it closes for annual holidays in mid-summer – seriously.

🍴 SORZA *International* €€

☎ 01 43 54 78 62; www.restaurant -sorza.fr in French; 51 rue St-Louis en l'Île, 4e; ⏱ noon-10.30pm; Ⓜ Pont Marie

The Île St-Louis has an air of being frozen in time, but this minimalist black-and-red geomaetric cube with a neon-orange bar sitting in the back corner is a striking exception. Contemporary fare ranges from octopus salad to foie gras risotto, and prices are reasonable given the location and lack of competition on this small island.

🍸 DRINK

🍸 LA CHARLOTTE EN L'ÎLE
Salon de Thé

☎ 01 43 54 25 83; 24 rue St-Louis en l'Île; ⏱ 2-8pm Thu-Sun; Ⓜ Pont Marie

The most enchanting of the Île St-Louis' tea rooms, this fairytale place serves Turkish coffee and hot chocolate along with dozens of varieties of tea.

🍸 TAVERNE HENRI IV *Bar*

☎ 01 43 54 27 90; 13 place du Pont Neuf, 1er; ⏱ 11.30am-9.30pm Mon-Fri, noon-5pm Sat, closed Aug; Ⓜ Pont Neuf

Popular with Paris' legal eagles from the Palais de Justice nearby, this small, old-fashioned wine bar serves inexpensive and tasty bistro fare such as quiches and cheese-*charcuterie* platters, all of which go well with a glass of beaujolais; or you can just stop by for a drink. Hours can fluctuate.

⭐ PLAY

Aside from Ste-Chapelle's classical concerts there's not a lot doing on these little islands, though they're a good spot to catch buskers, particularly musicians on the Pont St-Louis and street performers in front of Notre Dame.

>LATIN QUARTER

So named because university students here communicated in Latin until the French Revolution and renowned worldwide as an intellectual incubator, the Latin Quarter remains the centre of academic life in Paris.

The quarter centres on the Sorbonne's main university campus, which is graced by fountains and lime trees. In the surrounding area you'll encounter students and professors lingering at its late-opening bookshops and secondhand record shops on and around the 'boul Mich' (blvd St-Michel). You'll also encounter them researching in its museums like the Musée National du Moyen Âge (aka Cluny); at the library within its exquisite art deco–Moorish mosque; in its botanic gardens, the Jardin des Plantes – or simply relaxing in its pigeon-filled squares and gardens.

To really take the area's pulse, head to its liveliest commercial street, medieval rue Mouffetard, a colourful jumble of student bars, cheap eateries, market stalls and inexpensive clothing and homewares shops.

LATIN QUARTER

⊙ SEE

Catacombes	1	A5
Galerie d'Anatomie Comparée et de Paléontologie	2	D3
Galerie de Minéralogie et de Géologie	3	C4
Grande Galerie de l'Évolution	4	C3
Institut du Monde Arabe	5	C2
Jardin des Plantes	6	D3
Ménagerie du Jardin des Plantes	7	D3
Mosquée de Paris	8	C4
Musée National du Moyen Âge	9	B2
Panthéon	10	B3
Rue Mouffetard	11	B3
Sorbonne	12	B2

⌂ SHOP

Abbey Bookshop	13	B2
Mouffetard Folie's	14	C3
Shakespeare & Company	15	B2

🍴 EAT

Chez Nicos	16	B3
La Tour d'Argent	17	C2
L'Ourcine	18	B5
Marché Maubert	19	B2
Marché Monge	20	C3
Mouffetard Food Market	21	C4
Pho 67	22	B2

▾ DRINK

Café Panis	23	B2
Le Pantalon	24	B3
Le Vieux Chêne	25	C3

★ PLAY

Le Caveau de la Huchette	26	B2
Le Champo	27	B2

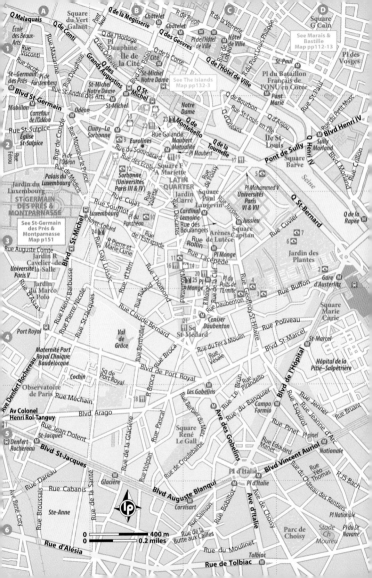

SEE

CATACOMBES

☎ 01 43 22 47 63; www.catacombes
.paris.fr in French; 1 av Colonel Henri
Rol-Tanguy, 14e; admission €7/5.50;
🕙 10am-5pm Tue-Sun; Ⓜ Denfert
Rochereau

Paris' most macabre sight is its
series of underground passages
lined with skulls and bones ex-
humed from the city's overflowing
cemeteries and packed in here
in 1785. From the *belle époque*
building on av Colonel Henri Roi-
Tanguy (formerly place Denfert
Rochereau), descend 130 steps to
prowl 1.7km of claustrophobia-
inducing tunnels. Rug up as tem-
peratures are quite chilly below
ground.

INSTITUT DU MONDE ARABE

☎ 01 40 51 38 38; www.imarabe.org;
place Mohammed V, 5e; museum €5/4,
temporary exhibitions extra; 🕙 museum
10am-6pm Tue-Sun; Ⓜ Cardinal Lemoine
or Jussieu; ♿

The building that established the
reputation of French architect Jean
Nouvel (opposite) blends modern
and traditional Arab elements with
western influences, such as photo-
sensitive apertures in the glass
walls, inspired by latticed wooden
windows. Museum exhibits en-

Institut du Monde Arabe

BRAVE NOUVEL WORLD

No architect has made as much of a splash on Paris' contemporary landscape as Jean Nouvel. The 1945-born Nouvel trained at Paris' École des Beaux-Art, going on to design icons including the **Institut du Monde Arabe** (opposite), **Fondation Cartier Pour l'Art Contemporain** (p154), **Musée de la Publicité** (p74), and **Musée du Quai Branly** (p43). His most famous edifice never built was his competition-winning Tour Sans Fin (ironically meaning 'never-ending tower') at **La Défense** (p52), which bankrupted his first architectural practice. Undeterred, his latest La Défense competition winner is the landmark Tour Signal, designed like four immense stacked cubes with technicolour screens.

compass 9th- to 19th-century Arab arts. Incredible views stretch across the Seine and Notre Dame as far as Sacré-Cœur from the 9th floor. Also here is a library, café (open 11am to 7pm Tuesday to Sunday), caféteria, Le Moucharabieh (lunch Tuesday to Sunday), and restaurant, Le Ziryab (lunch Tuesday to Sunday, dinner by reservation only; set *menus* around €50).

JARDIN DES PLANTES
☎ 01 40 79 56 01; www.mnhn.fr; 57 rue Cuvier, 5e; admission €1/0.50, some sections free; ☽ 8am-5.30pm to 8pm depending on season; Ⓜ Gare d'Austerlitz, Censier Daubenton or Jussieu; ⓹
Founded in 1626 as Louis XIII's herb garden, Paris' botanical gardens are a serious institute rather than a leisure destination, but fascinating all the same. Sections include a winter garden, tropical greenhouses and an alpine garden, as well as the school of botany, and a menagerie (right).

MÉNAGERIE DU JARDIN DES PLANTES
☎ 01 40 79 37 94; www.mnhn.fr; 57 rue Cuvier & 3 quai St-Bernard, 5e; admission €7/5 ☽ 9am-5pm; Ⓜ Gare d'Austerlitz, Censier Daubenton or Jussieu; ⓹
Like the Jardin des Plantes (left), in which it's located, this 1000-animal zoo is more than a tourist attraction, also doubling as a research centre for the reproduction of rare and endangered species. Its animals were themselves endangered during the Prussian siege of 1870, when almost all were eaten by the starving Parisians.

MOSQUÉE DE PARIS
☎ 01 45 35 97 33; www.la-mosquee.com; 2bis place du Puits de l'Ermite, 5e; admission €3/2; ☽ mosque 9am-noon & 2-6pm Sat-Thu, tearoom 9am-11.30pm daily, restaurant lunch & dinner daily, hammam 10am-9pm Mon, Wed, Thu, Sat & Sun, 2-9pm Tue & Fri, souk 11am-7pm daily; Ⓜ Censier Daubenton or Place Monge; ⓹

PARIS FOR FREE

If you can, time your trip to be here on the first Sunday of the month when you can visit the **musées nationaux** (national museums; www.rmn.fr in French) for free, including those listed below (some during certain months only as noted). Temporary exhibitions still incur a charge.

Arc de Triomphe (p52) November to March
Château de Vincennes dungeons (p118) November to March
La Conciergerie (p134) November to March
Musée de l'Orangerie (p72)
Musée d'Orsay (p42)
Musée du Louvre (p73)
Musée du Quai Branly (p43)
Musée Guimet des Arts Asiatiques (p56)
Musée National d'Art Moderne (p55)
Musée National du Moyen Âge (Musée de Cluny; opposite)
Musée National Eugéne Delacroix (p154)
Musée Picasso (p116)
Musée Rodin (p43)
Notre Dame towers (p131) November to March
Panthéon (opposite) November to March
Ste-Chapelle (p134) November to March

Anytime, you can visit the permanent collections of selected **musées municipaux** (city-run museums; www.paris.fr) for free, including those listed here. Temporary exhibitions also incur a charge.

Maison de Balzac (p54)
Maison de Victor Hugo (p115)
Musée Carnavalet (p115)
Musée Cognacq-Jay (p115)
Musée d'Art Moderne de la Ville de Paris (p55)

In addition to a clutch of other free exhibits, such as the **Musée du Parfum** (p55), the **Pavillon de l'Arsenal** (p117) and the **Musée de La Défense** (p52), there are plenty of alternate ways to soak up the city without spending a *centime*. See p42 for free resident-led tours, p181 for info on the city's beautiful parks and gardens, p191 for the best areas to stroll, p183 for architecture to check out along the way, and p178 for shopping (well, window shopping never goes out of style).

A *hammam* (Turkish steam bath), body scrub, massage, mint tea and couscous or *tajine* (North African stew) at Paris' exquisite central mosque (see p15) are cheapest if you select a €58 'Oriental Formula' package but you can take any of the above treats separately. Note that visitors are not admitted inside the prayer hall; and that the *hammam* is open to women only on Mondays, Wednesdays, Thursdays and Saturdays, and men only on Tuesdays and Sundays.

○ MUSÉE NATIONAL D'HISTOIRE NATURELLE

☎ 01 40 79 30 00; www.mnhn.fr; 57 rue Cuvier, 5e; 🕑 10am-5pm Wed-Mon, some sections close 6pm; Ⓜ Censier Daubenton or Gare d'Austerlitz; ♿
France's National Museum of Natural History incorporates three separate centres that each adjoin the Jardin des Plantes (p141): the **Galerie de Minéralogie et de Géologie** (admission €7/5), which deals with minerals and geology; the **Galerie d'Anatomie Comparée et de Paléontologie** (admission €6/4), which focusses on anatomy and fossils; and the most interesting, the **Grande Galerie de l'Évolution** (admission €8/6), with topical exhibits about humanity's effect on the ecosystem and global warming, and an interactive 'discovery space' for kids.

○ MUSÉE NATIONAL DU MOYEN ÂGE

☎ 01 53 73 78 16; www.musee-moyen age.fr; 6 place Paul Painlevé, 5e; admission €7.50/5.50, audioguide €1; 🕑 9.15am-5.45pm Wed-Mon; Ⓜ Cluny–La Sorbonne or St-Michel; ♿
The National Museum of the Middle Ages (often called the Musée de Cluny, or just Cluny) is fittingly housed in both the remains of Gallo-Roman baths (c AD 200), and the 15th-century Hôtel de Cluny, Paris' finest civil medieval building. The highlight is the series of 15th-century tapestries, *The Lady with the Unicorn*. Its foliage inspired the forest planted outside.

○ PANTHÉON

☎ 01 44 32 18 00; www.monum.fr; place du Panthéon; admission €7.50/4.80; 🕑 10am-6.30pm Apr-Sep, to 6pm Oct-Mar; Ⓜ Luxembourg
Commissioned by Louis XV as an abbey, this domed neoclassical building had the misfortune of reaching completion in 1789. The Revolutionary climate saw it converted into a mausoleum, housing leading lights including Victor Hugo, Voltaire, Louis Braille and Emile Zola among 80 or so others. Its first female resident, Marie Curie (who is accompanied by husband Pierre), only arrived in 1995.

SEINE SAILING

Watching the city float past from Paris' most beautiful boulevard of all, the Seine, offers one of the most peaceful perspectives of the city, during the day, sunset, or floodlit night.

The Seine's sightseeing boats are colloquially called Bateaux Mouches (literally 'fly boats', though the name originates from the Mouche area of Lyon). While 'Bateaux Mouches' refers specifically to the original and best-known operator (p214), you'll find a raft of other companies with departure docks and ticket kiosks along both banks of the river.

See p214 for cruise info, and p209 for details of Paris' new 'metro boat' service.

SORBONNE
☎ 01 40 46 20 25; www.sorbonne
.fr in French; 12 rue de la Sorbonne, 5e;
Ⓜ Luxembourg or Cluny–La Sorbonne

One of the world's most prestigious universities, 'La Sorbonne' was founded in 1253 by Robert de Sorbon as a theological college for just 16 pupils, going on to have its own government and laws. The main campus' imposing buildings, domed chapel and lime tree–shaded squares dominate the Latin Quarter, while its students dominate the local bars and cafés. The campus is undergoing a series of renovations until 2015.

Sorbonne

🛍 SHOP

📗 ABBEY BOOKSHOP *Books*
☎ 01 46 33 16 24; www.abbeybookshop
.net; 29 rue de la Parcheminerie, 5e;
🕙 10am-7pm Mon-Sat; Ⓜ St-Michel or
Cluny–La Sorbonne

In a heritage-listed townhouse, this welcoming Canadian-run bookshop serves free coffee (sweetened with maple syrup) to sip while you browse tens of thousands of new and used books, and hosts literary events where wine and conversation flow in equal measure.

🏠 MOUFFETARD FOLIE'S
Homewares

☎ 01 45 87 00 12; 51 rue Mouffetard, 5e; ⏰ 9am-9pm ; Ⓜ Censier Daubenton
Step down from the bustling rue Mouffetard into this shop located in a basement that is crammed with kitsch new items, such as battery-powered flying Fresian-cow mobiles and gumdrop-coloured lamps.

📖 SHAKESPEARE & COMPANY
Books

☎ 01 43 26 96 50; http://shakespeareco.org; 37 rue de la Bûcherie, 5e; ⏰ 10am-11pm; Ⓜ St-Michel
Fossicking through this 'wonderland of books' (as Henry Miller described it) unearths bargains, but it's equally fabled for its long history of nurturing writers (see p16). Readings by emerging to illustrious authors take place at 7pm most Mondays. Shakespeare & Co also hosts regular writers' workshops, and high-profile literary festivals (see www.festivalandco.com).

🍴 EAT

🍴 CHEZ NICOS *Crêperie* €
44 rue Mouffetard, 5e; ⏰ 11am-1am; Ⓜ Censier Daubenton
The signboard outside crêpe artist Nicos' unassuming little

ALL ABOARD
To sightsee while resting your feet, a cheaper and more authentic alternative to tourist buses (p214) is to hop on a regular public bus. Particularly scenic routes include the following:
Line 21 or 27 Opéra–Panthéon
Line 29 Opéra–Gare de Lyon
Line 47 Centre Pompidou–Gobelins
Line 63 Musée d'Orsay–Trocadéro
Line 73 Concorde–Arc de Triomphe
Line 82 Montparnasse–Eiffel Tower

See p209 for ticket info.

shop chalks up an overwhelming variety of fillings but ask by name for his masterpiece, 'La Crêpe du Chef', stuffed with aubergines, feta, mozzarella, lettuce, tomatoes and onions. There's a handful of tables inside; otherwise head to a nearby park.

🍴 LA TOUR D'ARGENT
Gastronomic €€€

☎ 01 43 54 23 31; www.latourdargent.com; 15 quai de la Tournelle, 5e; ⏰ lunch Wed-Sun, dinner Tue-Sun; Ⓜ Cardinal Lemoine or Pont Marie
Since it opened in 1582 (no typo!), the 'Silver Tower' has refined every facet of fine dining. Its signature pressed duck still mesmerises diners, as do its glimmering views over Notre Dame and the Seine. Book well ahead.

WORTH THE TRIP – SOUTHEAST PARIS

Paris' southeast is an eclectic mix of quarters that makes for a fascinating half-day stroll if you've stood in one tourist queue too many.

Cinephiles won't want to miss the **Cinémathèque Française** (☎ 01 71 19 33 33; www .cinemathequefrancaise.com; 51 rue de Bercy, entry place Leonard Bernstein, 12e; permanent collection €5/4, temporary exhibitions €8/6.50; ◷ noon-7pm Mon, Wed, Fri & Sat, to 10pm Thu, to 8pm Sun; Ⓜ Bercy). These stunning Frank Gehry–designed premises showcase the history of French cinema and screen black-and-white classics and edgy new films.

There are more cinemas at **Bercy Village** (☎ 01 40 02 90 80; www.bercyvillage.com; 28 rue François Truffaut; ◷ shops 11am-9pm, restaurants to 2am; Ⓜ Cour St-Émilion), converted from former wine stores, but the main draw here is the cobblestone strip of branché (trendy) designer shops, bars and restaurants.

From Bercy, the oak-and-steel footbridge Passerelle Simone de Beauvoir leads, appropriately enough, to the **Bibliothèque Nationale de France** (National Library; ☎ 01 53 79 53 79, 01 53 79 40 41; www.bnf.fr; 11 quai François Mauriac, 13e; temporary exhibitions from €5/3.50, library €3.30; ◷ 10am-7pm Tue-Sat, 1-7pm Sun; Ⓜ Bibliothèque), which has four glass towers shaped like open books and subterranean reading rooms wrapped around a rainforest, and hosts excellent exhibitions. On the river out front is a **floating swimming pool** (Piscine Joséphine Baker; ☎ 01 56 61 96 50; www.paris.fr in French; admission €2.60/1.50; ◷ vary; Ⓜ Quai de la Gare or Bibliothèque). Two of Paris' best floating nightclubs are also here: **Le Batofar** (☎ 01 56 29 10 33; www.batofar.org in French; opposite 11 quai François Mauriac, 13e; admission free-€15; ◷ 9pm or 10pm-midnight Mon & Tue, to 4am or later Wed-Sun; Ⓜ Quai de la Gare or Bibliothèque), a fire engine–red tugboat with a bar on its upper deck and an electro-oriented club beneath; and **La Dame de Canton** (☎ 01 53 61 08 49; www.damecanton.com in French; opposite 11 quai François Mauriac, 13e; admission €12; ◷ 7pm-2am Tue-Thu, to dawn Fri & Sat; Ⓜ Quai de la Gare or Bibliothèque), aboard a three-mast Chinese junk.

Just north of the library, the 20,000-sq-metre, 1907-built **Docks en Seine** (30 quai d'Austerlitz, 13e; Ⓜ Gare d'Austerlitz) warehouses, a long-time industrial wasteland, has been transformed beyond recognition by architects Dominique Jacob and Brendan MacFarlane. By the time you're reading this, they'll house the **Cité de la Mode et du Design**, incorporating Paris' premier fashion school, the Institut Français de la Mode, plus bars, restaurants, boutiques, and a 24-hour Seine-side terrace. A Voguéo (p209) metro-boat ride offers amazing views of its Salvador Dalí–like lurid-lime glass façade. The docks are part of the sprawling 130-hectare ZAC Paris Rive Gauche redevelopment zone, which will ultimately encompass a 30,000-strong university campus.

Heading southwest, Paris' largest Chinatown (Ⓜ Tolbiac or Porte d'Ivry) feels like another continent with its high-rises, malls, Asian supermarkets and dozens of authentic restaurants where you can twirl a pair of baguettes (chopsticks) in a bowl of noodles.

Otherwise, dine sans tourists a few blocks west on café-clad rue de la Butte aux Cailles (Ⓜ Corvisart), or northeast towards place d'Italie (Ⓜ place d'Italie).

L'OURCINE Bistro €€€
☎ 01 47 07 13 65; 92 Rue Broca, 13e; ⏱ lunch & dinner Tue-Fri, closed approx late Jul-late Aug; Ⓜ Les Gobelins

A prime example of a 'neo bistro' (p174), this intimate place may be casual (no dress code), but it takes its food seriously. The focus is on the flavours of the French Basque Country, including pan-fried baby squid with fiery Espelette peppers.

MARCHÉ MAUBERT Market
place Maubert, 5e; ⏱ 7am-2.30pm Tue & Thu, to 3pm Sat; Ⓜ Maubert Mutualité

St-Germain's bohemian soul lives on at this colourful market.

MARCHÉ MONGE Market
place Monge, 5e; ⏱ 7am-2.30pm Wed & Fri, to 3pm Sun; Ⓜ Place Monge

This open-air market is laden with wonderful cheeses, baked goods and a host of other temptations.

PHO 67 Vietnamese €
☎ 01 43 25 56 69; 59 rue Galande, 5e; ⏱ lunch & dinner; Ⓜ Maubert Mutualité

Tuck into delicious Vietnamese dishes such as fried boned eel, crusty lacquered duck, rare tender goat with ginger and North Vietnamese soup amid the burgundy walls and suspended rattan lamps of this unpretentious little gem where everything is cooked to order. It is hidden away in a small backstreet of the Latin Quarter, but is fortunately located away from the over-touristy little maze of restaurants that surrounds rue de la Huchette.

🍸 DRINK

🍸 CAFÉ PANIS Café
☎ 01 43 54 19 71; 21 quai de Montebello, 5e; ⏱ 8am-midnight; Ⓜ St-Michel

This rather elegant-looking café might seem an unlikely spot

RUE MOUFFETARD

This narrow, sloping cobblestone street is one of Paris' earliest, beginning its life as a Roman road to Rome via Lyon. It acquired its current name in the 18th century, when the then-nearby River Bievre (now piped underground) became the communal waste-disposal for local tanners and wood-pulpers. The resulting odours gave rise to the name Moffettes (French for 'skunk'), which was transmuted over the years to Mouffetard.

Nicknamed 'La Mouffe', the street is lined with ancient shopfronts housing cheap, student-oriented cafés and bars, as well as the **Mouffetard food market** (⏱ 8am-7.30pm Tue-Sat, to noon Sun; Ⓜ Censier Daubenton).

STAYING ON TRACK

Throughout central Paris, the ultraefficient metro (underground rail) network has 373 stations, spaced an average of 500m apart. If you get lost, track down the nearest metro station, where large-scale maps of the immediate district are normally posted outside the entrance. Hopping on a metro will easily connect you back to where you planned to be. See p207 for ticket info.

Vélib' stations (p208) also display maps of the local area.

for the studenty-types you see scribbling in notebooks here, but it's close to Shakespeare & Co (p145), and waiters benevolently let impoverished writers sit on a coffee, salad or warming soup for an hour or two.

☆ LE PANTALON *Bar*
7 rue Royer-Collard, 5e; ❄ 5.30pm-2am; Ⓜ Cluny–La Sorbonne or RER Luxembourg
Ripped vinyl seats, coloured-glass light fittings and old stickers plastered on the walls make this hidden local bar a favourite hangout of Parisian musicians.

☆ LE VIEUX CHÊNE *Bar*
☎ 01 43 37 71 51; 69 rue Mouffetard, 5e; ❄ 4pm-2am Sun-Thu, to 5am Fri & Sat; Ⓜ Place Monge
Hosting Revolutionary meetings in 1848, today this ancient bar is frequented by a buzzing student crowd. You can catch live jazz here on the weekends.

⭐ PLAY

⭐ LE CAVEAU DE LA HUCHETTE *Jazz*
☎ 01 43 26 65 05; www.caveaudelahuchette.fr; 5 rue de la Huchette, 5e; adult €11-13, student €9; ❄ 9.30pm-2.30am Sun-Thu, to 4am Fri & Sat; Ⓜ St-Michel
Count Basie, Memphis Slim and Sacha Distel are among the greats who've played in this former medieval cellar (later French Revolution torture chambers). It now hosts a diverse line-up of swing bands, South American jazz and more.

⭐ LE CHAMPO *Cinema*
☎ 01 43 54 51 60; www.lechampo.com in French; 51 rue des Écoles, 5e; Ⓜ St-Michel or Cluny–La Sorbonne
The place to catch retrospectives of Hitchcock and Woody Allen as well as French directors. Behind the art deco façade of this cinema are two screens, one of which has wheelchair access.

>ST-GERMAIN DES PRÉS & MONTPARNASSE

Literary lovers, antique collectors and fashionistas all flock to this mythological part of Paris.

Legendary writers such as Sartre, de Beauvoir, Camus, Hemingway, Fitzgerald, Pound, Stein and Joyce hung out in the cafés of St-Germain des Prés, drinking, scribbling and engaging in earnest debate. Now decidedly upmarket, today's St-Germain des Prés accommodates exclusive homewares and clothing boutiques, though the original literary cafés still exist.

ST-GERMAIN DES PRÉS & MONTPARNASSE

◉ SEE
Cimetière du Montparnasse	1	B5
Église St-Germain des Prés	2	C2
Église St-Sulpice	3	C3
Fondation Cartier pour l'Art Contemporain	4	C5
Jardin du Luxembourg	5	C3
Musée de la Poste	6	A4
Musée du Luxembourg	7	C3
Musée National Eugène Delacroix	8	C2
Tour Montparnasse	9	B4

🏃 DO
Pari-Roller	10	B4

🏠 SHOP
A La Recherche De Jane	11	D2
Alexandra Sojfer	12	B2
Au Plat d'Étain	13	C2
Carré Rive Gauche	14	C1
Cine Reflet	15	D3
Gérard Durand	16	B2
La Fromagerie 31	17	C2
La Grande Épicerie de Paris	18	B3
Le Bon Marché	19	B2
Max Maroquinerie Bagagerie et Accessoires	20	D2
Plastiques	21	C3
Sonia Rykiel	22	C2
Village Voice	23	C2

🍴 EAT
Brasserie Lipp	24	C2
L'Atelier de Joël Robuchon	25	B1
Le Dôme	26	B4
Le Procope	27	D2
Le Salon d'Hélène	28	B3
Le Sévéro	29	B6

Marché Brancusi	30	A5
Marché Raspail	31	B3
Péres et Filles	32	C2
Poilâne	33	C2

🍷 DRINK
Bar Signature	(see 25)	
Bistro des Augustins	34	D2
Café de Flore	35	C2
La Closerie des Lilas	36	C5
La Palette	37	C2
Le Pré	38	C2
Le Select	39	B4
Les Deux Magots	40	C2
Les Etages St-Germain	41	D2

⭐ PLAY
La Coupole	42	B4
Théâtre du Luxembourg	43	C3
Théâtre du Vieux Colombier	44	C2

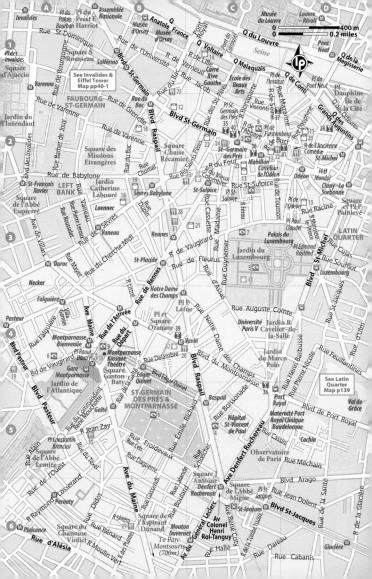

QUARTERS

ST-GERMAIN DES PRÉS & MONTPARNASSE

Gentrification saw the bohemians shift south to Montparnasse, where the literary community, along with artists including Chagall, Modigliani, Léger, Soutine, Miró, Kandinsky and Picasso, and political exiles Lenin and Trotsky, all spent time at some point. Following the Nazi occupation of Paris, late-20th-century developments such as the vast Gare Montparnasse train station and the '70s Tour Montparnasse skyscraper altered the landscape irrevocably. But you'll find reminders of Montparnasse's heyday in its surviving brasseries, newly re-energised backstreets, and its cemetery, where Sartre, de Beauvoir and other Left Bank legends are buried.

👁 SEE

📷 CIMETIÈRE DU MONTPARNASSE

☎ conservation office 01 44 10 86 50; blvd Edgar Quinet & rue Froidevaux, 14e; admission free; 🕐 8am-6pm Mon-Fri, 8.30am-6pm Sat, 9am-6pm Sun mid-Mar–early Nov, 8am-5.30pm Mon-Fri, 8.30am-5.30pm Sat, 9am-5.30pm Sun early Nov–mid-Mar; 🇲 Edgar Quinet or Raspail

Celebs laid to rest here include writers Charles Baudelaire, Guy de Maupassant, Jean-Paul Sartre and Simone de Beauvoir; playwright Samuel Beckett; and photographer Man Ray. Montparnasse's tomb traditions include fans leaving metro tickets on the grave of singer Serge Gainsbourg in reference to his song, 'Le Poinçonneur des Lilas' (see below). Free maps are available from the conservation office.

📷 ÉGLISE ST-GERMAIN DES PRÉS

☎ 01 55 42 81 33; 3 place St-Germain des Prés; 🕐 8am-7pm Mon-Sat, 9am-8pm Sun; 🇲 St-Germain des Prés; ♿ Built in the 11th century on the site of an abbey, this charming Romanesque church is Paris' oldest, and the city's main centre

SERGE GAINSBOURG

Born Lucien Ginsburg in Paris in 1928 to a musician father fleeing turmoil in Russia, Serge Gainsbourg started out painting advertising signs before landing a cabaret pianist slot. His 1958 track 'Le Poinçonneur des Lilas' depicts work-a-day monotony through the eyes of a metro ticket-puncher. Gainsbourg enacted the soul-destroying job (since eclipsed by machines) on film when recording the song in the Porte des Lilas station.

Gainsbourg parlayed his bohemian Left Bank following into widespread fame fuelled by scandal, excess and high-profile liaisons, most famously with Bridget Bardot, with whom he recorded his biggest international hits. He died in 1991.

PULLING STRINGS

You don't have to be a kid and you don't have to speak French to be delighted by marionette shows, which have entertained audiences in France since the Middle Ages.

The stringed puppets perform in the Jardin du Luxembourg's little **Théâtre du Luxembourg** (☎ 01 43 26 46 47; tickets €4.40; ⏱ 11am & 3.15pm Sat & Sun, 3.15pm Wed, school holidays daily; Ⓜ RER Luxembourg). There are also marionette shows at the **Parc du Champ de Mars** (Map pp40-1; ☎ 01 48 56 01 44; tickets €3; ⏱ 3.15pm & 4.15pm Wed, Sat & Sun; Ⓜ École Militaire).

Or you can buy your own puppets at the enchanting **Clair de Rêve** (p134).

of Catholic worship until it was eclipsed by Notre Dame. It's the (rumoured) resting place of its namesake, Saint Germain (AD 496–576), the city's first bishop.

Ⓒ ÉGLISE ST-SULPICE
☎ 01 46 33 21 78; place St-Sulpice, 6e; ⏱ 7.30am-7.30pm; Ⓜ St-Sulpice

Until recently, the few visitors to this delightful church, constructed over 150 years from 1646,

were fans of artist Eugène Delacroix, who painted the frescoes in the Chapelle des Stes-Agnes. But once Dan Brown set a murderous scene of *The Da Vinci Code* here, pivoting around the Rose Line (to the right of the middle of the nave), people turned up in their thousands. The hype over *da code* has, fortunately, died down, but it's now resolutely on the tourist map.

Interior of Église St-Sulpice, Paris' second-largest church

FONDATION CARTIER POUR L'ART CONTEMPORAIN

☎ 01 42 18 56 50; www.fondation.cartier .fr; 261 blvd Raspail; admission €6.50/4.50, 2-6pm Wed free; ⏰ 11am-10pm Tue, to 8pm Wed-Sun; M Raspail; &

Designed by Pritzker prize–winning architect Jean Nouvel (see p141), this light-flooded space is worth checking out for the building alone, but it also hosts temporary exhibits spanning all facets of contemporary art from the 1980s on, including paintings, photography, video and fashion.

JARDIN DU LUXEMBOURG

⏰ 7.30am to 8.15am-5pm to 10pm; M RER Luxembourg

One of the city's most beloved parks (see p13), the Jardin du Luxembourg is also home to orchards and even its own apiary (see p26). The northern end is dominated by the Palais du Luxembourg. Built in the 1620s and now housing the French senate, it is occasionally visitable by guided tour – call ☎ 01 44 54 19 49. The park also shelters the Musée du Luxembourg (right).

MUSÉE DE LA POSTE

☎ 01 42 79 24 24; www.museedelaposte .fr in French; 34 blvd de Vaugirard, 15e; permanent exhibits €5/3.50, permanent & temporary exhibits €6.50/5; ⏰ 10am-6pm Mon-Sat; M Montparnasse Bienvenüe or Pasteur

Not only posties and philatelists but anyone inspired by travel and communications will enjoy this postal museum. Exhibits span antique postal equipment and early French stamps and telecommunication. Imaginative temporary exhibitions could be anything from artistic letter boxes to wartime postal services.

MUSÉE DU LUXEMBOURG

☎ 01 42 34 25 95; www.museeduluxem bourg.fr in French; 19 rue de Vaugirard, 6e; most exhibitions around €11/9; ⏰ 10.30am-10pm Mon & Fri, to 7pm Tue-Thu & Sat & Sun; M RER Luxembourg

Prestigious temporary art exhibitions take place in this beautiful former *orangerie* in the Jardin du Luxembourg (left).

MUSÉE NATIONAL EUGÈNE DELACROIX

☎ 01 44 41 86 50; www.musee-delacroix .fr; 6 rue de Furstemberg, 6e; admission €5; ⏰ 9.30am-5pm Wed-Mon; M Mabillon or St-Germain des Prés; &

The father of French romanticism lived at this courtyard studio off a magnolia-shaded square until his death in 1863. Although his most famous works are at the Louvre (p73), Musée d'Orsay (p42) and St-Sulpice (p153), this much more intimate museum's collection includes oils, watercolours, pastels and drawings.

PARC MONTSOURIS

blvd Jourdan & av Reille; ☼ **sunrise to sunset;** Ⓜ **RER Cité-Universitaire**

The name of this sprawling lake-side park – planted with horse-chestnut, yew, cedar, weeping beech and buttonwood trees – derives from *moque souris* ('mice mockery') because the area was once overrun with rodents. Today it's a delightful spot for a picnic, and has some endearing play-ground areas such as a concrete 'road system' where littlies can trundle matchbox cars (BYO cars). The park adjoins the groundbreaking 1920s-built Cité Universitaire (student halls of residence); you're free to wander around the campus.

TOUR MONTPARNASSE

☎ **01 45 38 52 56; www.tourmontparnasse56.com; rue de l'Arrivée, 15e; admission €10/7;** ☼ **9.30am-11.30pm Apr-Sep, to 10.30pm Sun-Thu, to 11pm Fri & Sat Oct-Mar;** Ⓜ **Montparnasse Bienvenüe**

In a built-up city, this early-'70s 210m skyscraper would blend into the skyline but in low-rise Paris it sticks out like a painfully sore thumb. On the upside, its 56th-floor exhibition centre and bar (reached in 38 seconds in Europe's fastest lift/elevator) and

GOING UP?

The outrage following the construction of Tour Montparnasse (left) saw a clampdown on skyscrapers. But more could be looming. Given Paris' housing and office space shortage, in 2008 the Socialist city council voted to consider erecting high-rises towering above the current 37m limit up to 200m (two-thirds the height of the Eiffel Tower) in six designated zones on city's rim. Aghast Parisians include the Greens (Green deputy mayor Denis Baupin likened high-rises to 4WDs, claiming they require excessive energy to build and maintain), who found unlikely alliance with centre-right politicians. Architects, however, are upbeat – see p183.

59th-floor observation terrace (reached by stairs) are about the only spots in Paris where you can't see this unsightly smoked-glass office block. The last lift departs 30 minutes prior to closing; admission includes a 20-minute aerial-photography film. Other high-rises could soon be on the Parisian horizon – see above.

🏃 DO

🛼 PARI-ROLLER *Mass-skate*

☎ **01 43 36 89 81; www.pari-roller.com; to/from place Raoul Dautry, 14e;** ☼ **Fri 10pm-1am, arrive 9.30pm;** Ⓜ **Montparnasse Bienvenüe**

This fast-paced skate (see p129) covers a different 30km-odd route each week.

🛍 SHOP

Rue d'Alésia (14e; A6) has some great discounted designer outlets. Abstract landscape artist Rorcha (opposite) can receive buyers by appointment at his atelier; contact atelier.rorcha@gmail.com. To view his work, visit www.museepaulde louvrier.fr (in French).

🏠 A LA RECHERCHE DE JANE
Accessories
☎ 01 43 25 26 46; 41 rue Dauphine, 6e; 🕙 11.30am-7.30pm Thu-Sat, 12.30-7pm Sun; Ⓜ St-Germain des Prés
The amiable owners of this *chapelier* (milliner) have literally thousands of handcrafted hats on hand for both men and women, and can also make them to order.

🏠 ALEXANDRA SOJFER
Accessories
☎ 01 42 22 17 02; www.alexandrasojfer.fr; 218 blvd St-Germain; 🕙 9am-7pm Mon-Sat, by appt Sun; Ⓜ St-Germain des Prés
Parapluies and *ombrelles* (parasols and umbrellas) don't come more elegant than Alexandra Sojfer's creations, which have been hand-made here since 1834. If nothing on display catches your fancy, you can have one custom-made.

🏠 AU PLAT D'ÉTAIN *Toys*
☎ 01 43 54 32 06; http://auplatdetain.com in French; 16 rue Guisarde, 6e; 🕙 11am-12.30pm & 2-7pm Tue-Sat; Ⓜ Odéon
Tiny tin and lead soldiers have been sold at this little shop since 1775.

🏠 CINE REFLET *Books*
☎ 01 40 46 02 72; www.myspace.com/cinereflet; 14 rue Monsieur-le-Prince, 6e; 🕙 1-8pm Mon-Sat & sometimes Sunday; Ⓜ Odéon
An old projector takes pride of place at this welcoming cinema-dedicated bookshop.

🏠 GÉRARD DURAND
Accessories
☎ 01 45 44 98 55; www.accessoires-mode .com in French; 75-77 rue du Bac, 7e; 🕙 9am-7pm Tue-Sat; Ⓜ Rue du Bac
Brightly coloured, boldly printed *collants* and *bas* (tights and stockings) are the specialty of this boutique, which also stocks equally vibrant socks, scarves and gloves.

🏠 LA FROMAGERIE 31
Food & Drink
☎ 01 43 26 50 31; 64 rue de Seine, 6e; 🕙 10am-8pm Tue-Sat, to 1pm Sun; Ⓜ Mabillon
This stretch of rue de Seine is home to some tempting food shops including this small, heady *fromagerie*. Friendly staff can guide you through its lush selection of cheeses.

Rorcha
Painter

Why the pseudonym 'Rorcha'? From Rorschach's ink blots. I like the idea of undefined 'floating' forms…the viewer can see what he/she desires, and discover his/her own picture. **Path to becoming a full-time painter?** After graduating from landscape architecture I started painting and never stopped. I took my work around to some galleries in the Marais and was represented by one the same day; the owner later became my agent (for Rorcha's annual exhibitions and permanent exhibits). **Colour experimentation?** Paris has fabulous, diverse shades of grey, so I explore the *gris coloré* (the colours within the greys). **Inspiration?** Jogging in Parc Montsouris (p155); passing by the ateliers of artists like Giacometti who worked nearby; museums like Fondation Cartier (p154) and the Louvre (p73), which challenge me – they show me the way to a higher level. **Favourite aspect of Parisian life?** The culture reachable within 10 minutes…it's so rich.

QUARTERS

ST-GERMAIN DES PRÉS & MONTPARNASSE

Sonia Rykiel

this glorious grocery store within Le Bon Marché (below) are a sight to behold even if you're not here to buy.

☐ LE BON MARCHÉ
Department Store

☎ 01 44 39 80 00; www.bonmarche.fr; 24 rue de Sèvres, 7e; ⏱ 9.30am-7pm Mon-Wed & Fri, 10am-9pm Thu, 9.30am-8pm Sat; Ⓜ Sèvres Babylone

The name's a misnomer – *bon marché* is a French expression for 'bargain' and this beautifully laid-out store definitely isn't. But it is a Paris institution, built by Gustave Eiffel in 1852 as the city's first department store, and housing designer salons and a fantastical food hall, La Grande Épicerie de Paris (left).

☐ LA GRANDE ÉPICERIE DE PARIS *Food & Drink*

☎ 01 44 39 81 00; www.lagrandeepicerie .fr; 36 rue de Sèvres, 7e; ⏱ 8.30am-9pm Mon-Sat; Ⓜ Sèvres Babylone

The exquisitely presented chocolates, pastries, tins of biscuits, fruit and vegetables, seafood, cheeses, wines and other luxury goods in

☐ MAX MAROQUINERIE BAGAGERIE ET ACCESSOIRES *Accessories*

☎ 01 43 54 59 87; 45 rue Dauphine, 6e; ⏱ 11am-7.30pm Mon-Sat; Ⓜ St-Germain des Prés

ART NOUVEAU INFLUENCE

Art nouveau swept the Parisian cityscape from the mid- to late 19th century until WWI, leaving its mark on architecture, interior design, furniture and graphics. Sinuous swirls, curls and floral tendrils characterise this 'new art' movement. Materials that supported its signature motifs included wrought iron, glass, richly grained timbers and marble. Art nouveau splendours include Guimard's **metro entrances** (p75) and **synagogue** (p115); the train station housing the **Musée d'Orsay** (p42); department stores like **Le Bon Marché** (above) and **Galeries Lafayette** (p61); ornate brasseries such as **Bofinger** (p122); and Paris' 'iron lady' herself, the **Eiffel Tower** (p39).

Among the wares of this handbag boutique are small-run, limited-edition Frederic T totes for extremely reasonable prices.

PLASTIQUES *Homewares*
☎ 01 45 48 75 88; 103 rue de Rennes, 6e; ☺ 10.15am-7pm Mon-Fri, to 7.30pm Sat; M Rennes

Lollypop-coloured tableware (trays, serving bowls, dinner settings etc) and cookware (whisks, mixing bowls and much more) fill this original, inexpensive boutique.

SONIA RYKIEL *Fashion*
☎ 01 49 54 60 60; www.soniarykiel.com; 175 blvd St-Germain, 6e; ☺ 11am-7pm Mon-Sat; M St-Germain des Prés

In the heady days of May 1968 amid Paris's student uprisings, Sonia Rykiel opened her inaugural Left Bank boutique here, and went on to revolutionise garments with inverted seams, 'no hems' and 'no lining'. Her diffusion labels are housed in separate boutiques nearby, with other outlets around Paris.

VILLAGE VOICE *Books*
☎ 01 46 33 36 47; www.villagevoice bookshop.com; 6 rue Princesse, 6e; ☺ 2-7.30pm Mon, 10am-7.30pm Tue-Sat, noon-6pm Sun; M Mabillon

On a quaint backstreet, this English-language bookshop specialises in North American litera-

CARRÉ RIVE GAUCHE
Art and antiques gather under the umbrella of **Carré Rive Gauche** (☎ 01 42 60 70 10; www.carrerivegauche.com; M Rue du Bac or Solférino), just east of the Musée d'Orsay, bounded by quai Voltaire, rue de l'Université, rue des St-Pères & rue du Bac. Within this 'Left Bank square' are more than 120 highly specialised merchants, along with half a dozen restaurants. Antiques fairs (usually held in spring) trigger a flurry of professional buyers, and a program of exhibitions (such as an exhibition on masks: carnival masks, Australian Aboriginal and Native American masks and so on) unfolds during the year.

ture (great for picking up obscure Hemingway novellas), and has an excellent range of French literature in translation. It hosts regular readings and literary events.

🍴 EAT

BRASSERIE LIPP
Brasserie   €€€
☎ 01 45 48 53 91; www.brasserie-lipp.fr; 151 blvd St-Germain, 6e; ☺ 9am-1am; M St-Germain des Prés

Elegantly poured beers in tall glasses and brasserie fare like pork knuckle are served by waiters in black waistcoats, bow ties and long white aprons at this historic haunt. Hemingway sang its praises in *A Moveable Feast* and today its faded glamour is neither too faded nor too glamorous but simply perfect.

🍴 L'ATELIER DE JOËL ROBOUCHON *International* €€€
☎ 01 42 22 56 56; www.hotel-pont-royal.com; 5 rue de Montalembert, 7e; ⏱ lunch & dinner; Ⓜ Rue du Bac

Joël Robouchon's contemporary cuisine is served at long counters rather than separate tables, reflecting the increasing numbers of Parisians dining alone – or with their dogs; see p121 – who still want to eat *very* well.

🍴 LE DÔME *Seafood* €€€
☎ 01 43 35 25 81; 108 blvd du Montparnasse, 14e; ⏱ lunch & dinner to 12.30am; Ⓜ Vavin

So the stories go, it was here in this magnificent brasserie that Gertrude Stein allegedly convinced Henri Matisse to open his artists' academy – only for Matisse to add his voice to the *Testimony against Gertrude Stein* over her 1933 *Autobiography of*

Seafood in style at Le Dôme

Alice B Toklas. Le Dôme is still one of the swishest places around for a seafood extravaganza.

🍴 LE PROCOPE *French* €€
☎ 01 40 46 79 00; www.procope.com; 13 rue de l'Ancienne Comédie, 6e; ⏰ 11.30am-1am; Ⓜ Odéon
Founded in 1686, the world's oldest café was once frequented by Voltaire, Molière, Beaumarchais, Balzac, Verlaine and Victor Hugo, among others; paintings of many of them hang in the book-lined interior. Today it serves traditional fare like coq au vin.

🍴 LE SALON D'HÉLÈNE
French €€€
☎ 01 42 22 00 11; www.helenedarroze .com; 4 rue d'Assas, 6e; ⏰ lunch & dinner Tue-Sat; Ⓜ Sèvres Babylone
Female star chefs are a rarity in Paris, but Hélène Darroze is a stellar exception. These premises house both her twin Michelin-starred restaurant upstairs and this relaxed downstairs salon. Renowned for its multicourse tasting menus, Le Salon d'Hélène's dishes reflect Darroze's native southwestern France, such as wood-grilled foie gras.

🍴 LE SÉVÉRO *Bistro* €€
☎ 01 45 40 40 91; 8 rue des Plantes, 14e; ⏰ lunch & dinner Mon-Fri; Ⓜ Mouton Duvernet

Meat is the mainstay of this cosy neighbourhood bistro (it's run by an ex-butcher), washed down with any number of excellent wines, which are chalked on an entire wall. It seats just 20 people, but there's a nearby annex.

🍴 MARCHÉ BRANCUSI *Market*
place Constantin Brancusi, 14e; ⏰ 9am-3pm Sat; Ⓜ Gaîté
Overdose on organic produce at this weekly open-air market.

🍴 MARCHÉ RASPAIL *Market*
blvd Raspail btwn rue de Rennes & rue du Cherche Midi, 6e; ⏰ regular market 7am-2.30pm Tue & Fri, organic market 9am-3pm Sun; Ⓜ Rennes
A traditional open-air market on Tuesday and Friday, Marché Raspail is especially popular on Sundays when it's filled with organic produce.

🍴 PÈRES ET FILLES
Café, Restaurant €€
☎ 01 43 25 00 28; 81 rue de Seine, 6e; ⏰ lunch & dinner; Ⓜ Mabillon
Retractable timber-framed glass doors opening out to the street make this a good spot for people-watching while dining on classic French fare (steak, sole and so on) or stopping by for a drink and banter with the fun-loving staff. Inside black-and-white photos and books line the walls of the spacious ground floor and mezzanine.

🍴 POILÂNE *Bakery* €
☎ 01 45 48 42 59; www.poilane.fr;
8 rue du Cherche Midi, 6e; ⏰ 7.15am-8.15pm Mon-Sat; Ⓜ Sèvres Babylone
Pierre Poilâne opened this *boulangerie* (bakery) upon arriving from Normandy in 1932. Today his granddaughter runs the company, which also includes a second shop in the 15e (p46), a London outlet, and a healthy supply trade to high-quality establishments.

🍸 DRINK

🍸 BAR SIGNATURE *Bar*
☎ 01 42 22 56 56; www.hotel-pont-royal.com; 5 rue de Montalembert, 7e; ⏰ daily; Ⓜ Rue du Bac
Under the same roof at the Hôtel Pont Royal as L'Atelier de Joël Robouchon (p160), this mahogany-panelled bar was once the hangout of Aldous Huxley, Henry Miller, Truman Capote and TS Eliot.

🍸 BISTRO DES AUGUSTINS
Bar, Bistro
☎ 01 43 54 04 41; 39 quai des Grands Augustins, 6e; ⏰ 11am-10pm Mon-Sat; Ⓜ St-Michel
Plastered with old advertising posters from the *bouquiniste* (booksellers) stalls opposite, this authentic bistro-bar is a cosy spot for a glass of red. The aromas of home cooking wafting from the kitchen may

tempt you to stay for its simple but scrumptious bistro fare.

🍸 CAFÉ DE FLORE *Café*
☎ 01 45 48 55 26; 172 blvd St-Germain, 6e; ⏰ 7.30-1.30am; Ⓜ St-Germain des Prés
This 1880s café is where Sartre and de Beauvoir essentially set up office, writing in its warmth during the Nazi occupation. It's actually less touristy than neighbouring Les Deux Magots (opposite), but, alas, its prices are just as lofty.

🍸 LA CLOSERIE DES LILAS
Brasserie, Bar
☎ 01 40 51 34 50; www.closeriedeslilas.fr; 171 blvd du Montparnasse, 6e; ⏰ bar 11am-1.30am, brasserie noon-1am, restaurant lunch & dinner; Ⓜ Port Royal
With a legacy stretching back to Baudelaire, 'the Lilac Enclosure' is where Hemingway wrote much of *The Sun Also Rises* while he was living around the corner. Brass plaques tell you where he and luminaries such as Picasso, Apollinaire, Man Ray, Jean-Paul Sartre and Samuel Beckett imbibed. In addition to the bar, there's a hedged terrace adjoining the brasserie, and an upmarket restaurant.

🍸 LA PALETTE *Café*
☎ 01 43 26 68 15; 43 rue de Seine, 6e; ⏰ 8am-2am Mon-Sat; Ⓜ Mabillon
One of Henry Miller's faves, this mirror-lined café was also a haunt

Café de Flore -- historical hangout for great philosophical minds

of Cézanne and Braque, and these days is popular with art dealers.

▼ LE PRÉ *Bar*
☎ 01 40 46 93 22; 4-6 rue du Four;
🕒 7am-4am; Ⓜ Mabillon
Mauve-and-orange wicker chairs line the terrace of this hip drinking spot, while inside the chrome-and-laminex bar resembles a '50s Airstream trailer.

▼ LE SELECT *Café*
☎ 01 42 22 65 27; 99 blvd du Montparnasse, 6e; 🕒 7.30am-2.30am; Ⓜ Vavin
This Montparnasse institution was the first of the area's grand cafés to open late into the night in its 1920s

heyday, and still draws everyone from beer-swigging students to whisky-swilling politicians.

▼ LES DEUX MAGOTS *Café*
☎ 01 45 48 55 25; 170 blvd St-Germain, 6e; 🕒 7am-1am; Ⓜ St-Germain des Prés
If ever there were a café that summed up St-Germain des Prés' early-20th-century literary scene, it's this former hangout of anyone who was anyone. You will spend *beaucoup* to sip a coffee or hot chocolate in a wicker chair on the terrace shaded by dark-green awnings and geraniums spilling from window boxes, but it's an undeniable piece of Parisian history.

ST-GERMAIN DES PRÉS & MONTPARNASSE

Y **LES ETAGES ST-GERMAIN**
Bar
☎ 01 46 34 26 26; 5 rue de Buci, 6e;
🕒 3.30pm-2am; Ⓜ Odéon
Spilling from its dark-red interior,
Les Etages' terrace wraps around
two bustling streets in the heart
of St-Germain des Prés and is
positively hopping on a sunny
afternoon or balmy night.

⭐ PLAY

⭐ **LA COUPOLE** *Club*
☎ 01 43 27 56 00; 102 blvd du Montparnasse, 14e; admission €12-16; 🕒 club
9.30pm-3am Thu, 11.30pm-5.30am Fri,
10am-5pm Sat, brasserie 8am-1am Sun-
Thu, to 1.30am Fri & Sat; Ⓜ Vavin

Since the roaring '20s, this
showpiece has set Paris' trends (it
heralded electronica and salsa),
and now hosts diverse genres
including reggae and funk. Its
brasserie, with muraled columns
painted by artists including
Chagall, is favoured by young,
serious French writers drawing
inspiration from de Beauvoir, who
worked on *L'Invitée (The Guest)*
here in 1940.

⭐ **THÉÂTRE DU VIEUX
COLOMBIER** *Theatre*
☎ 01 44 39 87 00; rue du Vieux
Colombier, 6e
This theatre is one of the three
venues of Comédie Française
(p83).

>FURTHER AFIELD

Daffodils near Monet's Japanese bridge in the gardens at Giverny (p168)

VERSAILLES

When it comes to over-the-top opulence, the **Château de Versailles** is in a class of its own, even for France.

Set in the leafy, very bourgeois suburb of Versailles, this baroque palace was the kingdom's political capital and the seat of the royal court from 1682 up until the fateful events of 1789. In that year, revolutionaries massacred the palace guard and dragged Louis XVI and Marie Antoinette back to Paris, where they were ingloriously guillotined.

Louis XIV (1643–1715) transformed his father's hunting lodge into the colossal Château de Versailles in the mid-17th century. His palace, sprawling over 900 hectares of fountain-graced gardens, pond-filled parks and woods, boasted 700 rooms, 2153 windows, 352 chimneys and 28 acres of roof. It housed the entire court of 6000 (plus an additional 5000 servants), emblemising the power of the French monarchy. The grandstanding king hired the finest talent of the day, including architects Louis Le Vau and later Jules Hardouin-Mansart; landscape artist André Le Nôtre; and painter/decorator Charles Le Brun, who, with his team of hundreds of artisans, lavished every interior moulding, cornice, ceiling and doorway with some 6300 paintings, 2000 sculptures and statues, 15,000 engravings, and 5000 ostentatious furnishings and *objets d'art*.

Interior highlights include the **Grand Appartement du Roi** (King's Suite), with rooms dedicated to Hercules, Venus, Diana, Mars and Mercury; and the *pièce de résistance*, the **Galerie des Glaces** (Hall of Mirrors), a 75m-long ballroom with 17 massive mirrors, facing an equal number of windows overlooking the luxuriant gardens.

INFORMATION

Location 21km southwest of Paris

Getting there RER line C5 (€2.80, 35 minutes) from Left Bank RER stations travels to/from Versailles–Rive Gauche station; trains run every 15 minutes (fewer on Sunday)

Contact www.chateauversailles.fr

Costs Admission from €16 to €25 depending on day/access; skip queues by purchasing your ticket ahead of time from Fnac (p211), or, from April to September (Tuesday to Friday) or October (Saturday and Sunday) purchase a combined train/palace Forfait Loisirs Château de Versailles SNCF pass from train station ticket windows (Tuesday to Friday €21.65, Saturday and Sunday €25.95), which includes metro connections within Paris

When to go 🕑 9am to 6.30pm Tuesday to Sunday April to October, 9am to 5.30pm November to March

Left The sun god Apollo and his chariot rise from the depths of the Bassin d'Apollon **Right** The vast Galerie des Batailles (Hall of Battles) is lined with huge canvases depicting French military glory

GIVERNY

After viewing Monet's gardens and floating water lilies in Paris' galleries, from spring to autumn you can see them flourish in living colour in the gardens of his former home in the village of Giverny.

The 'Painter of Light' and his family lived at the **Maison de Claude Monet** from 1883 to 1926, during which time he dug a pool, planted a seasonally blooming garden, and constructed the Japanese bridge that features in many of his paintings (it has since been rebuilt). Entwined with purple wisteria, the footbridge blends into the asymmetrical foreground and background, creating the intimate effect for which Monet was famous.

Yellow daffodils and a rainbow of tulips, rhododendrons, wisteria, irises, poppies and lilies create a spectacle in spring. Nasturtiums, roses and sweet peas blossom in summer, while dahlias, sunflowers and hollyhocks flower in autumn.

The northern part of the property shelters Monet's famous pastel pink-and-green house and the **Atelier des Nymphéas** (Waterlilies Studio), now the home's entrance hall, hung with reproductions of his works (though you'll have to head back to Paris to see any originals).

Just 100m northwest of the Maison de Claude Monet, the modern **Musée d'Art Américain** (American Art Museum; www.maag.org; admission €5.50; ☼ 10am-6pm Tue-Sun Apr-Oct) contains works by many of the American impressionist painters who flocked to France in the late 19th and early 20th centuries.

INFORMATION

Location 76km northwest of Paris
Getting there From Paris' Gare St-Lazare there are two early-morning trains to Vernon (€11.90) from where shuttle buses (☎ 02 32 71 06 39; €4) link with Giverny, 7km to the northwest; there's roughly one train an hour back to Paris from 5pm to 9pm
Contact www.fondation-monet.com in French
Costs Admission €5.50
When to go ☼ 9.30am to 6pm Tuesday to Sunday April to October

CHAMPAGNE

Popping over to the stately city of **Reims**, in the vineyard-ribboned Champagne region, makes a refreshing change from Paris' busier day-tripper destinations (Chartres, Chantilly, Fontainebleau et al).

Reims was the site of jubilant celebrations when WWII ended in Europe here. This city of 215,000 residents is graced with pedestrianised streets; exceptional museums, most notably the Musée des Beaux-Arts; and a stained-glass Gothic cathedral, Cathédrale Notre Dame.

Moreover, it's where you'll find the region's eponymous sparkling wines. According to French law, only bubbly from the region – grown, aged and bottled to exacting standards – can be labelled as true champagne.

Eight of Reims' champagne *maisons* (houses/producers) and their cellars can be visited on guided tours. Among the most central are **Mumm** (☎ 03 26 49 59 70; www.mumm.com; 34 rue du Champ de Mars); **Pommery** (☎ 03 26 61 62 55; www.pommery.fr; 5 place du Général Gouraud); and **Taittinger** (☎ 03 26 85 84 33; www.taittinger.com; 9 place St-Niçaise), which occupies 4th-century stone quarries, with sections added in the 13th century by Benedictine monks. Tours end, *naturellement,* with a tasting.

INFORMATION

Location 144km northeast of Paris
Getting there The TGV Est Européen line whisks you to/from Paris' Gare de l'Est in 45 minutes seven times daily (around €29.30 one way; check www.voyages-sncf.com in French for times and discounted train tickets); in Reims you can walk to most sights including champagne houses
Contact www.reims-tourisme.com
Costs Champagne house tours generally cost around €10
When to go The champagne houses open year-round but you need to reserve ahead for tours

Paris' iconic sights justify their hype. But the real magic of Paris lies in the unexpected: hidden parks, small, specialised museums and galleries, and tucked-away bistros, boutiques and bars. This thematically arranged chapter provides a starting point for discovering both Paris' star attractions and its secrets based on your interests.

> Accommodation	172
> Food	174
> Drinking & Nightlife	176
> Shopping	178
> Artistic Paris	180
> Parks & Gardens	181
> Literary Paris	182
> Architecture	183
> Romantic Paris	184
> Panoramas	185
> Mondial Paris	186
> Jazz, Chansons & Cabaret	187
> Cooking & Wine-tasting Courses	188
> Classical Music, Opera, Dance & Theatre	189
> Gay & Lesbian	190
> Walking *(flâneurie)*	191
> Cycling	192
> Kids	193
> Cinema	194

Shopping (p178) along rue des Francs Bourgeois

ACCOMMODATION

Paris has an extensive array of sleeping options – in theory. In practice, although Paris counts no fewer than 76,500 beds in 1480 establishments, they're often *complet* (full) well in advance. Reservations are recommended at any time of year, and are essential during the high season (Easter to October and Christmas/New Year) and the fashion shows (January to March). If you get stuck, the tourist office (p215) can help find you a room.

Accommodation outside central Paris is marginally cheaper than within the city itself, but it's almost always a false economy. Travelling into the city will eat up precious time, can be expensive, and if there's a transport strike, you will be hamstrung. Your best bet is to choose somewhere within Paris' 20 *arrondissements* (administrative districts), where you can experience Parisian life the moment you step out the door.

If you're coming to Paris to kick up your heels, the Marais and Bastille, Montmartre and its surrounds, the Latin Quarter, St-Germain des Prés and Montparnasse, and the Louvre and Les Halles are all in the heart of the action. And if you're coming to shop, you won't go wrong in either these areas or the glamorous Arc de Triomphe, Champs-Élysées and Grands Boulevards precinct. Consider the Invalides and Eiffel Tower area or the Île St-Louis if you're seeking a bit more serenity.

Paris levies a *taxe de séjour* (tourist tax) that costs from €0.20 up to €1.50 per person per night, which is normally added to your bill. Internet access often incurs an additional fee. France's new nonsmoking laws (p215) don't extend to hotel rooms, which are considered private rentals, so you'll still need to specifically request a smoke-free room.

lonely planet Hotels & Hostels

Need a place to stay? Find and book it at lonelyplanet.com. More than 60 properties are featured for Paris – each personally visited, thoroughly reviewed and happily recommended by a Lonely Planet author. From hostels to high-end hotels, we've hunted out the places that will bring you unique and special experiences. Read independent reviews by authors and other travellers, and get practical information including amenities, maps and photos. Then reserve your room simply and securely via our online booking service. It's all at www.lonelyplanet.com/hotels.

To live like a Parisian, rent a short-stay apartment. The best apartment-booking services are below. Beware of disreputable rentals: check http://parishousingscamwatch.wordpress.com/tag/housing-scams/.

Paris has lagged behind other major European capitals when it comes to quality independent hostels, but things are looking up with the opening of the shiny new, purpose-built **St Christopher's Paris Hostel** (19e, www.st-christophers.co.uk). Info on Paris' HI (Hostelling International) hostels is online at www.fuaj.org; stays require a membership card. Under 35s can also try central hostels run by two youth organisations: www.bvjhotel.com (15 days' advance booking required); or www.mije.com.

Online hostel and budget accommodation specialists include www.hostelbookers.com, www.hostelworld.com, and www.gomio.com. For hotels in all categories, including many boutique gems, try www.hotels-paris.fr or www.parishotelservice.com.

BEST BUDGET HOTELS

> Hôtel du Nord – Le Pari-Vélo, 10e (www.hoteldunord-leparivelo.com)
> Port Royal Hotel, 5e (www.hotelportroyal.fr)
> Hôtel de Blois, 14e (www.hoteldeblois.com)
> Hôtel Eldorado, 17e (www.eldoradohotel.fr)
> Hôtel de Lille, 1er (www.hotel-paris-lille.com)

BEST DESIGNER DIGS

> Hôtel Sezz, 16e (www.hotelsezz.com)
> Murano Urban Resort, 3e (www.muranoresort.com)
> Hôtel du Petit Moulin, 3e (www.paris-hotel-petitmoulin.com)
> Hôtel Le A, 8e (www.paris-hotel-a.com)
> Kube, 18e (www.kubehotel.com)

BEST SPOTS TO RUB SHOULDERS WITH STARS

> Hôtel Ritz Paris, 1er (www.ritzparis.com)
> Hôtel de Crillon, 8e (www.crillon.com)
> Hôtel Plaza Athénée, 8e (www.plaza-athenee-paris.com)
> Hôtel Costes, 1er (www.hotelcostes.com)
> L'Hôtel, 6e (www.l-hotel.com)

BEST PARISIAN APARTMENTS

> Paris Attitude (www.parisattitude.com)
> A La Carte Paris Apartments (www.alacarte-paris-apartments.com)
> Paris Accommodation Service (www.paris-accommodation-service.com)
> Paris Apartments Services (www.paris-apts.com)
> Paris Stay (www.paristay.com)

FOOD

For Parisians, how food looks on the plate is just as important as how it tastes. Colours, textures and garnishes are impeccably arranged – not only at *haute cuisine* establishments, but small, simple restaurants where even a humble hot chocolate is sometimes poured in a heart shape on the cup's inside edge.

Parisians relish talking about, shopping for, preparing and, above all, enjoying food. The city doesn't have its own local cuisine per se, but is the crossroads for the regional produce and flavours of France. In addition to classical French fare, also look out for cuisines from around the globe (see p186).

One of the most enduring culinary trends of recent times is *bistronomique* – bistros offering pared-down regional fare by big-name chefs with pared-down prices. Such venues are often referred to as 'neo-bistros'. Overall, the skilful combination of fresh ingredients is more important than any fad – whether for a Michelin-starred meal or a picnic built from the markets.

Breakfast isn't a priority in Paris – most locals stick to a baguette (p90) with butter and jam (croissants are usually weekend treats) and strong coffee (served espresso-style in a short cup unless you specify otherwise – see p107). It's seen as a mere precursor to lunch, which remains the traditional main meal; smaller shops and businesses often close for a couple of hours at this time. Lunch generally starts around 12.30pm with an aperitif, and is almost always washed down with wine – which costs less than soft drink or bottled water. Tap water is safe to drink in Paris, and is free; ask for *une carafe de l'eau*.

Restaurants usually serve a *plat du jour* (dish of the day) or *formule* (fixed main course plus starter or dessert) at lunch (and occasionally at dinner), as well as *menus* (fixed-price meals) of an entrée, *plat* (main course), and *fromage* (cheese) or dessert or both. These offer infinitely better value than ordering à la carte. Meals are often considerably cheaper at lunch than dinner (making lunch a good way to experience *haute cuisine* dining if you're on a budget).

The North American convention of diners taking away a doggy bag or 'box' of leftovers is nonexistent here – even if portion sizes permitted it, local culture doesn't (as the dining experience and the food itself are considered inseparable).

Most restaurants open for dinner at about 7pm or 7.30pm, but don't really get busy until an hour or so later; many serve late into the night. Note that some high-end restaurants close on weekends, and many close during August (see p201).

Booking ahead – which may just mean popping in to make dinner reservations at a place that looks appealing as you pass by at lunchtime – is usually a good idea. By law, all restaurants are required to post their menus outside, allowing you to check the prices. Popular places, such as *haute cuisine* establishments, should be booked as far ahead as possible – anything from a couple of weeks up to a couple of months.

Exclusively vegetarian eateries are almost unheard of in Paris, and while some traditional places do have meatless dishes, the French love of chicken and meat stocks can make these a dicey proposition. Aquatarians (fish eaters) will be fine, however, with fish and/or seafood a mainstay on most menus. One of the best bets for vegetarians is Paris' burgeoning array of North African, Middle Eastern, Indian and Asian restaurants, which all have at least some meat-free dishes on the menu. See p186 for info on where to find international cuisines.

Edible Paris (www.edible-paris.com) creates personalised 'food itineraries' and has links for food-themed guided tours.

To learn how to whip up delicious dishes yourself, see p188 for courses.

The blog *Chocolate & Zucchini* (http://chocolateandzucchini.com), by native Parisian food writer Clotilde Dusoulier (p81), has a treasure trove of information for foodies.

See p193 for information on dining with kids.

Left Creamy cheese for sale in the Latin Quarter's Mouffetard food market (p148)

DRINKING & NIGHTLIFE

Deciding where to drink or to party in Paris can be bewildering given the cross-over of venues.

For Parisians, drinking and eating go together like wine and cheese, and the line between what constitutes a café, bistro, brasserie, bar and even a seemingly self-explanatory *bar à vins* (wine bar) is blurred – especially after a *verre* (glass) or two. All usually serve at least light meals (sometimes full menus), and it's normally fine to order a coffee or alcohol if you're not dining. Many drinking establishments have a tiered pricing structure based on where you sit, with the coveted terrace seats more expensive than perching at the counter.

Paris' cafés have long been the city's communal lounge rooms: places to meet friends, read, write, philosophise (p126), flirt and fall in – and out of – love. As such, they've played a central role in the city's history over the centuries. Many are gilded, dark-wood-panelled *belle époque* treasures, where past patrons from Picasso to Sartre still haunt the air. See p182 for some of the most celebrated literary cafés. Just as atmospheric, and more down-to-earth, are tucked-away *cafés quartiers* (local cafés). If you're craving a cuppa, there are some charming *salons de thé* (tearooms) serving hot chocolate as well as tea, a beverage that's gaining ground in this city of coffee drinkers. Coffee terminology is decoded on p107. To learn more about French wines the best way there is, by tasting them, see p188. Places that are primarily drinking, rather than eating, establishments are listed under Drink in the Quarters chapters.

If the line between eating and drinking is blurred, the line between drinking and clubbing is often nonexistent. A café that looks quiet early in the afternoon, for example, might groove to a DJ set in the evening and see dancers getting sweaty later on.

When it comes to hardcore clubbing, however, Paris is no Berlin, as everyone from first-time visitors through to industry insiders like Benoît Rousseau, artistic director of music at Point Éphemère (p108) will attest. This is due to Paris' residential make-up (see p199), combined with the fact that parties in private apartments – either *une soirée posée* (an intimate gathering of friends) or *une grosse soirée* (a bigger, louder affair) – mean Parisians often stay in rather than heading out and about.

Determined Parisian clubbers generally divide their night into several parts. First, *la before,* usually drinks in a bar with a DJ playing. Next, a club for *la soirée,* which rarely kicks off before 1am or 2am. When the party continues (or begins) at around 5am and goes until midday, it's called *l'after*. Often, however, the before and the after blend into one without any real 'during'. Meanwhile '*after d'afters*' are increasingly held in bars and clubs on Sunday afternoons and evenings, with a mix of strung-out clubbers kicking on and people out for a party that doesn't take place in the middle of the night.

Electronica, laced with funk and groove, remains the French capital's strong suit. DJs tend to have short stints in venues – look out for flyers in shops and cafés. Salsa and Latino tunes also maintain a strong following. R&B and hip-hop get less of a run. Admission to clubs generally costs €5 to €20 and often includes a drink. Entry is usually cheaper before 1am.

Nightlife venues are spread around the city (see the Play sections of the Quarters chapters); good bets are the Marais and Bastille, the Arc de Triomphe, Champs-Élysées and Grands Boulevards area, Louvre and Les Halles, Montmartre and Pigalle, and Belleville and its surrounds. The website www.gogoparis.com is a fount of info on gigs, clubbing events and venues.

See p190 for info on gay and lesbian nightlife; p187 for jazz, *chansons* and cabarets; and p189 for classical music, opera, dance and theatre.

Left The warm inviting glow of the circus-themed Le Clown Bar (p123) in the Marais and Bastille area

SHOPPING

Shopping spreads throughout the city's quarters and Parisians will cross town for a *bonne adresse* (good address).

Like anywhere, Paris has its international chains, but what sets the city apart is its incredible array of specialist shops. Instead of stocking up at a supermarket, Parisians will buy their bread at a *boulangerie,* cheese at a *fromagerie,* meat at a *charcuterie,* and fruit and vegetables at the street-market stalls (p14) etc. It takes longer, but the food is better and fresher, and the social interaction between shopkeepers and regulars forms part of the city's village atmosphere. The website www.paris.fr lists every market in Paris, including opening hours, by *arrondissement.* The same site also has details of Paris' speciality markets, which include bird markets, a stamp market, craft markets, and flower markets filled with buckets of blooms.

It's not only food shops that are specialised. There are shops that sell just hats, others that sell just umbrellas. Even Parisian dogs (p121) are in on the act, with shops selling nothing but dog outfits and accessories.

Fashion shopping is Paris' forte. Numerous luxury labels that originated here are anchored by flagship stores, particularly in the 8e's Triangle d'Or (Golden Triangle; p63), which is bordered by avs Georges V, Champs-Élysées and Montaigne. Discount designer outlets are found along rue Alésia (p156). Edgier, experimental designers are also a fashion force. Rue Étienne Marcel in the 2e (Map pp70–1, G4), the emerging 'haut Marais' (p120), and Canal St-Martin (p21) are all fertile ground for up-and-coming talent. Unless you're splashing out on made-to-measure *haute couture,* it pays to try before you buy, as size conversions are complex – see p60. If you're happy browsing, feel free to tell any overenthusiastic sales staff '*Je regarde*' – 'I'm just looking'.

Vintage and new clothes along with accessories, antiques and all sorts of bric-a-brac are laid out at Paris' flea markets (p14), which are always buzzing with activity. They're also buzzing with pickpockets – stay alert. It's a good idea to use cash rather than credit cards at the flea markets, as scams aren't uncommon. In any case, cash is your best bet for haggling, and there are some genuine bargains.

Paris' covered arcades (see p62) are treasure chests of small, exquisite boutiques. These marble-floored, glass-roofed shopping passages, streaming with natural light, were the elegant forerunners to department stores and malls. The *grande dame* department stores – Le Bon Marché (p158), Galeries Lafayette (p61) and Le Printemps (p63), as well as La Samaritaine (closed for structural renovations until c 2011) – are filled with specialist sections, and are beautiful to wander around. If you're watching your *centimes,* **Monoprix** (www.monoprix.fr in French) has branches located all around town selling well-made clothes and gourmet goods at affordable prices.

What's somewhat ironic for a city so dedicated to shopping is that Paris doesn't have a consumer culture as such. Shopping here is about style and quality, rather than status or acquisition. While a few shops are open '*7 jours sur 7*' (sometimes written 7j/7; seven days out of seven), most close at least one or two days a week, ensuring that shopping itself stays a luxury.

Left Pretty-in-pink accessories at Kenzo (p77) on rue du Pont Neuf

SNAPSHOTS

ARTISTIC PARIS

Paris is one of the great art repositories of the world, harbouring treasures from throughout the ages. Viewing art is an integral part of Parisians' leisure activities from childhood on, which is fostered by all levels of government (see p142), and accounts for Parisians' keen sense of aesthetics (p199). A roll-call of masters – whose works are displayed in Paris' museums – have painted the City of Light over the centuries. Today, new waves of artists follow in their footsteps. Artists still set up their easels all over the city, particularly in Montmartre (p88), and in the ateliers of Belleville and its surrounds (p101). The website www.ivyparisnews.com is a great resource for artists and art enthusiasts.

But art also flourishes in unexpected places: parks and public spaces are filled with sculptures; metro stations act as de facto galleries (see p75); and the twice-yearly fashion shows (p24) are arguably more about art than garments. Artisan workshops are found throughout the city, such as in the Viaduc des Arts (p121), while cutting-edge venues mount multimedia exhibitions. Artist squats are hotbeds of creativity – the website www.fraap.org/mot46.html (in French) has info. And where else but Paris would you find specialised museums such as the Musée de d'Érotisme (p87), where sex toys sit alongside works by Degas?

See p210 for information on museum passes. For a behind-the-scenes glimpse into a Parisian painter's atelier, see p157.

BEST IMPRESSIONIST COLLECTIONS
> Musée de l'Orangerie (p72)
> Musée d'Orsay (p42)
> Musée Marmottan (p57)
> Musée d'Art
  Américain (p168)

BEST MODERN & CONTEMPORARY COLLECTIONS
> Musée Picasso (p116)
> Musée National d'Art Moderne (p69)
> Musée d'Art Moderne
  de la Ville de Paris (p55)
> Dalí Espace Montmartre (p87)

PARKS & GARDENS

Paris' elegantly laid out parks and gardens are idyllic for strolling or simply soaking up the sunshine, with plenty of seating as well as kiosks and cafés. The loveliest of the traditional parks in central Paris are the Jardin du Luxembourg (p13) and the Jardin des Tuileries (p72), as well as the sprawling lawns of the Parc du Champ de Mars (Map pp40–1, D3). Some sections of Paris' botanical gardens, the Jardin des Plantes (p141), are free. Sweeping views over Paris unfold from the steep Parc de Belleville (p100). Lush large-scale parks also include the hilly, forested Parc des Buttes–Chaumont (p101), Parc de Monceau (p57) and Parc Montsouris (p155).

One of Paris' charms is its small, secreted gardens tucked between its gracious old buildings, or even perched in the middle of the Seine (see Map pp132–3). A comprehensive list of parks and gardens by *arrondissement* is available at www.paris-walking-tours.com/parisgardens.html.

Recent innovations include the fantastical Parc de la Villette (p101) and the disused railway viaduct that has been transformed into a walking path, the Promenade Plantée (p19). Further out, the Bois de Boulogne (p59), on the western edge of Paris, and the Bois de Vincennes (p118), on the eastern edge, are easily reached by metro, as is the hi-tech urban environment of La Défense (p52), incorporating walking paths, sculptures and art.

Ecominded city initiatives will see Paris become even greener, with many more open spaces in the works.

Above Unwind in one of the historic green metal chairs in Jardin du Luxembourg (p13)

LITERARY PARIS

Flicking through a street directory reveals just how much Paris honours its literary history, with listings including place Colette, square Charles Dickens, avs Marcel Proust and Emile Zola, and rues Balzac, George-Sand, George Bernard Shaw and Ernest Hemingway. The city has nurtured countless French authors over the centuries, who, together with expat writers who've made the pilgrimage here, have sealed Paris' literary reputation.

You can leaf through Paris' literary heritage in atmospheric bookshops and libraries, and haggle at the open-air *bouquiniste* (p134) stalls lining the banks of the Seine. You can hang out in cafés and swish literary bars frequented by luminaries, visit their former-homes-turned-museums (see www.paris.fr), or sleep in hotels where they holed up, such as L'Hôtel (p172), where Oscar Wilde fought a duel to the death with his wallpaper. You can pay your respects to Wilde and other departed writers at the city's cemeteries (p97, p152 and p86). And you can work on your own novel at cafés patronised by contemporary writers, such as Le Progrès (p127). And we could go on. But as Hemingway wrote in *A Moveable Feast*, 'There is never any ending to Paris.'

Our pick of Paris' English-language bookshops (below) have details of literary events throughout the year, many of which are held at the shops themselves. They also sell stacks of books on Paris' literary connections, such as Noël Riley Fitch's timeless *Walks in Hemingway's Paris: A Guide to Paris for the Literary Travele*r (1990).

See p202 for books set in Paris.

BEST BOOKSHOPS	MOST HISTORIC LITERARY CAFÉS
> Shakespeare & Co (p145)	> Les Deux Magots (p163)
> Abbey Bookshop (p144)	> Café de Flore (p162)
> Red Wheelbarrow Bookstore (p120)	> La Closerie des Lilas (p162)
> Village Voice (p159)	> Brasserie Lipp (p159)

ARCHITECTURE

Several key eras are woven into Paris' contemporary fabric. Magnificent stained-glass cathedrals and palaces were built from the 11th century onwards. Baron Haussmann's late-19th-century 'renovation' of the medieval city's disease-ridden streets demolished more than 20,000 homes, making way for wide boulevards lined by 40,000-plus new apartments in neoclassical creamy stone, grey-metal-roofed buildings. And the turn-of-the-20th-century art nouveau movement (see p158) ushered in signature sights including Paris' ornate brasseries and wrought-iron metro entrances.

Additions in the late 20th century centred on the French presidents' bold *grands projets* or *grands travaux* (great projects or works). President Georges Pompidou's Centre Pompidou (p69), unveiled in 1977, prompted a furore, as did President François Mitterrand's Louvre glass pyramid (p73) in 1989 (both are now widely admired). Mitterrand oversaw a slew of other costly *projets*, including the Opéra Bastille (p129) and the Bibliothèque Nationale de France (p146). In 1995 the presidential baton passed to Jacques Chirac; his pet *projet,* the Musée du Quai Branly (p43), recently opened in a stunning building designed by Jean Nouvel (p141). Chirac's 2007-elected successor, Nicolas Sarkozy, hasn't yet signalled his own architectural *projets,* but the cityscape is still set for changes. Along with architects such as Michel Angevin, Nouvel is among the advocates of controversial new legislation to raise Paris' building height limits (see p155), declaring the need to 'stop thinking of Paris as a museum city'.

Architecture buffs shouldn't miss the Cité de l'Architecture et du Patrimoine (p56), Pavillon de l'Arsenal (p117) and Musée La Défense (p52).

Above The distinctive colour-coded air vents and plumbing pipes of Centre Pompidou (p69)

ROMANTIC PARIS

Seduction emanates from the smallest details in Paris – a drift of perfume wafting from a *parfumerie* or a perfectly arranged bunch of flowers (p135), a piano tinkling from an open apartment window, or the sky turning kaleidoscopic pink, amber and violet hues as the sun starts its descent.

Even if you're falling madly *out* of love, this is one of the most memorable places to do it. (Only Paris could make breaking up feel romantic.)

But yes, if you're in love, strolling over the bridges at dusk as the wrought-iron lamps cast a sepia glow on the darkened water, sipping champagne in olde-worlde hotel bars (or plastic cupfuls of wine in parks), and dining *à deux* (as a couple) in candlelit bistros make you feel as if you've stepped into a giant film set – with nonchalant waiters the supporting actors and buskers providing the soundtrack.

Lovers come to Paris for all sorts of reasons, not the least of which is to propose. Proposing in Paris is almost a cliché but like all good clichés, there's a reason it became one in the first place. To wit, an Eiffel Tower lift operator confirms a busy day can see two or three proposals per hour. The tower's probably more romantic in retrospect, however, as the top platform is tiny and teeming with visitors – see below for alternatives.

The best part of Paris' seductiveness is that it isn't contrived. And after your trip's over, you'll always have Paris. Clichéd but true.

MOST PERSUASIVE PROPOSAL SPOTS (EIFFEL TOWER ASIDE)
> The steps of Sacré-Cœur (p22) at sunrise
> Bridges such as the Pont Neuf (p134) at sunset
> The Jardin des Tuileries (p72) at twilight
> The Louvre's illuminated cour Carrée (p18) at night

BEST ANTIDOTES TO ROMANCE
> A spa treatment at Guerlain (p61)
> A *baba rhum* (rum-drenched brioche) from Stohrer (p80)
> A shopping spree in the Triangle d'Or (p63)

PANORAMAS

Paris is a photographer's dream. Capturing the city on camera is only limited to the size of your memory card or the number of rolls of film in your bags. In addition to close-up shots of local street life, there are spectacular vantage points where you can snap vistas of the city – from the top of monuments, on hilltops, in vast squares and on bridges. Even without a camera, the views are unforgettable.

We've listed our top viewing spots here and throughout this book, but there are many more, and as you stroll around you'll no doubt find your own favourite panoramas of Paris.

TOP BUILDINGS WITH A VIEW
> Eiffel Tower (p39)
> Tour Montparnasse (view pictured above; p155)
> Arc de Triomphe (p52)
> Grande Arche (p52)
> Centre Pompidou (p69)

MOST ICONIC CHURCHES WITH A VIEW
> Sacré-Cœur (p86)
> Notre Dame (p131)
> Église de la Madeleine (p53)

BEST DINING ROOMS WITH A VIEW
> Les Ombres (p46)
> La Tour d'Argent (p145)
> Georges (p79)
> Café des Hauteurs (p46)
> Le Jules Verne (p45)

BEST TRANSPORT WITH A VIEW
> Riding a riverboat (p214)
> Cruising the canals (p214)
> Catching a cross-town bus (p145)

MONDIAL PARIS

Paris might be 'very French' (see p199), but these days that definition incorporates myriad nationalities who call this cosmopolitan city home.

Unlike France's second-largest metropolis, Marseille, where communities of all backgrounds blend throughout the entire city, specific quarters of Paris are vibrant hubs of cultural life. Visiting the grocery stores, delis, markets, shops and places of worship in these areas offers a mini world-tour.

Around the 10e's metro stations La Chapelle (Map pp98–9, C2) and Château d'Eau (Map pp98–9, C4) you'll find a concentration of Indian, Pakistani and Turkish communities. The largest Chinatown district (p146) is in the 13e, with establishments including vast supermarkets stocking goods from all over Asia. Rue Ste-Anne, in the 2e (Map pp70–1, D2), is lined with Japanese restaurants and food shops. In the Marais, the Pletzl area (p115) is the heart of Jewish life in central Paris. North African–Jewish restaurants and Sephardic kosher shops also cluster just south of the Cadet metro station (Map p85, D6) in the 9e. And the area around metro stations Château Rouge and Barbès Rochechouart (Map pp98–9, B2) in the 18e is the colourful North African quarter.

See p202 for background information on Paris' multicultural make up.

BEST MULTICULTURAL MARKETS
> Marché Belleville (p105)
> Marché Beauvau (p124)

BEST MONDIAL MUSEUMS
> Cité Nationale de l'Histoire de l'Immigration (p118)
> Musée du Quai Branly (pictured right; p43)
> Institut du Monde Arabe (p140)
> Musée d'Art et d'Histoire du Judaïsme (p116)

JAZZ, CHANSONS & CABARET

Catching a jazz or *chanson* session or a show-stopping cabaret will leave you in little doubt that you're in Paris.

Jazz greats have long flocked to Paris, playing alongside local musos, and the city remains a standout on the international scene, with some fantastically atmospheric jazz clubs. Though once dark and smoky, by law all are now smoke free (see p215). During June and July, free jazz concerts are held on Saturday and Sunday in parks across the city during the Paris Jazz Festival; see www.paris.fr for information.

While *chanson* literally means 'song' in French, it also specifically refers to a style of heartfelt, lyric-driven music typified by Édith Piaf, Maurice Chevalier, Charles Aznavour et al. You'll come across some stirring live covers of their most famous songs at venues like Chez Louisette (p92), plus contemporary twists on the genre such as the fusion of dance beats with traditional *chanson* melodies. The term also covers intimate cabarets such as Montmartre's Au Lapin Agile. For a peek behind the scenes of this legendary venue, see p93.

Whirling lines of feather boa–clad, high-kicking dancers at grand-scale cabarets like the can-can creator, the Moulin Rouge (p95), are a quintessential fixture on Paris' entertainment scene – for everyone but Parisians. Still, the dazzling sets, costumes and dancing guarantee an entertaining evening (or matinee). Tickets to these spectacles start from around €89 (from €125 with lunch, from €145 with dinner), and usually include a half-bottle of champagne.

Info on tickets is listed on p211.

Above Enjoy an extravagant production at the Moulin Rouge (p95)

COOKING & WINE-TASTING COURSES

France pioneered what is still the most influential style of cooking in the Western world, and Paris is its showcase *par excellence*. If dining in the city's restaurants whets your appetite, there are stacks of cookery schools – from famous institutions to private homes – offering courses for all levels, even if you're only here on a quick trip.

Where there's food in France, wine is never more than an arm's length away. Plenty of places in Paris offer wine tastings and instruction for all levels of ability and pockets. To taste champagne at the source, see p169. Within Paris, O-Château (p102) offers high-spirited champagne-tasting cruises on the Seine. François Audouze at www.wine-dinners.com organises regular events where 10 ultrarare vintages (such as a 1928 Château Filhot) are paired with gastronomic extravaganzas; connoisseurs can expect to shell out upwards of €1000 for the privilege.

Some cooking and wine-tasting courses are run in English, while those that are in French usually offer at least some level of English translation; confirm language requirements when you book.

Good resources for hands-on gourmet travellers include specialist bookshop Librairie Gourmande (p77), which stocks a fantastic array of cookbooks, oenology tomes and cocktail recipes. To stock up on quality cookware from shops where Paris' professional chefs have kitted out their kitchens for well over a century, see p78.

See p26 for food and wine festivals.

BEST CULINARY CLASSES FOR...

Budding chefs on a budget – Les Coulisses du Chef Cours de Cuisine Olivier Berté (p58)
Bragging rights – École Le Cordon Bleu (p44)
Lunch-hour lessons – Cuisine Fraîch' Attitude (p102)
Food-shopping secrets – Promenades Gourmandes (p118)

BEST WINE APPRECIATION SESSIONS FOR...

Losing your inhibitions – O-Château (p102)
Lesser-known drops – Legrand Filles & Fils (p63)
Historical context – Musée du Vin (p55)

CLASSICAL MUSIC, OPERA, DANCE & THEATRE

Paris plays a leading role on the world stage when it comes to the performing arts. In addition to renowned locally based companies, it's also a major stop on the international circuit, and boasts historic – even mythologised – venues.

France's national opera, the Opéra National de Paris, and national ballet company, the Ballet de l'Opéra National de Paris, perform at Paris' two opera houses: the Palais Garnier (p67) and the Opéra Bastille (p129).

A host of theatre productions tread the boards, such as the Comédie Française (p83). Virtually all theatre performances are in French but increasingly mainstream theatres project English-language subtitles on screens – check when you book.

Paris' beautiful, centuries-old stone churches, such as Ste-Chapelle (p134) and Église de la Madeleine (p53) have magnificent acoustics and provide a meditative backdrop for classical concerts. Posters outside churches advertise upcoming events with ticket information, or you can check www.ampconcerts.com. As of 2012, the Jean Nouvel–designed Philharmonie de Paris (Map pp98–9, F1) in Parc de la Villette will be the home of Orchestre de Paris (Paris Orchestra), with a 2400-seat auditorium.

In addition to the classics, Paris is a nerve-centre for creativity and fringe art. On any given day there are innumerable local performances and productions, often extremely avant-garde.

The 'What's On' section of www.parisinfo.com is a good source of info when planning your trip. See p23 for details of listings publications available for sale in Paris, and p211 for ticket outlets.

Above The colonnaded façade of France's oldest national theatre, home of the Comédie Française (p83)

GAY & LESBIAN

The city known as 'gay Paree' lives up to its name. Paris was the first-ever European capital to vote in an openly gay mayor when Bertrand Delanoë was first elected in 2001, and the city itself is very open – it's common to see same-sex couples displaying affection publicly. Gay couples are also unlikely to experience any problems when checking into a hotel room.

In fact, Paris is so open that there's less of a defined 'scene' here than other cities where it's more underground. As one baffled traveller told us after his trip: 'It was hard to tell where gay Paris ended and straight Paris started – everyone's so stylish and sexy. I found a gay café which was packed and had devastatingly cute staff. But once again, I could be mistaken – it might not actually be gay at all.'

The Marais (p110) – particularly around the intersection of rue Ste-Croix de la Bretonnerie and rue des Archives, and eastwards to rue Vieille du Temple – is the mainstay of gay and lesbian Parisian nightlife. But you'll find venues right throughout the city attracting a mixed straight and gay crowd. See the Drink and Play sections of the Quarters chapters for listings.

Gay pride peaks during the city's annual Gay Pride March (p26), with over-the-top floats and festivities.

Good online resources in English include www.legayparis.fr, www.paris-gay.com, www.girlports.com/lesbiantravel/destinations/paris/bars_nightclubs, and the website of the Centre Gai et Lesbien de Paris Île de France (Lesbian, Gay, Bisexual and Transsexual Centre), www.cglparis.org.

Above Disco drag at Le Queen (p67)

WALKING (*FLÂNEURIE*)

The single-best way to acquaint yourself with any city is walking, or in Paris' case, *flâneurie*. Writer Charles Baudelaire (1821–67) came up with the whimsical term *flâneur* to describe a 'gentleman stroller of city streets' or a 'detached pedestrian observer of a metropolis' (the metropolis being Baudelaire's native Paris). Paris' ornate glass-roofed arcades (p62) were closely tied to the concept of *flâneurie* in Walter Benjamin's Arcades Project. The term is now widely used, especially in the context of architecture and town planning. But Paris – with its villagelike backstreets, its riverbank paths (particularly down the steps along the water's edge), its parks and gardens (p181) and its arcades – remains the ultimate place for a *flâneur* to meander without any particular destination in mind.

The best quarters to simply get lost include the skein of streets in the Marais and Bastille, the Latin Quarter, and St-Germain des Prés and Montparnasse, as well as Montmartre – see p87 for ideas. (If you do get lost, it's easy to find your way back – see p149.) And Paris' compact layout, prevalence of footpaths and mainly flat terrain makes the entire city ideal for discovering on foot. Just be sure to wear comfortable shoes (you'll be glad you did!).

Many of the itineraries in this book (p29) can be followed as walking tours. See p42 for free walks with local volunteers and p214 for organised walking tours of the city.

Above Wander the streets for hours in Montmartre (p87)

CYCLING

Until recently, cycling through central Paris was a terrifying exercise. But new efforts by the city to reduce the number of cars on the road have cut the fear factor considerably. Upwards of 370km of permanent *pistes cyclables* (cycling lanes) now criss-cross the city. And, under the scheme Paris Respire ('Paris Breathes'), cars are banned on Sunday and public holidays in favour of pedestrians, cyclists and skaters in popular locations, including large sections around the Seine, Montmartre, Bastille and Canal St-Martin (p21). For updated coverage of these areas and maps of every cycling path in Paris, visit www.velo.paris.fr. Alternatively, bookshops sell the detailed *Paris de Poche: Cycliste et Piéton* (Pocket Paris: Cyclist and Pedestrian; €3.50).

In tandem with these measures, the City has revolutionised pedal-powered transport via the Vélib' system. This pick-up, drop-off bicycle rental scheme operates across 1451 Vélib' stations citywide, spaced 300m apart. Accessible 24 hours, each station incorporates about 20 bike stands – over 20,600 bikes in all. Parisians of all walks of life now whiz around town on these sleek pearly-taupe-coloured machines. Although in essence it's low-cost or free, the system's designed as a means of getting from one place to another rather than sightseeing, and if you're not clear on how the fees are calculated, the cost of a ride can quickly blow out – see p208 to avoid the pitfalls.

See p208 for the nuts-and-bolts of using Vélib' bikes, plus alternate bike rental outlets; and p214 for organised bike tours.

KIDS

Parisians adore *les enfants* (children) and welcome them with open arms just about everywhere.

Many restaurants accept little diners (confirm ahead), but they're expected to behave (bring crayons/books). Children's menus aren't widespread, however, and most restaurants don't have highchairs. Department store cafeterias such as BHV (p121) and chain restaurants like **Flunch** (www.flunch.fr) offer kid-friendly fare. In fine weather, good options include picking up sandwiches and crêpes from a street stall or packing a market-fresh picnic and heading to gardens such as the Jardin du Luxembourg (see p13), where they can play to their hearts' content.

Children under four travel free on public transport and generally receive free admission to sights. For older kids, discounts vary from place to place – anything from a euro off for over fours to free up to the age of 18.

When booking accommodation, check availability and costs for a *lit bébé* (cot).

Central Paris' residential make-up (p199) means you'll find playground equipment in parks all over the city. The Jardin d'Acclimatation (p59) is great for tiny tots; bigger kids will enjoy Parc de la Villette (p101). Further afield, you might consider a full-day trip to the **Disneyland Resort Paris** (www.disneylandparis.com) or much more **French Parc Astérix** (www.parcasterix.fr) theme parks.

Kids are by no means forgotten when it comes to French fashion. Home-grown labels like **Petit Bateau** (www.petit-bateau.fr) and **Bonpoint** (www.bonpoint.com) cost less than abroad, while cutting-edge designers such as agnès b (p74) produce their own children's lines.

We've mentioned in reviews where places are especially good for children.

SNAPSHOTS

CINEMA

Paris' love affair with cinema stretches back to 1895, when Lyon's Lumière brothers, who invented 'moving pictures', organised the world's first paying public film-screening: a series of two-minute reels in Paris' long-since-closed **Grand Café** (14 blvd des Capucines, 9e, corner rue Scribe; marked by an inscription on the building's exterior).

France remains Europe's leading producer, making over 200 films each year. Weekly entertainment guides *Pariscope* and *L'Officiel des Spectacles* (p23) list screening times across the city. First-run tickets cost around €10 per adult. Students and seniors receive discounts of around 40 percent to most (but not all) sessions. There are across-the-board discounts on Wednesdays. Foreign films (including English-language films) that are screened in their original language with French subtitles are labelled 'VO' (*version originale*). Films labelled 'VF' – *version française* – are dubbed in French.

Parisians' passion for cinema is borne out by some unique cinemas throughout the city – from a 19th-century Chinese pagoda (p47) to the art deco Le Grand Rex (p83) and summertime screens beneath the stars (p28). Other venues where you'll see just how seriously Parisians take films are the avant-garde Cinéma des Cinéastes (p94); Le Champo (p149), showing retrospectives and classics; the Parisian archive Forum des Images (p83); and, most seriously of all, the national institute, the Cinémathèque Française (p146). Cinema-specialist bookshop Cine Reflet (p156) has countless titles on the '7th art'.

Our pick of films set in Paris are listed on p203.

>BACKGROUND

An Egyptian obelisk towers over figures spouting water in La Fontaine des Mers at Place de la Concorde (p58)

BACKGROUND
HISTORY

Throughout Paris' illustrious history, political rebellion has remained a constant theme. For a montage of the city's evolution, head to the Musée Carnavalet (p115).

THE BEGINNINGS TO THE RENAISSANCE

Paris was born in the 3rd century BC, when a tribe of Celtic Gauls known as the Parisii settled on what is now the Île de la Cité. Centuries of conflict between the Gauls and Romans ended in 52 BC, when Julius Caesar's legions crushed a Celtic revolt. Christianity was introduced in the 2nd century AD, and Roman rule ended in the 5th century with the arrival of the Germanic Franks. In 508 Frankish king Clovis I united Gaul and made Paris his seat.

France's west coast was beset in the 9th century by Scandinavian Vikings (also known as Norsemen and, later, as Normans) who, three centuries later, started pushing towards Paris, which had risen rapidly in importance; construction began on the cathedral of Notre Dame in the 12th century, the Louvre began life as a riverside fortress around 1200, the beautiful Ste-Chapelle was consecrated in 1248 and the Sorbonne opened in 1253. The Vikings' incursions heralded the Hundred Years' War between Norman England and Paris' Capetian dynasty, bringing the French defeat in 1415 and English control of the capital in 1420. In 1429 the 17-year-old Jeanne d'Arc (Joan of Arc) rallied the French troops to defeat the English at Orléans. With the exception of Calais, the English were eventually expelled from France in 1453.

The Renaissance helped Paris get back on its feet in the late 15th century. Less than a century later, however, turmoil ensued as clashes between Huguenot (Protestant) and Catholic groups culminated in the St Bartholomew's Day massacre in 1572, in which 3000 Huguenots died.

THE REVOLUTION TO A NEW REPUBLIC

A five-year-old Louis XIV ascended the throne in 1643 and ruled until 1715, virtually emptying the national coffers with his ambitious battling and building, including his extravagant palace at Versailles (p166). The excesses of the grandiose king and his heirs led to an uprising of Parisians on 14 July 1789, kick-starting the French Revolution. Within four years, the so-called Reign of Terror was in full swing.

The unstable postrevolutionary government was consolidated in 1799 under Napoleon Bonaparte, who declared himself first consul. In 1804 he had the Pope crown him emperor of the French, going on to conquer most of Europe before his defeat at Waterloo in present-day Belgium in 1815. He was exiled and died in 1821.

France struggled under a string of mostly inept rulers until a coup d'état in 1851 brought Emperor Napoleon III to power. At his behest, Baron Haussmann (see p183) razed whole tracts of the city, replacing them with sculptured parks, a hygienic sewer system and – strategically – boulevards too broad for rebels to barricade. Napoleon III embroiled France in a costly war with Prussia in 1870, which ended within months with the French army's defeat and the capture of the emperor. When the masses in Paris heard the news, they took to the streets, demanding that a republic be declared.

Despite its bloody beginnings, the Third Republic gave rise to the glittering belle époque, celebrated for its advances made in the arts and sciences.

20TH-CENTURY HISTORY

Out of WWI's conflict came increased industrialisation, confirming Paris' place as a major commercial as well as artistic centre and establishing its reputation among freethinking intellectuals. This was halted by WWII and the Nazi occupation of 1940; Paris would remain under direct German rule until 25 August 1944. After the war, Paris regained its position as a creative nucleus and nurtured a revitalised liberalism that peaked with the student-led uprisings of May 1968 – the Sorbonne was occupied, the Latin Quarter blockaded, and a general strike paralysed the country.

The second half of the century saw major architectural additions – see p183. Under centre-right President Jacques Chirac's watch, the late 1990s saw Paris seize the international spotlight with the rumour-plagued death of Princess Di in 1997, and France's first-ever World Cup victory in July 1998, at the Stade de France (p95).

THE NEW MILLENNIUM

In May 2001 Socialist Bertrand Delanoë was elected mayor, becoming widely popular for making Paris more liveable through improved infrastructure and green spaces. Chirac (himself a former Paris mayor) named Dominique de Villepin as prime minister in 2005. In October that year, the deaths of two teenagers who were electrocuted while allegedly hiding from police in an electricity substation sparked riots that quickly spread across Paris, and then across France. Consequently, the government promised to address the disenfranchisement felt by unemployed French youth, but one of Villepin's first efforts – the introduction of two-year work contracts for workers under 26 years old – was met by street protests and transport strikes by sympathetic unions around the country, sparking comparisons with May '68. Backed by a reputed 70% of the French public, Chirac overrode Villepin, scrapping the week-old law. Chirac retired in 2007.

RECENT HISTORY

With Dominique de Villepin's political career blighted, Chirac's centre-right successor, Nicolas 'Sarko' Sarkozy, beat Socialist Ségolène 'Ségo' Royal in the 2007 presidential elections, and appointed François Fillon prime minister. Sarkozy's win was widely attributed to his platform of economic reform, with many French claiming it was time for 'modernisation'. In his first year of office, Sarkozy complied, though not in the way people anticipated: within months he divorced his second wife, model-turned–PR exec Cécilia Ciganer-Albéniz, then began a high-profile romance with Italian model-turned-singer Carla Bruni, whom he wed in early 2008, 11 weeks after they met. The French, who consider private lives to be emphatically that, were unimpressed at the *peopolisation* (media/celebrity hype) surrounding the presidency, dubbing him 'President Bling-Bling'. The right subsequently suffered heavily at France's March 2008 municipal elections, including Paris mayor Delanoë's comfortable re-election.

Since then, Sarkozy's personal life has attracted less press than his political endeavours, particularly July 2008's constitutional reform, which squeaked through by two votes. These changes to President Charles de Gaulle's 1958 constitution include a two-term limit for presidents, pave the way for a longer working week (see p201), and, most controversially, give the president an annual parliamentary address – something barred for the French head of state since 1875 to separate executive and legislative powers. Opponents believe this to be a 'coronation' of the president (a contentious concept in France).

The next presidential elections will take place in 2012, with Socialist Delanoë tipped to be a contender.

One thing remains certain: if Parisians aren't happy with changes, they're not afraid to protest.

LIFE AS A PARISIAN

'Wow,' a fresh-off-the-plane traveller once exclaimed to us, 'Paris is so French!' But, startling lack of irony aside, he's right. It is.

Paris is defined by its walls (that is, the *Périphérique*, or ring road), the interior of which spans 105 sq kilometres. *Intra-muros* (Latin for 'within the walls'), the city has a population of just under 2.2 million, while the greater metropolitan area – the Île de France *région*, encircled by rivers – has over 12 million inhabitants, about 19% of France's total population. This makes Paris – the capital of both the *région* and the country – in effect an 'island within an island' (or, as residents of other regions might say, a bubble).

In this highly centralised country, Paris is the principal place where the national identity is defined and embraced.

VILLAGE LIVING

Paris' dense inner-city population defines city life. Paris isn't merely a commuter destination; instead, its shops, street markets, parks and other facets of day-to-day living evoke a village atmosphere, and its lack of high-rises gives it a human scale.

Single-occupant dwellings make up more than half of all households in central Paris. On top of this, space shortages mean residential apartments are often miniscule. As a result, communal spaces are the living and dining rooms and backyards of many Parisians, while neighbourhood shops (see p178) are the cornerstones of community life.

This high concentration of city dwellers is why most bars and cafés close around 2am, due to noise restrictions, and why nightclubs in the inner city are few.

It's also why so many domestic dogs (some 200,000) live in Paris – and why there's so much dirt on the streets. But the days when dog owners wouldn't deign to clean up are fading into the past (boosted by the introduction of hefty fines), and the pavements are the cleanest they've ever been. Still, watch your step.

WALKING THE WALK

Parisians have a finely tuned sense of aesthetics, and take meticulous care in the presentation of everything from food to fashion to private and public domains. This extends to personal presentation on the streets – you'll never see a Parisian leave their apartment with just-out-of-the-shower wet hair or wearing running shoes with a business suit. For both men and women, shorts (save for on a football pitch) or a jumper tied around the waist (rather than the shoulders) identify a person as a tourist as surely as an unfolded map and a camera.

Smart casual is a fail-safe form of dress, but it's nearly impossible to overdress in this fashion-conscious city, which at times looks and feels like a giant catwalk.

TALKING THE TALK

Etiquette – itself a French word – is extremely important in Paris, which is central to understanding how the city and its residents operate.

It's customary to greet anyone you interact with, such as a shopkeeper, with 'Bonjour Madame/Monsieur'. Substitute bonjour (good day) for bonsoir (good evening) once the sun goes down. Similarly, when leaving, conclude with 'Au revoir Madame/Monsieur' (increasingly, though, bonjour/au revoir alone suffices). Particularly in smaller shops, shopkeepers generally don't appreciate you touching the merchandise until they invite you to do so.

People who know each other well greet one another with bises (kisses), usually one glancing peck on each cheek (starting with the left). People always stand up when meeting one another for the first time (and usually shake hands), including women with women.

An important distinction is made in French between tu and vous, which both mean 'you'. Tu is only used with people you know very well, children or animals. When addressing an adult who isn't a personal friend, vous should be used until the person invites you to use tu. In general, younger people insist less on this distinction with each other (but always use vous with an elder). If this sounds confusing, take heart that French people can find it hard to distinguish when to use tu and vous, too, especially in today's society as communication becomes more informal overall. If in doubt, use vous.

PARLEZ-VOUS FRANÇAIS?

Parisians have long had a reputation for being unable or unwilling to speak English, but this has changed dramatically in recent years, particularly since the internet became commonplace. Street signs, menus, establishment names and buzz words incorporate ever more English. Indeed, if you've come here to practice your French, you may find little opportunity to use it. On detecting an accent, Parisians will often automatically switch to English to facilitate conversation. Feel free to say if you prefer to converse in French.

Conversations between locals often revolve around philosophy, art and sports such as rugby, football, cycling and tennis. Talking about money (salaries or spending outlays, for example) is generally taboo in public.

Although non-French speakers will have few problems (see opposite), you'll earn greater respect (and have a more rewarding experience) by addressing locals in French, even if the only phrase you use is '*Parlez-vous anglais?*' (Do you speak English?). Often what is mistaken for Parisian arrogance is the result of foreigners not acknowledging the local language (the same as a stranger addressing you in a foreign language in your home country). Another potential cause for misunderstanding is the directness of French communication. Whereas in English it's common to say, for example, 'Can I have a coffee, please?', the French '*Un café s'il vous plaît.*' (A coffee, please.) cuts to the chase, but can sound abrupt to an anglophone ear. Likewise, the French tendency to frame a question as 'You would like a coffee?' rather than 'Would you like a coffee?' can seem forward though it isn't intended as such. One more quirk: if someone accidentally bumps into you, it's routine for you (and them) to say *pardon* (sorry), even if it's entirely their fault, as a way of saying 'it's OK'.

WORKING TO LIVE

By and large, the French work to live rather than live to work.

In 2000 a 35-hour working week became French law. Hence *les anglais* (the French term for anyone from the English-speaking world, including the US, Australia and so on) are often caught off-guard to find most shops and services shut at least one or two days per week (usually Sunday and/or Monday). In addition to this and long annual leave (which for Parisians might be anything up to nine weeks), France is blessed with a *lot* of public holidays, when shops and services generally shut (see p211). The upside is that without the impetus to make and spend money 24/7/365, friends, family and leisure activities all take on greater importance.

However, while the 35-hour week created new (mostly part-time) jobs, its restrictions also left some people feeling that although they had time on their hands they couldn't earn enough income to enjoy it. The associated tax penalties also deterred entrepreneurs and freelancers. Following 2008's constitutional reform, staff and employers are allowed to negotiate individual working hours (though the 35-hour week is retained as a standard). The reform also allows for extended trial periods and negotiable termination of employment, and waives tax on overtime. How significantly this will change the Parisian tempo remains to be seen.

MULTICULTURAL MOSAICS

Waves of immigration over the centuries, including a large number of immigrants from France's former colonies since the middle of last century, make Paris an exhilarating mix of ethnicities.

The resulting array of cuisines, music, shops and services now available continues to change Parisian tastes in many things; and gives rise to generations of Parisians with immigrant ancestry (including President Sarkozy himself, whose father emigrated from Hungary). It's also given rise to debates like the 2004 ban at state-run schools on Muslim headscarves (and all other religious symbols, such as crucifixes) in favour of secularism.

Under French law, censuses can't ask questions regarding ethnicity or religion, but they do collect country-of-birth statistics, which confirm Paris as one of the most multicultural cities in Europe.

To discover multicultural Paris, see p186.

FURTHER READING

Paris has inspired endless literature over the centuries.

Almost French: A New Life in Paris (Sarah Turnbull; 2003) An unpretentious insight into the Parisian psyche. Australian journalist Turnbull meets and marries a Parisian and struggles over eight years to adapt to the city's unwritten social rules.

Down and Out in Paris and London (George Orwell; 1933) Eric Blair's (aka Orwell's) first published book is a humorous, no-holds-barred account of early-20th-century Paris recounting his days as a downtrodden dishwasher in the bowels of a Parisian hotel.

The Elegance of the Hedgehog (Muriel Barbery; 2008) Sharp social satire about a secretly cultured Left Bank concierge.

The Flâneur: A Stroll Through the Paradoxes of Paris (Edmund White; 2001) A small, absorbing collection of random observations from American novelist White as he ambles Paris' quarters, musing on the city's Jewish history, gay community, literary luminaries and jazz heritage.

Just Like Tomorrow (Faiza Guene; 2004) Surprisingly uplifting novel about a 15-year-old girl's grim life in the *banlieues,* incorporating *verlan* (back-rhyming Parisian slang mixing Arabic, Caribbean and old French words).

Les Misérables (Victor Hugo; 1862) Epic novel adapted to the stage and screen, tracing 20 years in the life of convict Jean Valjean through the battles and barricades of early-19th-century Paris.

Life: A User's Manual (Georges Perec; 1978) Intricately structured novel distilling Parisian life through the parade of characters inhabiting a 10-storey apartment block between 1833 and 1975.

A Moveable Feast (Ernest Hemingway; 1964) Witty, wry work recalling the author's early writing career in 1920s Paris – a lifestyle that expat writers continue to emulate.

Perfume: The Story of a Murderer (Patrick Süskind; 1985) Protagonist Jean-Baptiste Grenouille is born in the fish-market filth of 18th-century Paris with a rare olfactory gift, and goes on to become a macabre perfume creator. *Perfume* was made into a film in 2006.

The Phantom of the Opera (Gaston Leroux; 1910) The basis for the longest-running Broadway musical in history, this dark novel evokes the ghostlike figure who lurks in the Garnier opera house.

Satori in Paris (Jack Kerouac; 1966) Frenetic novella based on Kerouac's whirlwind foray to France to discover his roots.

This is Paris (Miroslav Sasek; 1959) A delight for nostalgia buffs, this iconic 'children's guidebook' was re-released in 2004 with its illustrations and text intact, and a little list of updates at the back.

FILMS

This seductive city is at least as much a star as the actors who compete with it on the big screen.

2 Days in Paris (2007) Julie Delpy wrote, directed and acts in this poignant comedy about a native Parisian (Delpy) and her American partner (Adam Goldberg) attempting to rekindle their relationship in the face of her string of exes and her overbearing parents (played by Delpy's real-life parents).

À Bout de Souffle (Breathless; 1960) Filmed with hand-held cameras, this new-wave film about a car thief who kills a policeman revolutionised cinema in its day.

Before Sunset (2004) Together with Ethan Hawke, Julie Delpy also co-wrote and starred in this Oscar-nominated arthouse film, which follows the star-crossed lovers on a real-time stroll around Paris.

The Bourne Identity (2002) Featuring Matt Damon as an amnesiac government-agent-turned-target, this fast-moving action flick twists and turns against a fabulous Parisian backdrop.

Frantic (1988) Stylish thriller set in and around the city's seedier quarters. Harrison Ford enlists the help of a feisty Emmanuelle Seigner to help him track down his kidnapped wife.

La Haine (Hate; 1995) Raw, angst-ridden (and violence-ridden) film powerfully shot in black-and-white. Three teenagers from Paris' *banlieues* are trapped by crime, poverty and xenophobia while trapped in the city waiting for a train overnight.

La Môme (La Vie en Rose; 2007) Acclaimed biopic of 'little sparrow' Édith Piaf, uncannily played by Marion Cotillard, who scored the first French Best Actress Oscar in nearly half a century for the role. Most songs use Piaf's own voice.

Last Tango in Paris (1972) Marlon Brando steams up the screen as a US businessman embroiled in a sordid affair with a young Parisian woman.

Le Fabuleux Destin d'Amélie Poulain (Amélie; 2001) Quirky contemporary fable starring Audrey Tautou as a Montmartre café (p92) waitress. The colours red and green saturate the film to create a dreamlike quality, enhanced by an emotive soundtrack.

Les Amants du Pont-Neuf (1991) Haunting romance between two young homeless Parisians, set against the city's oldest bridge.

Paris, je t'aime (2006) A roll call of actors (including Gérard Depardieu and Willem Dafoe) and directors (Wes Craven, the Coen brothers, among others) contribute to this ensemble of five-minute films set in 18 of Paris' *arrondissements* (the 11e and 15e, though made, were dropped last-minute).

Ratatouille (2007) Winsome animated film about a rat who dreams of becoming a top Parisian chef.

DIRECTORY
TRANSPORT
ARRIVAL & DEPARTURE
AIR

Most international airlines serve Paris. The Aéroports de Paris website (www.adp.fr) has information on flights, routes and carriers.

Paris' two major international airports, Aéroport Roissy Charles de Gaulle and the smaller Aéroport d'Orly, both have numerous options for travelling to/from central Paris; we've listed the most expedient.

Further out, Paris-Beauvais, used by Ryanair, is served by buses.

Aéroport Roissy Charles de Gaulle

Paris' largest international airport, **Charles de Gaulle** (☎ 01 70 36 39 50; www.adp.fr), is 30km northeast of the city centre in the suburb of Roissy. Its terminals are linked by free *navettes* (shuttle buses) and free CDGVAL shuttle trains – check www.easycdg.com for info. Terminals are served by RER line B3 (follow the signs 'Paris by Train').

Train

Both terminals are served by RoissyRail on RER line B3. Trains leave every 15 minutes from 5.30am to midnight (€8.20 one way) and take 40 minutes to the centre of Paris.

Bus

Air France bus (☎ 08 92 35 08 20; www.cars-airfrance.com; one-way/return tickets from €13/18) Runs services to several locations in central Paris.

Noctilien night bus (☎ 08 92 68 77 14; tickets €7.50) Buses run every hour from 12.30am to 5.30am; Buses 120 and 121 go to Montparnasse, Châtelet, Gare du Nord; Bus 140 goes to Gare du Nord and Gare de l'Est.

Roissybus (☎ 08 92 68 77 14; one-way €8.60) Links the airport with rue Scribe, place de l'Opéra (Map pp50–1, G3). Buses take 45 minutes and run from 5.45am to 11pm.

CLIMATE CHANGE & TRAVEL

Travel – especially air travel – is a significant contributor to global climate change. At Lonely Planet, we believe that all who travel have a responsibility to limit their personal impact. As a result, we have teamed with Rough Guides and other concerned industry partners to support Climate Care, which allows people to offset the greenhouse gases they are responsible for with contributions to energy-saving projects and other climate-friendly initiatives in the developing world. Lonely Planet offsets all staff and author travel.

For more information, turn to the responsible travel pages on www.lonelyplanet.com. For details on offsetting your carbon emissions and a carbon calculator, go to www.climatecare.org.

Shuttle Bus

Prebook private door-to-door shuttles such as **Paris Airports Service** (☎ 01 55 98 10 80; www.parisairportservice .com; from €25/40 day/night per person for Charles de Gaulle or Orly). Allow time for numerous pick-ups and drop-offs.

Taxi

The tariff to the city is €40 to €60. The journey takes 30 to 50 minutes, depending on traffic.

Aéroport d'Orly

Situated 18km south of the city centre, **Orly** (☎ 01 49 75 15 15; www .adp.fr) has two terminals – Ouest (West; mainly domestic flights) and Sud (South; mainly international flights), linked for free by the Orlyval shuttle train.

Train

The **Orlyval shuttle train** (☎ 08 92 68 77 14; one-way €9.05) links Orly with RER line B at Antony (eight minutes), at least every seven minutes from 6am to 11pm. From Antony it's a 35-minute trip to central Paris.

Bus

Noctilien night bus (☎ 08 92 68 77 14, 08 92 68 41 14 in English; tickets €6) Bus 31 runs every hour from 12.30am to 5.30am, linking Gare de Lyon, Place d'Italie and Gare d'Austerlitz with Orly-Sud.

Orlybus (☎ 08 92 68 77 14; one-way €6.10) Links Place Denfert Rochereau, 14e with the airport. Buses take 30 minutes; buses run every 15 to 20 minutes from 6am to 11.50pm from the airport, from 5.35am to 11.25pm to the airport.

Shuttle Bus

Take **Air France Bus No 1** (☎ 08 92 35 08 20; one-way/return €9/14) from the airport to the eastern side of Gare Montparnasse (Map p151, A4), and Aérogare des Invalides (Map pp40–1, F1). Buses takes 30 to 45 minutes, and run every 15 minutes from 6am to 11.30pm from the airport; 5.45am to 11pm to the airport.

See p205 for door-to-door services.

Taxi

The tariff to the city is €40 to €50 (depending on time of day). The journey takes upwards of 30 minutes.

Aéroport Paris-Beauvais

Paris-Beauvais (☎ 03 44 11 46 86, general inquiries 08 92 68 20 64; www.aeroportbeauvais.com) is located 80km north of Paris.

Bus

Express services leave the airport about 20 to 30 minutes after each flight's arrival from 5.45am to 7.15pm and drop passengers on Paris' place de la Porte Maillot (Map pp50–1, A2). Buses leave Paris for the airport three hours and 15 minutes before flight departures at **Parking Pershing** (Map pp50-1, A1; 1 blvd Pershing, 17e; Ⓜ Porte Maillot). Tickets for the 75-minute trip (one-way €13) can be purchased (cash only) from **Ryanair** (☎ 03 44 11 41 41) located at the airport or a kiosk in the parking lot; or online up to 24 hours ahead at http://ticket.aeroport-beauvais.com.

Taxi

Between the city and Beauvais, taxis cost from €110 (day) and

€150 (night and all day Sunday) – probably more than the cost of your flight.

TRAIN

Paris has six stations for long-distance trains – contact **SNCF** (Societé Nationale des Chemins de Fer; ☎ 08 92 35 35 35; www.sncf.com), each with its own metro station: Gare d'Austerlitz (Map p139, D3), Gare de l'Est (Map pp98–9, C3), Gare de Lyon (Map pp112–13, F6), Gare du Nord (Map pp98–9, C3), Gare Montparnasse (Map p151, A4) and Gare St-Lazare (Map pp50–1, F2).

The highly civilised **Eurostar** (☎ 08 36 35 35 39, UK 09 90 186 186; www.eurostar.com) whisks you between Paris' Gare du Nord and London's St-Pancras Station in around two hours, 20 minutes. Through-ticketing is available to/from many regional UK stations.

Thalys (www.thalys.com) links Paris' Gare du Nord to Brussels-Midi, Amsterdam CS, Cologne's Haupt-bahnhof, and Marseille's Gare St-Charles.

BUS

Eurolines (Map p139, B2; ☎ 01 43 54 11 99; www.eurolines.com; 55 rue St-Jacques, 5e; Ⓜ Cluny-La Sorbonne) has services throughout Europe. The **Gare Routière Internationale de Paris-Galliéni** (Map pp98-9, H5; ☎ 08 92 89 90 91; 28 av du Général de Gaulle; Ⓜ Gallieni), the city's international bus terminal, is in the inner suburb of Bagnolet.

GETTING AROUND

Walking and, increasingly, cycling (p192) – is the best way to see Paris, but the city also has a fast, efficient and safe public transit system operated by **RATP** (Régie Autonome des Transports Parisiens; www.ratp.fr). This book indicates the nearest metro station after the Ⓜ in each listing.

TRAVEL PASSES

Mobilis and Paris Visite passes are valid on the metro, RER, SNCF's suburban lines, buses, night buses, trams and Montmartre's funicular railway – though a regular *carnet* (book) of transport tickets may work out cheaper.

Mobilis allows unlimited travel for one day (from €5.60 for zone 1-2). It's available at all metro, RER and SNCF stations in the Paris region.

Paris Visite (www.parisvisite.com) gives users unlimited travel, as well as discounted entry to certain museums, and other discounts/ bonuses. Passes are valid for either three, five or eight zones. The zone 1-3 pass costs €8.50/14/19/27.50 for one/two/three/five days. Passes are sold at larger metro and RER stations, Paris' SNCF offices and airports.

METRO, RER & TRAM

Paris' underground rail network has two separate but linked systems: the metro, with 14 lines and 373 stations to date; and the RER (Réseau Express Régional), a network of five suburban services (designated A to E) that pass through the city centre.

Each metro line is marked by a number, colour and final destination. Most services begin about 5.30am with the last train leaving between 12.35am and 1am (2.15am on Friday and Saturday nights).

Of Paris' four tram lines, the most central, the T3, connects the 13e, 14e and 15e south of the Seine. A fifth tram line is in the works.

For transport information, contact **RATP** (☎ 3246, 08 92 69 32 46; www.ratp.fr; ⏰ 7am-9pm Mon-Fri, 9am-5pm Sat & Sun). Tram information is available at www.tramway.paris.fr in French.

Tickets for travel within Paris' city limits cost €1.50, or €11.10 for a *carnet* of 10.

One ticket allows you to travel between any two metro stations for a period of 1½ hours, no matter how many transfers are required. A ticket can also be used on the RER for travel within zone 1; on the bus; or on the tram (but you cannot transfer between them). You can now also make bus transfers for up to 90 minutes (not

FREE WHEELING?

Beware: Paris' **Vélib'** (below) system is geared for short pick-up, drop-off hops, not all-day rental.

Let's say you sign up for a one-day €1 subscription. Scenario A: you pick up a bike just after 8am, drop it off at a station outside a café in under 30 minutes, pick up *another* bike after having your coffee, drop it off at a station outside a museum in under 30 minutes and so on, returning your final bike of the day just after 11.30pm. That €1 subscription is all you'll pay all day. Great. However, costs for an identical day's outing spiral out of control during scenario B: you pick up a bike just after 8am, lock it outside a café, ride that *same* bike to a museum, lock it there and so on, eventually dropping it off just after 11.30pm. Bearing in mind that you're charged for unused portions of half-hour blocks (ie 31 minutes costs the same as 59 minutes), your bike rental for the day has now cost a whopping €120.

But by maximising your minutes and returning bikes whenever you don't need one, it's the nearest thing to free wheeling there is. Just watch out for traffic — and traffic cops!

roundtrip; different routes are OK), provided tickets are bought from a metro station (not on the bus).

Keep your ticket until you exit the station or you risk a fine.

If you're staying in Paris for a week or more, ask at metro station offices about rechargeable **Navigo** (www.navigo.fr in French) passes.

BICYCLE

Using the new **Vélib'** (p192; ☎ 01 30 79 79 30; www.velib.paris.fr; day/week/year subscription €1/5/29, bike hire 1st/2nd/3rd & each additional half-hr free/€2/4) system is simple. Start by setting up a Vélib' account at any bike station's multilingual terminal using any major credit card, providing it has a microchip and pin number. You'll need to pre-authorise a direct debit of €150 as a deposit. If the station where you're return-

ing your bike is full, swipe your card across the terminal to get 15 free minutes to find another station. The multigeared bikes are designed for cyclists aged from 14, and are fitted with an antitheft lock and front/rear lights but not helmets (bring your own). See above to avoid escalating costs.

Note that North American credit cards, which don't have a chip-and-pin, can't access the Vélib' system – although we've had anecdotal reports that American Express cards from North America do work, despite being chip-less. We've also had reports of some international, non–North American cards not working, even ones that do have a chip.

For longer rentals, and/or if your credit card doesn't work with the Vélib' system, Fat Tire

Bike Tours (p214) has one-hour/day/weekend/week rentals for €2.50/15/25/50; you'll need to leave a €250 deposit plus photo ID. Alternatively try **Maison Roue Libre** (Map pp70-1, G4; ☎ 01 44 76 86 43; www.rouelibre.fr; 1 Passage Mondétour, 1er; 1hr/4hr/weekend €4/10/28, electric bikes 1hr/4hr/weekday/Sat or Sun €6.50/16/16/26; ☻ 9am-7pm mid-Jan–mid-Dec; Ⓜ Les Halles), which requires a €150 deposit plus photo ID; additional outlets are listed on its website.

Guided bicycle tours are listed on p214.

BOAT

The Voguéo *métro fluvial* ('metro boat') launched in the city's south-east in mid-2008, and is expected to service one end of Paris to the other within two years. Single tickets cost €3; Navigo passes (p207) of one week or longer are valid. RATP (p207) has timetables and route information.

BUS

Frequent bus services run from 5.45am to 8.30pm, but the number of routes is reduced at night and on Sundays. Timetables and route information is available from RATP (p207).

Noctilien (www.noctilien.fr) night buses operate after the metro closes; the website has information and maps. Routes cover most of the city; look for blue 'N'

or 'Noctilien' signs at bus stops. Tickets cost the same as one metro/bus ticket for short journeys; longer journeys require two or more tickets.

TAXI

You'll find ranks around major intersections, or you can hail taxis in the street. The *prise en charge* (flagfall) is €2.10. Within the city limits, it costs €0.82 per kilometre for travel between 10am and 5pm Monday to Saturday (*Tarif A;* white light on meter). At night (5pm to 10am), on Sunday from 7am to midnight, and in the inner suburbs the rate is €1.10 per km (*Tarif B;* orange light on meter). Travel in the outer suburbs is at *Tarif C,* €1.33 per kilometre. There's a €2.75 surcharge for taking a fourth passenger, but drivers may refuse for insurance reasons. The first piece of baggage is free; additional pieces over 5kg cost €1 extra.

Avoid 'freelance' – ie illegal – cabs.

To order a taxi, call Paris' **central taxi switchboard** (☎ 01 45 30 30 30, passengers with reduced mobility 01 47 39 00 91; ☻ 24hr), or reserve by phone or online with the following:

Alpha Taxis (☎ 01 45 85 85 85; www.alpha taxis.com)

Taxis Bleus (☎ 01 49 36 29 48, 08 91 70 10 10; www.taxis-bleus.com)

Taxis G7 (☎ 01 47 39 47 39; www.taxisg7 .fr in French)

PRACTICALITIES
BUSINESS HOURS

Opening hours fluctuate constantly – call ahead to be sure. In general, shops and business close on Sunday and either Monday or Tuesday; many also close for lunch (12.30pm to 2.30pm), and some also close on Saturday afternoons. Larger shops often open to 10pm once a week, usually Thursday. Most banks are open from 9am to 4pm (some close for lunch).

Restaurants generally serve lunch from noon to 3pm and dinner from 7pm or 7.30pm until at least 9.30pm. Restaurants that vary from these times by more than an hour have been noted in reviews.

Final entry to attractions such as monuments, museums and galleries is generally half an hour to an hour before the official closing times including times given in this book.

DISCOUNTS

Concessions (usually 30% to 50%) abound for youth, students and seniors on everything from transport to museums. Bring whatever concession ID you have from home and flash it every time you pull out your wallet. See p193 for information about reduced rates for kids.

If you plan to visit a lot of museums, your best bet is a **Paris Museum Pass** (www.parismuseumpass.fr), available for two, four or six days (€30/45/60). It gives you entry to more than 60 museums and allows you to skip the queues and head straight in. Pick it up from tourist offices, participating museums and monuments, or branches of Fnac. (Forget ordering it ahead online, which costs extra for postage.)

See opposite for ways to save on theatre tickets.

ELECTRICITY

Plugs in France have two round pins. Voltage is 220V AC, 50Hz. Appliances rated US 110V need a transformer to work safely. Transformers and adaptors can be bought at shops including most Fnac (p76) branches, and BHV (p119).

EMERGENCIES

Pickpockets prey on busy places; *always* stay alert to the possibility of someone surreptitiously reaching for your pockets or bags. A scam to look out for is when someone pretends to 'find' a gold ring on the ground (by dropping it on the ground) and picks it up to offer it to you. This could be a diversionary tactic for pickpocketing, or an opening to try to get money from you. It's especially prevalent around the Seine/Concorde/Tuileries area.

Many locals find the park above the Forum des Halles (p76) dodgy, especially at night.

Paris has a high incidence of beggars; if someone approaches you and you're not willing/able to give them money, simply say *désolé* (a compassionate form of 'sorry').

The metro is safe to use until it closes, including for women travelling alone, but stations best avoided late at night include the long passageways of Châtelet–Les Halles and Montparnasse Bienvenüe, as well as Château Rouge, Gare du Nord, Strasbourg St-Denis, Réaumur-Sébastopol and Stalingrad. *Bornes d'alarme* (alarm boxes) are located in the centre of each metro/RER platform and in some station corridors.

Emergency phone numbers:
Ambulance (☎ 15)
Fire Brigade (☎ 18)
Police (☎ 17)
Rape Crisis Hotline (☎ 08 00 05 95 95; 🕙 10am-7pm Mon-Fri)
SOS Helpline (☎ 01 47 23 80 80; 🕙 in English 3-11pm daily)

ENTERTAINMENT BOOKING AGENCIES

Tickets to concerts, theatre performances and sporting events are available from **Fnac** (www.fnac.fr in French), including its large branch in the Forum des Halles (p76).

Virgin Megastore (www.virginmega.fr in French), including its late-opening Champs-Élysées store (p64), also sells tickets. Otherwise try **Agence Perrossier & SOS Théâtres** (Map pp50-1, F4; ☎ 01 42 60 58 31, 01 44 77 88 55; www.agencedetheatresdeparis.fr; 6 place de la Madeleine, 8e; 🕙 10am-7pm Mon-Sat; Ⓜ Madeleine).

On the day of the performance, theatres across town often make unsold tickets available at half price (plus commission of about €2.50). The two main discount ticket outlets:

Kiosque Théâtre Madeleine (Map pp50-1, F3; opposite 15 place de la Madeleine, 8e; 🕙 12.30-8pm Tue-Sat, 12.30-4pm Sun; Ⓜ Madeleine)

Montparnasse Kiosque Théâtre (Map p151, B4; parvis Montparnasse, 15e; 🕙 12.30-8pm Tue-Sat, 12.30-4pm Sun; Ⓜ Montparnasse Bienvenüe)

Websites www.billetreduc.com and www.ticketac.com (both in French) sell discounted tickets online.

HOLIDAYS

New Year's Day (*Jour de l'An*) 1 January
Easter Sunday (*Pâques*) late March/April
Easter Monday (*Lundi de Pâques*) late March/April
May Day (*Fête du Travail*) 1 May
Victoire 1945 (Victory in Europe Day) 8 May
Ascension Thursday (*L'Ascension*) May

DIRECTORY

Whit Sunday/Whit Monday (*Pentecôte/ Lundi de Pentecôte*) May/June
Bastille Day (*Fête Nationale*) 14 July
Assumption Day (*L'Assomption*) 15 August
All Saints' Day (*La Toussaint*) 1 November
Armistice Day (*Le Onze Novembre*) 11 November
Christmas Day (*Noël*) 25 December

INTERNET

The City of Paris has set up 400 free daytime-only wi-fi points at popular locations including parks, libraries, local town halls and tourist hotspots. Many cafés and hotels offer wi-fi, although the latter may charge steeply for this service.

Internet cafés are prevalent throughout Paris; prices average around €4 per hour.

Useful websites:

Lonely Planet (www.lonelyplanet.com) Detailed information and links.

Paris Daily Photo (www.parisdailyphoto .com) Local photographer's daily snapshot with detailed comment.

Paris DJs (www.parisdjs.com) Groove around town with free weekly podcast compilations by northern *arrondissement* DJs.

Paris Notes (www.parisnotes.com) Paid subscription for in-depth newsletters, plus lots of handy info online for free.

Paris Pages (www.paris.org) Good coverage of cultural events.

Paris Tourist Office (www.parisinfo.com) Official tourism website with stacks of info in multiple languages.

Secrets of Paris (www.secretsofparis.com) Chock-full of up-to-date city info plus an excellent free newsletter.

Stuff Parisians Like (www.o-chateau.com /blog) On-the-money insight into Parisian life, covering topics such as 'not exercising', 'last-min flaking' & the camaraderie of 'urinating in the street' (for guys, not girls!).

LANGUAGE

BASICS

Hello.	*Bonjour.*
Good evening.	*Bonsoir.*
Goodbye.	*Au revoir.*
How are you?	*Comment allez-vous?*
How's it going?	*Ça va?*
I'm fine.	*Bien, merci.*
Please.	*S'il vous plaît.*
Thank you.	*Merci.*
Yes.	*Oui.*
No.	*Non.*
Excuse me/ Sorry.	*Excusez-moi/ Pardon.*
I (don't) understand.	*Je (ne) comprends (pas).*
Do you speak English?	*Parlez-vous anglais?*

EATING & DRINKING

Two beers/ a coffee/ a table for two, please.	*Deux bières/ un café/une table pour deux s'il vous plaît.*
That was delicious!	*C'était délicieux!*
I'm a vegetarian.	*Je suis végétarien/ végétarienne. (m/f)*
The bill, please.	*L'addition, s'il vous plaît.*
Cheers!	*Santé!*

SHOPPING

How much is it?	*C'est combien?*
It's too expensive.	*C'est trop cher.*

EMERGENCIES

I'm sick.	*Je suis malade.*
Help!	*Au secours!*
Call the police!	*Appelez la police!*
Call a doctor!	*Appelez un médecin!*
Call an ambulance.	*Appelez un ambulance!*

DAYS & NUMBERS

today	*aujourd'hui*
tomorrow	*demain*
yesterday	*hier*
0	*zéro*
1	*un*
2	*deux*
3	*trois*
4	*quatre*
5	*cinq*
6	*six*
7	*sept*
8	*huit*
9	*neuf*
10	*dix*
11	*onze*
12	*douze*
13	*treize*
14	*quatorze*
15	*quinze*
16	*seize*
17	*dix-sept*
18	*dix-huit*
19	*dix-neuf*
20	*vingt*
21	*vingt et un*
22	*vingt-deux*
30	*trente*
40	*quarante*
50	*cinquante*
60	*soixante*
70	*soixante-dix*
80	*quatre-vingts*
90	*quatre-vingt-dix*
100	*cent*
1000	*mille*

MONEY

Budget travellers sticking to simple meals, hitting a museum or two and having a couple of drinks might get by on around €50 per person per day in addition to accommodation expenses. If you're dining at midrange places, doing a fair bit of sightseeing and going out on the town, count on spending around €85 to €150 per person, per day on top of your hotel bill (much more if you're planning on *haute cuisine* and/or *haute couture*).

For currency exchange rates, see the inside front cover.

ATMS & CREDIT CARDS

Visa is the most widely accepted credit card, followed by MasterCard. American Express and Diners Club cards are only accepted at more exclusive establishments. Some restaurants still don't accept credit cards.

Many automated services, such as ticket machines, require a chip-and-pin credit card. ATMs generally won't accept PIN codes with more than four digits.

Ask your bank for advice before you leave.

NEWSPAPERS
Paris' main daily newspapers are the conservative *Le Figaro,* the sombre, centre-left *Le Monde,* and the arty, left-leaning *Libération.*

ORGANISED TOURS
In addition to the open-topped hop-on, hop-off bus tours prevalent everywhere (see http://paris-open-tour.com), some excellent tours are available by bike, boat or foot.

BICYCLE TOURS
Fat Tire Bike Tours (Map pp40–1, D3; ☎ 01 56 58 10 54; www.fattirebiketoursparis .com; 24 rue Edgar Faure, 15e; ❥ office 9am–7pm; Ⓜ La Motte-Picquet Grenelle) Popular day- and night-time city tours; prices start from €24. Ask about its entertaining 'segway' tours on gyroscopic two-wheeled contraptions.

BOAT TOURS
Numerous companies cruise on *la ligne de vie de Paris* (the lifeline of Paris, aka the Seine) and Paris' canals. Our picks are listed here.

Canal Cruises
Canauxrama (☎ 01 42 39 15 00; www .canauxrama.com; Mon–Fri €15/11, Sat &

Sun €15; Ⓜ Jaurès or Bastille) Barges travel between Port de Plaisance de Paris-Arsenal, 12e, opposite 50 blvd de la Bastille, and the Parc de la Villette, 19e, along Canal St-Martin and Canal de l'Ourcq, including an illuminated underground section, taking 2½ hours. Departures are at 9.45am and 2.30pm from Port de Plaisance de Paris-Arsenal (Map pp112–13, E5) and at 9.45am from Bassin de la Villette from April to September and, in July and August, at 2.45pm from Bassin de la Villette. Cruises are often available from October to March by reservation.

River Cruises
See also p209.
Bateaux-Mouches (Map pp50–1, D5; ☎ 01 42 25 96 10; www.bateauxmouches .com; Port de la Conférence, 8e; tickets €9/4; ❥ every 30min 11am-10.30pm Apr–Sep, every 45min 10.15am-9pm Oct–Mar subject to demand; Ⓜ Alma-Marceau) Bilingual 70-minute cruises.
Batobus (☎ 08 25 05 01 01; www.batobus .com; day pass €12/8; ❥ 10am-9.30pm May–Aug, 10am-7pm Sep–mid-Nov & mid-Mar–Apr, 10.30am-4.30pm mid-Nov–mid-Dec & Feb–mid-Mar, 10.30am-5pm mid-Dec–Jan) Hop-on, hop-off waterbus making eight stops between the Eiffel Tower and the Jardin des Plantes; boats leave every 25 to 30 minutes from 10am; no boats run from early January to early February.

WALKING TOURS
See p42 for free local-led walks around Paris, and p101 for walks in the Belleville area.

Paris Walks (☎ 01 48 09 21 40; www.paris
-walks.com; walks from €10/8) Entertaining
and informative tours in English focussing on
various quarters/themes.

SMOKING

As of 2008, smoking is forbidden
in all public places throughout
France, as well as restaurants and
bars. This doesn't apply to hotel
rooms, however – see p172.

TELEPHONE

France uses the GSM 900/1800
cellular system, compatible with
phones from the UK, Australia
and most of Asia (and all tri-band
and quad-band phones), but not
GSM 1900 phones from North
America (GSM 1900/900 phones
are OK), or the separate Japanese
system.

Public telephones generally
require a phonecard (télécarte),
which can be purchased at post
offices, tabacs and anywhere displaying a blue 'télécarte en vente
ici' ('phonecards sold here') sticker.
Cards start from €7.50.

See the inside front cover for
country and city codes and useful
numbers.

TIME

Time format 24-hour clock (1.30pm = 13h30,
2.30pm = 14h30 etc)
Time zone Central European Time (one hour
ahead of/later than GMT)

TIPPING

French law requires that
restaurant, café and hotel bills
include a *service compris* (service
charge), usually 15%, so a tip is
neither necessary nor expected,
although people often round
restaurant bills up by a couple of
euros. Round taxi fares up to the
nearest €1.

TOURIST INFORMATION

The main branch of the **Paris
Convention & Visitors Bureau** (Office de
Tourisme et de Congrès de Paris; Map pp50-1,
G4; ☎ 08 92 68 30 00; www.parisinfo
.com; 25-27 rue des Pyramides, 1er; ☼ 9am-
7.30pm Jun-Oct, 10am-7pm Mon-Sat & 11am-
7pm Sun Nov-May; Ⓜ Pyramides) is 500m
northwest of the Louvre.

Elsewhere in Paris, telephone
numbers and websites are the
same as for the main office.
Anvers (Map p85, C4; opposite 72 blvd Roche-
chouart, 18e; ☼ 10am-6pm; Ⓜ Anvers)
Gare de Lyon (Map pp112-13, F6; Arrivals hall,
20 blvd Diderot, 12; ☼ 8am-6pm Mon-Sat;
Ⓜ Gare de Lyon) In the arrivals hall for
mainline trains.
Gare du Nord (Map pp98-9, C3; 18 rue de
Dunkerque, 10e; ☼ 8am-6pm; Ⓜ Gare du
Nord) At the station's eastern end.
Opéra-Grands Magasins (Map pp50-1, G3;
11 rue Scribe, 9e; ☼ 9am-6.30pm Mon-Sat;
Ⓜ Auber or Opéra)
Syndicate d'Initiative de Montmartre
(Map p85, C4; ☎ 01 42 62 21 21; 21 place
du Tertre, 18e; ☼ 10am-7pm; Ⓜ Abbesses)
Locally run office.

TRAVELLERS WITH DISABILITIES

Paris' antiquated architecture, including much of the metro, means unfortunately that *fauteuil roulent* (wheelchair) access is severely limited, and ramps are rare. Newer hotels, museums and public facilities must by law provide access. In this book, we've used the symbol ♿ to denote sights that are wheelchair accessible, but check ahead regarding specific requirements. Many restaurants may only have partial access and restaurant bathrooms may not accommodate wheelchairs or provide rails – ask when you book.

INFORMATION & ORGANISATIONS

The tourist office website (www .parisinfo.com) has excellent information for travellers with disabilities and impairments. Access-Able Travel Source (www.access-able .com) also has some good links for organisations that can provide advice about reduced mobility access in Paris.

For information on wheelchair accessibility for all forms of public transport, the *Guide Practique à l'Usage des Personnes à Mobilité Réduite* from the **Syndicat des Transports d'Île de France** (☎ 01 47 53 28 00; www .stif-idf.fr) is indispensable.

>INDEX

See also separate subindexes for See (p220), Do (p221), Shop (p221), Eat (p222), Drink (p223) and Play (p224).

A

accommodation 172-3
air travel 204-6
ambulance 211
Arc de Triomphe 52-3
Arc de Triomphe area 48-67,
  50-1
architecture 183
art 180
  art nouveau 12, 42-3, 158
  contemporary art 28
  impressionism 12, 42-3
  metro 75
  Montmartre artists 88
ATMs 213-14

B

baguettes 90
Balzac, Honoré de 54
Banlieues Bleues 25
bars, *see* Drink *subindex*
Basilique du Sacré-Cœur
  22, 86
Bastille 110-29, **112-13**
Bastille Day 26-7
Bateaux Mouches 144
Belleville 96-109, **98-9**
bicycling, *see* cycling
boat travel 209, 214
Bois de Boulogne 59
Bois de Vincennes 118
Bonaparte, Napoleon 197
books 182, 202
bookshops 182, *see also* Shop
  subindex
bread 90
brunches 124

bus travel 145, 206-7, 209
business hours 210

C

cabarets 187, *see also* Play
  subindex
cafés, *see* Eat, Drink
  subindexes
Canal St-Martin 21
Capitale de la Creation 24
Catacombes 140
Cathédrale de Notre Dame de
  Paris 131
cathedrals, *see* See *subindex*
cemeteries, *see* See *subindex*
Centre Pompidou 69-70
Champagne 169
Champs-Élysées, av des 53
Champs-Élysées area 48-67,
  50-1
chansons 94, 187, *see
  also* Play *subindex*
children, travel with 193
Chinatown 146
Chinese New Year 25
Chirac, Jacques 197-8
churches, *see* See *subindex*
Cimetière du Père Lachaise
  20, 97
cinema, *see* film
Cinéma au Clair de Lune 28
cinemas 194, *see also* Play
  subindex
classical music 189
clothing sizes 60
clubs, *see* Play *subindex*
cooking courses 44-5, 188,
  see also Do *subindex*

costs, *see inside front cover*
credit cards 213-14
cruises 144
cycling 27, 192, 208-9, 214

D

Dalí, Salvador 87
dance 189
Delanoë, Bertrand 197
Delpy, Julie 203
disabilities, travellers with 216
dogs 121
drinking 176-7, *see also* Drink
  subindex
  Arc de Triomphe area 65-6
  Bastille 125-8
  Belleville 106-7
  Champs-Élysées area 65-6
  Eiffel Tower area 46
  Grands Boulevards area
    65-6
  Île de la Cité 137
  Île St-Louis 137
  Invalides 46
  Latin Quarter 148-9
  Les Halles 80-3
  Louvre area 80-3
  Marais 125-8
  Montmartre 91-2
  Montparnasse 162-4
  St-Germain des Prés 162-4
Dusoulier, Clotilde 81

E

Eiffel Tower 10-11, 39
Eiffel Tower area 38-47, **40-1**
electricity 210

emergencies 210-11
entertainment booking
   agencies 211
European Heritage Days 28
events 23-8
exchange rates, *see inside
   front cover*

F
fashion, *see also* Shop
   subindex
      festivals 24
      shopping 63, 179
Festival d'Automne 28
Festival des Musiques du
   Nouvel An 24
festivals 23-8
Fête des Vendages de
   Montmartre 26
Fête du Beaujolais 26
Fête du Miel 26
film 194, 203
   festivals 27, 28
fire services 211
flowers 135
Foire du Trône 25
Foire Internationale d'Art
   Contemporain 28
food 174-5, 188, *see also* Eat,
   Shop *subindexes*
      Arc de Triomphe area 64-5
      Bastille 121-5
      Belleville 103-6
      Champs-Élysées area 64-5
      Eiffel Tower area 45-6
      festivals 26
      for children 193
      Grands Boulevards area
         64-5

000 map pages

Île de la Cité 136-7
Île St-Louis 136-7
Invalides 45-6
Latin Quarter 145-8
Les Halles 78-80
Louvre area 78-80
Montmartre 89-91
Montparnasse 159-62
St-Germain des Prés
   159-62
Forum des Halles 77

G
Gainsbourg, Serge 152
galleries 180, *see also* See
   subindex
gardens 181, *see also* See
   subindex
Gay Pride March 26
gay travellers 189, *see
   also* Drink, Play *subindexes*
Giverny 168
Grande Arche 52
Grands Boulevards area
   48-67, **50-1**
Guimard synagogue 115

H
Haussmann, Baron 197
Hemingway, Ernest 202
history 196-203
holidays 211-12
Hugo, Victor 115

I
ice cream 17, *see also* Eat
   subindex
ice skating 28
Île de la Cité 130-7, **132-3**
Île St-Louis 17, 130-7, **132-3**
impressionism 168, 180
Internationaux de France de
   Tennis 26
internet access 212

internet resources 212
Invalides 38-47, **40-1**
itineraries 29-33

J
Jardin du Luxembourg
   13, 154
jazz 82, 187, *see also* Play
   subindex

L
La Course des Garçons de
   Café 26
La Défense 52
La Goutte d'Or en Fête 26
language 200-1, 212-13
Latin Quarter 138-49, **139**
Le Grand Fooding de l'Été 26
Les Halles 68-83, **70-1**
Les Misérables 202
lesbian travellers 189, *see
   also* Drink, Play *subindexes*
lifestyle 199-200, 201
literature 182, 202
Louis XIV 166, 196
Louvre, the 18, 73
Louvre area 68-83, **70-1**

M
Marais 110-29, **112-13**
Marathon International de
   Paris 25
marionettes 153
markets 14, *see also* Shop,
   Eat *subindexes*
mass-skates 129, *see also* Do
   subindex
metro 149, 207-8
   art 75
   safety 211
Mois de la Photo 28
Mona Lisa 73, 74
Monet, Claude 73, 168

money 213-14
    discount cards 210
Montmartre 84-95, **85**
Montparnasse 150-64, **151**
Morrison, Jim 97
Mosquée de Paris 15, 141, 143
multiculturalism 186, 202
Musée d'Orsay 12, 42-3
Musée du Louvre 18, 73
museums 180, see also See subindex
    discount cards 210
    free entry 142
music, see also Play subindex
    chansons 94, 187
    classical music 189
    dance 189
    festivals 25, 26, 27
    jazz 187
    opera 189
    theatre 189

N
Napoleon III 197
New Year's Eve 28
newspapers 214
nightlife 176-7, see also Play subindex
Nouvel, Jean 141
Nuit Blanche 28

O
opera 189, see also Play subindex
Orwell, George 202

P
Paris, Capitale de la Creation 24
Paris Cinéma 27
Paris Greeter 42
Paris Jazz Festival 26

Paris Plages 27
parks 181, see also See subindex
    for children 193
Passage Brady 104
Patinoire de l'Hôtel de Ville 28
philocafés 126
photography 28
Picasso, Pablo 116-17
Place de la Concorde 58
planning 32
    discount cards 210
police 211
politics 197-8
Pont Neuf 134
Portes Ouvertes des Ateliers d'artistes de Belleville 101
Portes Ouvertes des Ateliers de Ménilmontant 101
Portes Ouvertes des Ateliers du Père Lachaise Associés 101
Promenade Plantée 19, 117

R
rape crisis hotline 211
Reims 169
RER travel 207-8
restaurants, see Eat subindex
river cruises 214
Rock en Seine 27-8
Rodin, Auguste 43-4
Rollerblading 129
Rorcha 157
Rousseau, Benoît 108
rue Cler 45
rue Montorgueil 79
rue Mouffetard 148

S
Sacré-Cœur 22, 86
safety 210-11

St-Germain des Prés 150-64, **151**
Ste-Chapelle 134
Salon International de l'Agriculture 26
Sarkozy, Nicolas 198
Seine 144
Shakespeare & Company 16, 145
shopping 178-9, see also Shop subindex
    Arc de Triomphe area 59-64
    Bastille 119-21
    Belleville 102-3
    Champs-Élysées area 59-64
    Eiffel Tower area 45
    Golden Triangle 63
    Grands Boulevards area 59-64
    Île de la Cité 134-6
    Île St-Louis 134-6
    Invalides 45
    Latin Quarter 144-5
    Les Halles 74-8
    Louvre area 74-8
    Marais 119-21
    Montmartre 88-9
    Montparnasse 156-9
    St-Germain des Prés 156-9
smoking 215
Sorbonne 144
Southeast Paris 146, **147**
sporting events
    Internationaux de France de Tennis 26
    Marathon International de Paris 25
    Tour de France 27
Stade de France 95
swimming 146

T

taxis 209
telephone services 215
theatres 189, *see also* Play *subindex*
Thomas, Frédéric 93
time 215
tipping 215
Tour de France 27
Tour Montparnasse 155
tourist information 215
tours 42, 214-15
train travel 206
tram travel 207-8
travel passes 207

V

Vélib' bicycle rental system 192, 208
Versailles 166-7
views 185
Villepin, Dominique de 197-8
Voguéo metro boat 209

W

walking 191, 214-15
Wilde, Oscar 182
wine 188
    festivals 26
    museums 55-6
wine-tasting courses 188, *see also* Do *subindex*

Z

zoos, *see* See *subindex*

SEE

Aquariums
Aquarium Tropical 118
Cinéaqua 53

000 map pages

Canals
Canal St-Martin 21

Cemeteries & Memorials
Catacombes 140
Cimetière de Montmartre 86-7
Cimetière du Montparnasse 152
Cimetière du Père Lachaise 20, 97

Champagne Houses
Mumm 169
Pommery 169
Taittinger 169

Châteaus & Palaces
Château de Bagatelle 59
Château de Versailles 166-7
Château de Vincennes 118
Conciergerie 134
Palais de Chaillot 56-7
Palais de Tokyo 57

Churches & Cathedrals
Basilique du Sacré-Cœur 22, 86
Cathédrale de Notre Dame de Paris 131
Église de la Madeleine 53-4
Église St-Germain des Prés 152-3
Église St-Sulpice 153
Ste-Chapelle 134

Libraries
Bibliothèque Nationale de France 146

Mosques
Mosquée de Paris 15, 141, 143

Museums & Galleries
Centre Pompidou 69-70
Cité de l'Architecture et du Patrimoine 57

Cité des Sciences et de l'Industrie 97
Cité Nationale de l'Histoire de l'Immigration 118
Dalí Espace Montmartre 87
Fondation Cartier Pour l'Art Contemporain 154
Galerie d'Architecture Moderne & Contemporaine 57
Galerie Musée Baccarat 54
Galeries du Panthéon Bouddhique du Japon et de la Chine 56
Hôtel de Sully 114
Hôtel de Ville 114
Institut du Monde Arabe 140-1
Jeu de Paume 72
Maison de Balzac 54
Maison de Claude Monet 168
Maison de l'Air 97, 100
Maison de Victor Hugo 115
Maison Européenne de la Photographie 115
Musée Carnavalet 115
Musée Cognacq-Jay 115-16
Musée d'Art et d'Histoire du Judaïsme 116
Musée d'Art Moderne de la Ville de Paris 55-6
Musée de la Marine 56-7
Musée de la Mode et du Textile 74
Musée de la Poste 154
Musée de la Publicité 74
Musée de l'Érotisme 87
Musée de l'Homme 56
Musée de l'Orangerie 72-3
Musée de Montmartre 87
Musée des Arts Décoratifs 74
Musée des Arts et Métiers 116
Musée des Égouts de Paris 42

Musée d'Orsay 12, 42-3
Musée du Louvre 18, 73
Musée du Luxembourg 154
Musée du Parfum 55
Musée du Quai Branly 43
Musée du Vin 55-6
Musée Édith Piaf 100
Musée Galliera de la Mode de la Ville de Paris 56
Musée Guimet des Arts Asiatiques 56
Musée Jacquemart-André 56
Musée Marmottan 57
Musée National d'Histoire Naturelle 143
Musée National du Moyen Âge 143
Musée National Eugène Delacroix 154-5
Musée Picasso 116-17
Musée Rodin 43-4
Palais de Chaillot 56-7
Palais de Tokyo 57
Pavillon de l'Arsenal 117
Tenniseum-Musée de Roland Garros 59

Notable Buildings & Structures
Arc de Triomphe 52-3
Arc de Triomphe du Carrousel 69
Ballon Eutelsat 39
Centre Pompidou 69-70
Château de Vincennes 118
Docks en Seine 146
Eiffel Tower 10-11, 39
Grande Arche 52
Hôtel de Sully 114
Hôtel de Ville 114
Hôtel des Invalides 42
Panthéon 143
Pont Neuf 134

Sorbonne 144
Tour Montparnasse 155

Notable Streets & Places
Champs-Élysées, av des 53
Place de la Bastille 117
Place de la Concorde 58
Place de la Madeleine 61
Place des Vosges 116
Place du Tertre 87-8
Place Vendôme 58

Parks & Gardens
Bois de Boulogne 59
Bois de Vincennes 118
Jardin d'Acclimatation 59
Jardin des Plantes 141
Jardin des Tuileries 72
Jardin du Luxembourg 13, 154
Jardin du Palais Royal 72
Parc de Bagatelle 59
Parc de Belleville 100-1
Parc de la Villette 101
Parc de Monceau 57
Parc des Buttes Chaumont 101
Parc Floral de Paris 118
Parc Montsouris 155
Promenade Plantée 19, 117
Tenniseum-Musée de Roland Garros 59

Zoos
Ménagerie du Jardin des Plantes 141
Paris Zoo 118

🏃 DO

Cooking Courses
Cuisine Fraîch' Attitude 102
École Le Cordon Bleu 44-5
Les Coulisses du Chef Cours de Cuisine Olivier Berté 58
Promenades Gourmandes 118

Mass-skates
Pari-Roller 155-6
Rollers & Coquillages 119

Walking Tours
Ça Se Visite! Belleville Walking Tours 101

Wine-tasting Courses
O-Château 102

🛍 SHOP

Accessories
A La Recherche De Jane 156
Alexandra Sojfer 156
Antoine 75
Colette 76
Gérard Durand 156
Lancel 62
Maroquinerie Saint-Honoré 77-8
Max Maroquinerie Bagagerie et Accessoires 158-9
Seven Seventies 103
Shine 120

Antiques
Village St-Paul 121
Zut! 89

Arcades
Galerie Véro Dodat 77
Galerie Vivienne 62
Passage des Panoramas 62
Passage du Grand Cerf 62
Passage Jouffroy 62
Passage Verdeau 62

Arts & Crafts
Boutique Paris-Musées 119
Viaduc des Arts 121
Village St-Paul 121

Books
Abbey Bookshop 144
Cine Reflet 156
Le Mots à La Bouche 119
Librairie Gourmande 77
Librairie Ulysse 135
Red Wheelbarrow Bookstore 120
Shakespeare & Company 145
Village Voice 159

Cookware Shops
A Simon 78
E Dehillerin 78
Mora 78

Department Stores
Bazar de l'Hôtel de Ville (BHV) 119
Drugstore Publicis 60
Galeries Lafayette 61
Le Bon March 158
Le Printemps 63
Tati 88

Fashion
agnès b 74-5
Antoine et Lili 102, 119
Chanel 63
Chloé 60
Christian Dior 63
Christian Lacroix 63
Colette 76
Commes des Garçons 63
Eres 60-1
Frivoli 102
Givenchy 63
Hermès 63
Jean-Paul Gaultier 63
Kenzo 77

Lanvin 63
L'Habilleur 119-20
Louis Vuitton 63
Seven Seventies 103
Shine 120
Sonia Rykiel 159
Stella Cadente 103
Un Chien dans le Marais 120
Yves Saint Laurent 63

Food & Drink
Boutique Maille 59
Fauchon 61
Fromagerie Alléosse 61
La Fromagerie 31 156
La Grande Épicerie de Paris 158
La Maison de la Truffe 62
La Maison du Miel 62
La Petite Scierie 135
Legrand Filles & Fils 63
Oliviers & Co 136

Homewares
Antoine et Lili 102, 119
Astier de Villatte 75
Mouffetard Folie's 145
Plastiques 159

Markets
flower market 61
Marché aux Fleurs 136
Marché aux Puces d'Aligre 120
Marché aux Puces de Montreuil 103
Marché aux Puces de St-Ouen 88

Music
Virgin Megastore 64

Perfumes
Guerlain 61-2
Kenzo 77

Sex Shops
Rebecca Rils 88

Shopping Centres & Malls
Carrousel du Louvre 75-6
Forum des Halles 76-7

Sports Equipment
Nomades 120

Toys
Au Plat d'Étain 156
Clair de Rêve 134-5

🍴 EAT

Bakeries
Arnaud Delmontel 89
Poilâne 162

Bistros
Le Chateaubriand 104
Le Sévéro 161
L'Ourcine 148

Brasseries
Brasserie Bofinger 122
Brasserie de l'Île St-Louis 136
Brasserie Lipp 159-60
Café le Flore en l'Île 136
Le Relais Gascon 91
Restaurant Musée d'Orsay 46

Breton
Crêperie Bretonne 122

Cafés
Le Loir dans la Théière 124
Le Look 105
Pères et Filles 161

Caféterias
Bazar de l'Hôtel de Ville (BHV) caféteria 121-2

000 map pages

Crêperies
Chez Nicos 145
Crêperie Bretonne 122

French
À la Cloche d'Or 89
Au Pied de Cochon 78
Aux Négociants 90
Café Marly 78-9
Chez Marie 90
Chez Toinette 90
Hôtel du Nord 103-4
La Maison Rose 91
Le Chansonnier 104
Le Clown Bar 123
Le Coude Fou 123
Le J'Go 65
Le Petit Bofinger 123-4
Le Procope 161
Le Roi du Pot au Feu 65
Le Salon d'Hélène 161
Le Train Bleu 124
Le Villaret 105
L'Escargot 80
Ripaille 91

Gastronomic
Alain Ducasse au Plaza
    Athénée 64
Comptoir de la Gastronomie 79
Guy Savoy 64
La Tour d'Argent 145
L'Arpège 45
Le Bistrot du Sommelier 65
Le Grand Véfour 79
Le Jules Verne 45
Les Ombres 46
Maison Prunier 65
Poilâne 46

Ice Cream
Café le Flore en l'Île 136
Maison Berthillon 137
Pozzetto 124

Indian
Bistro Indien 104
Krishna Bhavan 104

International
Georges 79
L'Atelier de Joël Robouchon
    160
Sorza 137

Japanese
Koba 64

Jewish
Chez Marianne 122
La Boutique Jeune 123
L'As de Felafel 123

Lyonais
Aux Lyonnais 64

Markets
Marché aux Enfants Rouges
    124
Marché Bastille 124
Marché Beauvau 124
Marché Belleville 105
Marché Brancusi 161
Marché des Batignolles
    91
Marché Maubert 148
Marché Monge 148
Marché Raspail 161
Marché St-Quentin 106

Notable Streets
rue Cler 45
rue Montorgueil 79
rue Mouffetard 148

Patisseries
Stohrer 80

Salons de Thé
Les Deux Abeilles 45-6

Seafood
Au Rocher de Cancale 78
Charlot, Roi des Coquillages 90
Le Dôme 160-1

Senegalese
Au Village 103

Thai
Le Krung Thep 105

Vegetarian
Grand Appétit 122

Vietnamese
Pho 67 148

🍸 DRINK

Bars
Andy Wahloo 126
Bar Hemingway 65
Bar Signature 162
Bistro des Augustins 162
Café Baroc 126
Café Chéri(e) 106
Curieux Spaghetti Bar 126
Harry's New York Bar 65
Kong 80, 82
La Closerie des Lilas 162
La Fourmi 92
Le Conchon à l'Oreille 82
Le Pantalon 149
Le Petit Château d'Eau 107
Le Pré 163
Le Tambour 82-3
Le Vieux Chêne 149
Les Etages St-Germain 164
Taverne Henri IV 137

Bistros
Bistro des Augustins 162
Le Conchon à l'Oreille 82
Le Tambour 82-3

INDEX

Brasseries
La Closerie des Lilas 162

Cafés
Café Bonnie 106
Café Branly 46
Café Charbon 106
Café de Flore 162
Café des Hauteurs 46
Café des Phares 126
Café La Fusée 80
Café Le Refuge 91
Café Panis 148-9
Chez Prune 106
La Palette 162-3
L'Atmosphère 106-7
Le Petit Château d'Eau 107
Le Progrès 127
Le Pure Café 127
Le Select 163
Le Viaduc Café 127
Les Deux Magots 163
Les Deux Moulins 92
L'Île Enchantée 107

Gay & Lesbian Venues
3W Kafé 125
Le Cox 127
Le Quetzal 127
Open Café 128

Salons de Thé
Angélina 80
Café Branly 46
Hédiard 66
La Charlotte en l'Île 137

Ladurée 66
Mariage Frères 127

Wine Bars
Le Baron Rouge 126-7

⭐ PLAY

Cabarets
Au Lapin Agile 92
Crazy Horse 66
Folies-Bergère 94
Le Lido 66-7
Moulin Rouge 95

Chansons
Au Limonaire 66
Chez Louisette 92
Le Vieux Belleville 109

Cinemas
Cinéma des Cinéastes 94
Cinémathèque Française 146
Forum des Images 83
La Pagode 47
Le Champo 149
Le Grand Rex 83

Clubs
La Coupole 164
La Dame de Canton 146
La Flèche d'Or 107
Le Balajo 128
Le Baron 66
Le Batofar 146
Le Divan du Monde 94
Point Éphemère 108, 109

Rex Club 83
Social Club 67

Gay & Lesbian Venues
Le Queen 67

Jazz Venues
Le Caveau de la Huchette 149
New Morning 109

Live Music Venues
La Cigale 94
La Java 107, 109
Le Baiser Salé 82
Le Duc des Lombards 82
Le Nouveau Casino 109
L'Élysée-Montmartre 95
L'Olympia 67
Point Éphemère 108, 109
Sunset & Sunside 82

Opera Houses
Opéra Bastille 129
Palais Garnier 67

Pool Halls
Académie de Billard 92

Salsa Bars
Barrio Latino 128

Sporting Venues
Stade de France 95

Theatres
Comédie Française 83
Théâtre du Luxembourg 153
Théâtre du Vieux Colombier 164